SYLVIA PANKHURST

Sylvia Pankhurst

From Artist to Anti-Fascist

Edited by

Ian Bullock
Lecturer in History
Brighton College of Technology

and

Richard Pankhurst
Professor of Ethiopian Studies
Addis Ababa University

St. Martin's Press　　　New York

First published in the United States of America in 1992

Printed in Hong Kong

ISBN 0–312–06840–9

Library of Congress Cataloging-in-Publication Data
Sylvia Pankhurst : from artist to anti-fascist
edited by Ian Bullock and Richard Pankhurst.
p.   cm.
Includes bibliographical references and index.
ISBN 0–312–06840–9
1. Pankhurst, E. Sylvia (Estelle Sylvia), 1882–1960.
2. Feminists—Great Britain—Biography.   3. Artists—Great Britain–
–Biography.   4. Socialists—Great Britain—Biography.
I. Pankhurst, Richard Keir Pethick, 1927– . II. Bullock, Ian,
1941– .
HQ1595.P34S95   1992
305.42'092—dc20   91–25785
                                                            CIP

Contents

List of Plates   vi

Acknowledgements   vii

Notes on the Contributors   viii

Preface   xi

Introduction   xv

1 Sylvia Pankhurst as an Art Student   1
   Hilary Cunliffe-Charlesworth

2 Sylvia Pankhurst as an Artist   36
   Jackie Duckworth

3 Suffragism and Socialism: Sylvia Pankhurst 1903–1914   58
   Les Garner

4 Sylvia Pankhurst and the Great War   86
   Barbara Winslow

5 Sylvia Pankhurst and the Russian Revolution: the   121
   making of a 'Left-Wing' Communist
   Ian Bullock

6 Sylvia and *New Times and Ethiopia News*   149
   Richard Pankhurst

7 Sylvia Pankhurst's Papers as a Source   192
   M. Wilhelmina H. Schreuder

Sylvia Pankhurst's Publications   199

Index   201

Acknowledgements

Many people have helped with the preparation of this book in a variety of ways. We would particularly like to thank William Alderson, Sue Bullock, Jacqueline Mulhallen, Rita Pankhurst and Margreet Schrevel. We are grateful for the assistance of the International Institute of Social History, the Fawcett Library and the Sylvia Pankhurst Society, and for the permission of the National Museum of Labour History and the Museum of London to reproduce illustrations.

The authors' royalties from this book have been assigned to the Institute of Ethiopian Studies at the University of Addis Ababa to assist in buying works of art for its museum and thus contributing to the preservation of Ethiopia's cultural heritage.

Ian Bullock
Richard Pankhurst

List of Plates

1. Untitled: portrait of a farm girl (National Museum of Labour History)

2. Untitled: a young woman painting decorations onto wooden ornamental plaques (National Museum of Labour History)

3. In a Glasgow Cotton Spinning Mill, changing a yarn package (National Museum of Labour History)

4. An Old-Fashioned Pottery: transferring the pattern onto the biscuit (National Museum of Labour History)

5. Untitled: study of a woman's head (National Museum of Labour History)

6. Untitled: full-length portrait of an old woman (National Museum of Labour History)

7. Illuminated Address for WSPU prisoners (Museum of London)

8. WSPU Membership Card (Museum of London)

Notes on the Contributors

Ian Bullock teaches history at Brighton College of Technology. His Sussex University D. Phil. thesis was on 'Socialists and Democratic Form in Britain, 1880–1914' and his interest in Sylvia Pankhurst developed out of further research on radical ideas of democracy. He is currently co-writing a book on democratic ideas in the British Labour movement, c. 1880–1914.

Hilary Cunliffe-Charlesworth lectures in design history at Sheffield City Polytechnic where she is involved with the Centre for Women's Studies. Her main area of research is the history of the Royal College of Art, London. Her first degree was in fine art at Ravensbourne College of Art and Design, Bromley, followed by MA research on the depiction of the British agrarian revolution at the RCA.

Jackie Duckworth won the Allen Lane Penguin Prize for her MA thesis on 'Arts and Crafts in the Suffragette Movement'. She is currently a part-time lecturer at the Chelsea School of Art and practises as a tapestry artist and a community textile artist.

Les Garner teaches at Thames Polytechnic, London. His interest in Sylvia Pankhurst developed from his research for his PhD thesis on the ideas of the women's suffrage movement. This was later published as *Stepping Stones to Women's Liberty – Feminist Ideas in the Women's Suffrage Movement 1900–1918*. He is also the author of *A Brave and Beautiful Spirit: Dora Marsden 1882–1960*.

Richard Pankhurst, Sylvia's son, is Professor of Ethiopian Studies at the Institute of Ethiopian Studies of Addis Ababa University. He is the author of *Sylvia Pankhurst, Artist and Crusader* and of several studies on early nineteenth-century British socialism, as well as of works on various aspects of Ethiopian history.

M. Wilhelmina H. Schreuder worked at the International Institute of Social History, Amsterdam, until her retirement in 1988. She managed and arranged the Sylvia Pankhurst collection there and co-authored the *Inventory of the E. Sylvia Pankhurst Papers 1863–1960*. At present she is working on Dutch Quaker history.

Barbara Winslow has been active in the women's movement in Britain and the United States for over twenty years. She teaches women's studies at Hunter College, New York. She is currently studying the women's liberation movement in the Pacific Northwest, 1965–75.

Preface

My mother never forgot her father's maxim that 'Life is nothing without enthusiasms'. Imbued, like her father (and before him his hero John Stuart Mill), with a belief in the possibility – and overriding need – for human betterment, she was passionately engaged over the years, as the following studies show, in several important, and, in their different ways, exciting movements. Though the causes she espoused may at first sight appear disconnected, she regarded each of them as part of a wider struggle against privilege and oppression, waged by and for the underdog; and in the various phases of her life she committed herself to each and all of the movements in which she was involved with more or less equal determination, perseverance and commitment.

Though imbued with the ambition to become an artist, and to devote her artistic abilities to the cause of human progress, she became an intimate participant in the suffragette movement, and was for a time a London representative of her mother Emmeline's then Manchester-based Women's Social and Political Union. She endured hunger, thirst and sleep strikes in the suffragette struggle against the refusal of Britain's then Liberal government to grant women the vote. Eventually, however, she broke with her mother and sister Christabel, and founded her own geographically narrower, but socially more broadly based as well as organisationally more democratic, East London Federation of the Suffragettes; and began to edit her own weekly newspaper.

Like her father, and her mother in the latter's early days, she was a pacifist for most of her life. She opposed World War I (which her mother and sister supported), devoted herself to welfare work and agitation in the East End of London, welcomed the Bolshevik Revolution in Russia (which she regarded as a major act of human emancipation), travelled, secretly and illegally, to Moscow to attend one of the first conferences of Lenin's Communist International, gained prominence as an internationally-minded socialist opposed to allied intervention against the newly-established Soviet Union, and, while criticised by the Russian leader in his monograph *Left Wing Communism*, was imprisoned in Britain for her convictions.

Soon disenchanted with the Communist movement which she had originally championed – one of the first to enter, she was also one of the first to leave – she nevertheless preserved the socialist, as well as the feminist and internationalist beliefs she had inherited from her father. Having acquired a deep interest in Italy, where she had lived as an art student and which she had subsequently visited as an international socialist, she was one of the earliest foreign critics of fascism, and, with a view to encouraging feminist and other opposition to it, founded an International Women's Matteotti Committee, named in memory of the Italian Socialist deputy murdered on Mussolini's orders.

Opposition to Italian fascism led her to become a keen defender of independent Ethiopia (then internationally better known as Abyssinia) which she regarded as Mussolini's second victim – Italy herself having been, in her view, the first. Appalled by the Duce's unprovoked attack on a defenceless independent African country, as well as by the fascist bombing of foreign Red Cross ambulances and the use of poison gas, she rallied to the cause of the League of Nations, and founded an anti-fascist weekly newspaper to defend the Ethiopian cause. There she castigated the appeasement policies of the then British and French governments, supported the Spanish Republic in its life and death struggle with Franco, was denounced by Mussolini's pen, and at the same time joined many then emerging African nationalist leaders in their denounciation of colonialism.

Though long a pacifist, she was an enthusiastic supporter of the British decision to go to war with Nazi Germany, urging that fascism should be 'fought to the finish'. The Gestapo placed her name on the list of persons to be arrested in the event of a German occupation of Britain. After Mussolini's declaration of hostilities against Britain and France, and the resultant defeat of the Italians in East Africa, she nevertheless felt duty-bound to support Ethiopia, the country whose cause she had espoused, against British attempts to reduce it virtually to the status of a protectorate. She subsequently laboured hard to raise funds to endow Ethiopia with its first modern hospital, named after Emperor Haile Sellassie's daughter Princess Tsehai (who had served as a nurse in London during the Blitz) and also worked against the return to Italy to its former African colonies, as well as to ensure Ethiopia access to the sea, without which, she was convinced, the country's development would be virtually impossible.

Subsequently, leaving London in 1956 at the age of seventy-four, she travelled enthusiastically to Ethiopia, where she founded and edited another journal, and was actively involved in establishing one of the country's first welfare societies.

My mother's career, it is apparent, does not fall easily into any simple pattern. It has nevertheless seemed by many to be worthy of further study, and it is for this reason that the present contributors – each a specialist in a different area of research – have banded together to examine some of the most important aspects of her life, her ideals and her work.

Richard Pankhurst

Introduction

This book has its origins in a conversation at the end of 1987. Why, we asked, was it so difficult for anyone to produce a satisfactory biography of Sylvia Pankhurst? We quickly came to the conclusion that the major problem was the diversity of her activities. Most people who knew anything about her were interested in one particular phase of her life. To be able to write about her life as a whole, one would need knowledge and expertise in early twentieth-century British art and art education; the complexities of not just the suffragette campaign but of the wider 'votes for women' and feminist movements at the beginning of the century; pre-1917 socialism; the early Communist movement and its dissident offshoots both in Britain and internationally; the rise of fascism and the struggle against it.

In all these things Sylvia Pankhurst had a part – sometimes a crucial one. Certainly, anyone aspiring to write her life story would need to be well-versed in all of these aspects of early twentieth-century history. But then the greater complications present themselves. Out of Sylvia's anti-fascism grew her involvement – which in one way or another occupied the last third of her life – with Ethiopia, and with the wider anti-imperialist movement. Later, such commitments, at least in a theoretical way, would become a standard part of being on the Left in Europe and the United States. But Sylvia was a pioneer in this as in several other fields. Furthermore, her commitment was total, involving as it did uprooting herself at an age when most people would regard themselves as retired and emigrating to a place which, much more truly than Czechoslovakia in 1938, could be described as 'a faraway country of which we know little'. Even to those with some knowledge of history, Ethiopia's past is often shadowy. It burst forth into the brilliant sunshine to defeat an attempt at Italian conquest in the late nineteenth century. In more tragic hues, it was an early victim of the brutal late imperialism of European fascism. But apart from the years 1896 and 1935–6 it remains for most of us hidden in the twilight, at least until the renewed attention of more recent years.

To find someone equally adept in the suffragist, socialist, Communist, and anti-fascist worlds over a period of more than thirty years was asking a great deal. To find such a person with sufficient understanding also of the Ethiopian background to make sense of

Sylvia's experiences with and in that country suggested needles and haystacks.

Yet on the other hand, there were many people who had or were researching and writing about one particular aspect of Sylvia Pankhurst's long career. The Sylvia Pankhurst papers in the International Institute of Social History in Amsterdam will never vie with the Rijksmuseum as a tourist attraction, but they are by the standards of such archives well visited. Instead of trying to produce a biography, why not try and put some of the results of these disparate labours together? The result is this book.

This is certainly not an attempt at a collectively-written biography. We have tried to look at the major areas of Sylvia's activities but we are well aware that we have left many gaps. Nor would any of the contributors claim to be giving either an exhaustive or a definitive account of their particular topic. What we can claim is that each contribution puts into print for the first time either new, previously unpublished material, such as the results of Hilary Cunliffe-Charlesworth's researches on Sylvia as an art student, or a new interpretation of some phase of her activities, or both. We are seeking to open, or continue, a series of debates both about a woman who was quite remarkable by anyone's standards, and about our understanding of the campaigns, movements and struggles which filled almost all of her waking hours from an early age until her death in 1960.

Ian Bullock

1

Sylvia Pankhurst as an Art Student

HILARY CUNLIFFE-CHARLESWORTH

The Pankhurst family involvement in art and design has been somewhat neglected. Sylvia Pankhurst's paternal grandfather was a valuer and auctioneer of fine art, while her maternal grandfather was a cotton printer and co-owner of a cotton factory, and therefore someone who would have been involved with both the design and production of textiles. Both Sylvia's parents were well-educated: her father studied law; they were both active in politics and became involved in the arts to the extent of opening a shop selling artistic objects.

As the Pankhursts lived in the large provincial city of Manchester they were not divorced from new ideas. The prosperity of Manchester's cotton trade encouraged the city to be a centre for artistic ideas and fashions, aware of the needs of design and art. The Manchester Art Museum was established in 1886 in Ancoats Hall, with the support of both Ruskin and Morris, and also reflected the ideas of Henry Cole (1808–82), the instigator of the Great Exhibition of 1851, who was concerned with the need to reform design education in order for Britain to successfully export her manufactured goods. The Manchester Art Museum contained reproductions of works of art but also included a model workman's cottage thought suitable for copying by ordinary workers.[1]

In 1885 Sylvia's father, Dr Pankhurst, stood for Parliament at Rotherhithe in London. The attempt was unsuccessful, but led to the family moving to rented premises in London at 165 Hampstead Road, near Euston Station. Here the Pankhursts opened a shop 'Emerson and Company' with Mrs Pankhurst in charge. It sold artistic items for the home.

The founding of such an establishment was a reflection of the ideals of John Ruskin and William Morris, whose examples led to the creation of a number of groups generically known as the Arts and Crafts Movement. The objective was that the designer could also be the maker, preventing the boredom of only being involved in manufacture, and also that the designers would understand the whole process of manufacture. This would lead to the production of better-designed and produced goods. This led to confusion as the result was that only the better-off could afford the objects designed for an ideal world. Also the attitude of *l'art pour l'art* and its connection with Oscar Wilde and aestheticism, combined with the theories of socialism and art, was challenging society in general, and although new styles of art and design were to become popular, the political overtones were not received with similar warmth.

Sylvia notes that her maternal grandfather disapproved of ideas such as those of William Morris who encouraged the crafts, and that her mother concurred with this view, for it was some ten years after the opening of Emerson and Company before Mrs Pankhurst came to appreciate the work of Morris and his circle. Indeed, Mrs Pankhurst considered Morris to be prejudiced against her because on their first meeting she was wearing a dress from Paris.

But there was a fashion for artistic furnishings and so it was not so surprising for the Pankhursts to open a shop selling crafted items: Emerson's sold objects such as milking stools decorated by Mrs Pankhurst and her sister Mary. But it was not near enough to the popular shopping area of Oxford Street, and financially the shop was a failure.

A large family house was rented at 8 Russell Square, to the south of Euston and near to the British Museum. This was decorated in the fashion of the period with Japanese blinds of reeds and coloured beads. Emerson's was reopened in Berners Street, not far from Oxford Circus, but due to the impending demolition of the premises the shop was moved once more, this time to the retailing centre of Regent Street with its high overheads. The aim was to present a smaller and less expensive shop in the style of the nearby Liberty's.[2] Emerson's sold white enamelled furniture, Japanese, Chinese and Indian goods, Turkish rugs, Persian ceramics, and textiles ranging from the fine silks made by Wardle's of Leek, to stout unglazed printed cottons designed by William Morris and his imitators. But Mrs Pankhurst seems not to have marked up her goods high enough. The position of the shop meant high overheads and it therefore continued to lose money and drain the family income.

The Pankhurst children thus grew up in a home aware of contemporary art and design as well as politics. Their education was home-based: in Manchester a Miss Pearson was engaged as a governess, but she eventually sent her sister, Miss Annie, who did little teaching but read aloud from novels. Mrs Pankhurst's sister, Aunt Mary, helped with the children's education, but they were predominantly self-taught, especially after the family moved to London. However, in the earliest months at Russell Square, Cecile Sowerby, an artist whom Aunt Mary had known in Paris, became their governess. No lessons took place, but the children were read to and taken on visits, notably to the British Museum, until Miss Sowerby returned to her painting. Aunt Mary was also something of an artist, and gave Sylvia help and encouragement leading to Dr Pankhurst recognising his daughters' artistic talent. But Aunt Mary left the household on marriage, and although Dr Pankhurst talked of sending the girls to a board school, they soon returned to teaching one another.

While in London the children came into contact with their parents' political friends, including some Fabians and William Morris. The Pankhursts had first met Keir Hardie in 1888. He was to remain a close family friend, with Dr Pankhurst joining the Independent Labour Party on its formation in 1893.

In the winter of 1892–3 the lease on the house in Russell Square ended, incurring heavy bills for dilapidation. These were duly paid, only for Dr Pankhurst to learn that the house was to be demolished. Dr Pankhurst found the commuting between Manchester and London a physical and financial strain, so Emerson's was wound up with the lease unsold, and the family moved to Southport in Lancashire. Here the Pankhurst children attended Southport High School for Girls for one term, with Sylvia gaining praise for her drawing skills. Though apparently bright students, the Pankhurst children endured teasing because of their non-attendance of classes in religious education on the orders of Dr Pankhurst.

The family then moved to Disley, in Cheshire, where they were rejoined by Aunt Mary during a temporary separation from her husband, though here the children were taught by a governess. It was only when the family returned to live in Manchester at 4 Buckingham Crescent, Daisy Bank Road, Victoria Park, that Sylvia began her formal art training. Art was a longstanding interest of Sylvia's, originating with her father buying the children books illustrated by Walter Crane, which together with the latter's socialist cartoons

aroused in me the longing to be a painter and draughtsman in the
service of the great movements for social betterment; and this
remained the lasting and fervent hope of my youth.[3]

Sylvia later described how at Russell Square she was always drawing from her imagination, and, ashamed of the standard of her work,
hid the sketchbooks under furniture. Later, art became the central
aim of her self-education, drawing figures building roads, or alche-
mists studying books. Now once more in Manchester, the sisters
attended the city's High School for Girls. The many different lessons
and homework proved a trial, with Sylvia using any pretext to
include drawing in her work. But she was already aware of the
divisions within society, seeing the social exclusion of the scholarship
pupils and experiencing the ridicule towards those students who
like herself did not attend religious education.

When Christabel was sixteen Dr Pankhurst wanted her to be
coached to take her matriculation (an examination in which all
subjects had to be passed). Mrs Pankhurst protested that she did
not want her daughters to train as high school teachers, and
hoped that Christabel would use her talent as a dancer. This incident
throws a somewhat unexpected light on Mrs Pankhurst's attitudes,
which were perhaps more conventional than might have been anticipated.

In Manchester the Pankhursts' nearest neighbours were the
Bancrofts: Elias Mollineaux Bancroft, an artist, his wife and only son.
In the winter of 1898 Sylvia began to take art lessons from Mr
Bancroft, and the lessons seem to have continued until 1900. When
Bancroft was teaching Sylvia he was at the end of his most fruitful
period. He had worked in London and exhibited at the Royal
Academy from 1874. He often worked in Wales and exhibited at the
Royal Cambrian Academy. Sylvia was amazed at the effect of drawing
with charcoal on good drawing paper and the use of bread as an
eraser. She continued her work at home, experimenting with water-
colours. This happy period was sadly interrupted by her father's
sudden death while her mother and Christabel were in Geneva.
Sylvia blamed herself, and perhaps in consequence suffered ill health.
A means of financial support had to be found for the family. Mrs
Pankhurst considered that a shop might have better fortune in
Manchester. Aided by her sister Mary, she made cushion covers and
opened a business. Assistants were employed and later when
Christabel (for whom Mrs Pankhurst claimed the shop had been

opened) returned from Geneva, Sylvia half-heartedly assisted her mother at the shop. The family could no longer afford the house in Victoria Park, and its belongings were sold to pay the debts. A family acquaintance, Charles Rowley, came to the Pankhurst home to advise on the value of pictures the family owned which were to be sold. On this visit Rowley saw some of Sylvia's work and this led to her paintings being sent to the Manchester Municipal School of Art. Rowley, a city councillor, together with the new headmaster of the art school, Richard Glazier, and the deputy master, Henry Cadness, encouraged the development of craft and design at the school. Rowley was a key figure in the art world of Manchester: a personal friend of the socialist artists and designers Walter Crane and William Morris, and of the Pre-Raphaelite painter Ford Maddox Brown. Rowley was the owner of several Manchester art shops which sold reproductions of the great masters. He also had a reputation as a philanthropist. Certainly he must have been impressed with Sylvia's work and appears to have been the catalyst which allowed her to enter art college. But Sylvia's work must have shown talent, no doubt developed by Bancroft's training, for she was given a free studentship to study design in 1900–2 at the Manchester Municipal School of Art.

Sylvia entered the Design School, which was headed by Henry Cadness. She remembered the kindness shown to her by the staff and students and her time at the school appears to have been very happy in comparison to the previous period of enclosed family life. Her work at the school included designing and illuminating one of the pages of an address for a royal visit, to open the nearby Whitworth Institute in Manchester. Her political beliefs were already sufficiently formed for her to spend the day of the visit selling £2-worth of pamphlets: Keir Hardie's *Open Letter to the King*, and one on unemployment.

Another event illustrates that her politics were at odds with those of most of her peers, especially as at this time the Boer War was at its height and jingoism was prevalent. Walter Crane came to lecture at the School of Art on ornament and design. His lecture included the drawing of Britannia's trident – which lead Crane to comment that he hoped Britain would respect the liberties of others as carefully as she safeguarded her own. Sylvia wrote a report of the lecture for the art school magazine. This led to a demand by a fellow student, Cicely Fox Smith, for the article to be excised. She also threatened to follow Sylvia home and smash her windows.[4]

Sylvia was dogged by ill health. She suffered from neuralgia which caused her to spend some time working at home, while working in the heat of the life room at the art school aggravated her chilblains to the point where relief was sought by dousing her feet with methylated spirits, used for fixing drawings. Her continued ill health during her first year induced a feeling of guilt at holding a free studentship. She also considered that, like her sister, she should do her share of work at Emerson's, where Christabel was showing some discontent. So in her second year, Sylvia persuaded her mother to pay the low fees for part-time attendance so that she could give half of her time to working at Emerson's. But other than writing price tickets for the window, there was actually little work for Sylvia to do at the shop.

In the summer of that year (1901) Sylvia was awarded the Lady Whitworth scholarship of £30 and fees, as the best woman student of the year. This meant that she had to revert to full-time study for her third year at the school of Art. She had considerable success in her final year. She won medals for Historic Ornament, Anatomy Design and Plant Drawing, gaining the top prize of the School, the Proctor Travelling Scholarship. She was also awarded a Primrose Silver Medal for Design, and a National Silver Medal for the designs of mosaic panels for a fountain, which came from success in the National Assessments of art and design. In November 1903 she became one of the first Associates of the Manchester Municipal School of Art. This was the first time this award had been given; it was instituted to provide post-diploma students with an opportunity for continued study, offering free use of studio facilities.[5]

Sylvia decided to use the Proctor Travelling Scholarship to study mosaics in Venice and Florence. In the summer of 1902 she set off with her mother for Venice, travelling via Bruges and Brussels, then to Switzerland to stay with her mother's friends, the Defaux. Here Monsieur Defaux painted Mrs Pankhurst's portrait while Sylvia drew. Mother and daughter continued to Venice with Madame Defaux, where at the end of one week her mother and friend departed, leaving Sylvia living with a Mancunian landlady. Sylvia overcame her loneliness at being parted from her mother by working, getting up at five in the morning and continuing until eight in the evening. In the mornings, she copied mosaics, and in the afternoon made paintings of Venice street life and its landscapes, often much inconvenienced by the attentions of onlookers, especially at first when she used '*avanti*' thinking it meant go away, rather than come forward.

Even her evenings were occupied by attempting to paint from her balcony by moonlight. In the winter of 1902 Sylvia enrolled at the Accademia di Belle Arti to work in the life class. As she was the only female student she was segregated in the antique room, but on the second day of her own accord entered the life room, where she was treated as just another student and without embarrassment. Though she pretended not to know any Italian, she comprehended her fellow students' chatter. She also attended a landscape class, and was awarded a diploma for her efforts.

In the spring of 1903 Christabel was preparing to train as a barrister by taking her matriculation examination, so Sylvia decided to return home. In Manchester Sylvia returned to her old tasks at home and in the shop, though her mother had also rented the attic over Emerson's as a studio for her where Sylvia designed cotton prints, and sold a number of her works done in Venice.

That summer the Pankhurst Hall, Salford, was completed. This was erected by the Independent Labour Party in memory of Sylvia's father, and she was invited to decorate the lecture hall. She happily began work on mural designs. The task was completed within the allotted three months. She was assisted in the heavier manual work by a decorator, R. C. Wallhead (later M P for Merthyr Tydfil), and also by one of the evening students from the Manchester Municipal School of Art. Walter Crane opened the hall, and Sylvia gave a lecture on the meaning of the decorations.

While Sylvia was working on the decoration of the hall, it was already in use, and to her amazement she found that women were not permitted to attend meetings of that branch of the Independent Labour Party. The reason given for this omission (which would seem extraordinary considering that Dr Pankhurst, in whose honour the hall was named, had been a strong defender of women's rights during his lifetime) was that the hall was attached to a social club, open to non-Independent Labour Party Members but not to women. This feeble excuse caused anger at its injustice, and triggered the formation of the Women's Social and Political Union by Sylvia's mother and sister in October 1903, which was intended to make the Labour Party support votes for women.

With Mrs Pankhurst's energy being put into the new women's movement, Emerson's inevitably declined. There was no work there for Sylvia. When her work on the Pankhurst Hall was completed Sylvia began to prepare for an examination to win a National Scholarship to the Royal College of Art, South Kensington, London. Although she does not record any further involvement with the Manchester Muncipal School of Art, the award of its Associateship in November 1903 would have provided her with free studio access to prepare for the National Scholarship series of examinations, which she took early in 1904.

The National Examinations Scheme was run by the Board of Education. All entrants sent work to London, where it was examined by the professors at the Royal College of Art, which was run by the Board of Education and funded by the Treasury. Students at art colleges took the National Examination to gain nationally recognised qualifications, but if a student gained enough marks a place could be awarded at the Royal College of Art for postgraduate study. Although there were some direct entrants to the Royal College of Art, the Board of Education's National Examinations Scheme was the most usual way to gain a place. The National Examinations gave a graduate from art school a qualification for use in industry, or more usually, education, notably school teaching. Though it was usually taken by senior students at schools of art, many entrants for the examination studied part-time while in full-time employment. If a place at the Royal College of Art was not obtained through the Board of Education's examination results, for one of the few Royal Exhibitioner or Free Studentship places, the Royal College of Art's own examination could be taken.

Sylvia had already taken some of the National Examinations in 1902 (for which she won the National Silver Medal for mosaic designs), but she was now aiming for a scholarship. There were six National Scholarships given to students to improve their design skills, plus fifteen Free Studentships without maintenance. Allowances were offered to students from industry (though in practice this rule was waived so that these places could be taken by fine arts students).

In the event, although Sylvia failed to complete any of the problems set in the geometry paper, when the results were announced she had gained a first-class certificate in all the other subjects, scored enough marks to win a scholarship, and furthermore was top of the list of all the candidates. She was awarded £50 a year to attend the Royal College of Art in London. This was paid at the rate of £5 a month during term time, and she also received travelling expenses from her home town. Sylvia was surprised and came to the conclusion that the standard of candidates could not have been high.

In 1900 there were nearly 400 students attending the Royal College of Art, but this was reduced to 200 in 1910 through reorganisation and a tightening of the entrance examinations procedure. In 1910 about 30 per cent of the students at the Royal College of Art received some form of award: each year there were ten Royal Exhibitioners, six National Scholars and fifteen Free Studentships. The majority of the students were between twenty and twenty-five years of age.[6]

The Diploma Course of the Royal College took three years to complete, but if a student had taken the Board of Education's Drawing Examination plus one other Board Examination, they could enter for the Schools Associateship Diploma Examination in two years, provided they were already nineteen on entering the College. This is why the award Sylvia received was for only two years, as she had enough qualifications to complete a Schools Diploma Course in two years. The Diploma made the students Associates of the Royal College of Art (ARCA). This qualification was accepted as a teaching qualification, was needed by all those who hoped to teach in an art school, and also made them eligible for headmasterships. The Diploma of Full Associateship was an alternative qualification for the headmaster of the school of art to the Board of Education's Art Master's Certificate.

Students at the Royal College of Art followed one of two routes: those intending to become teachers took the full course covering the work of all the schools, lasting at least three and usually four years, finally specialising in one of the areas, and receiving the Diploma of full Associateship of the Royal College of Art. Students such as National Scholars, for whom a shorter and more specialised course was suitable, spent all their time (after an introductory term of architecture) in one school of the College, and received a Diploma of the Schools Associateship of the Royal College of Art at the end of their course. This School's Associateship was intended for productive artists, and would be taken in two years, though the course often extended over three years. The latter route was the one taken by Sylvia.

Determined to become a painter, Sylvia was accepted into the School of Drawing and Painting, headed by Professor Gerald Moira (1867–1959). But when in the autumn of 1904 she began her studies at the Royal College of Art she, and all her contemporaries, could not study their specialism, but for the first six months had to undertake a compulsory course in architecture, with the only life drawing taking place in the evenings. To make matters worse, the quality of teaching in the life classes seemed poor, and seeing Sylvia's confident drawing skills, the other students asked for her help. Students who were at the College the previous year encouraged her to see the Principal, Augustus Spencer, over the issue. She asked for the days to be used for painting and life work, with architecture in the evenings. She had expected Spencer perhaps to reject her idea with the excuse that it was essential for a decorative painter to study some architecture. Instead Spencer was very angry and ordered her from the room. This was the start of conflict between the Principal and Sylvia, and from then on when the two met, scowls were exchanged.[7]

Sylvia found lodgings in a house off the Fulham Road for ten shillings (50p) per week. She joined the Fulham branch of the Independent Labour Party during her first year at college, and was asked to debate on votes for women. Through her political interests she met Margaret and Ramsay Macdonald. On Saturdays she sold designs for cotton prints, sending a pound of every guinea home, as she was concerned that her mother was continuing to pay the rent on her studio above Emerson's shop. Sylvia kept the remaining shilling (5p) for bus fares. On Sundays she would sometimes visit her Aunt Mary.

Before the end of 1904 Sylvia moved to a couple of rooms, one unfurnished, at Park Cottage on Park Walk, Chelsea. She encouraged her Tory landlady, Mrs Roe, to adopt the causes of votes for women, the Labour Party and socialism. At Park Cottage she felt more at home and could invite women students from her year to her lodgings for life painting, with one student acting as a model for the others, and herself as tutor.

Sylvia's interest centred around college life and her work. The students were divided into groups, with the female students usually sharing rooms with close women friends to economise on rent. To Sylvia it seemed that most also had a special male friend, but although acquainted with a number of students, she later learnt that the male students considered her haughty. Her friends at College included Austin Osman Spare (1888–1956). Younger than the other students, his work was considered strange which led to first year female students considering him rather daring, and thus attractive. When he announced his plan to publish a book of satirical and allegorical drawings entitled *Earth Inferno: Destiny, Humanity and the Chaos of Creation*, and when Sylvia announced that she was going to order one, several students got her to order copies for them.[8]

Every three weeks there was a college dance, as well as the annual fancy dress ball, which involved several months of preparation. Sylvia noted her attendance at only one college function: a concert attended by Sir Alfred Gilbert (1854–1934), the then Professor of Sculpture at the Royal Academy, and Edward Lanteri (1848–1917), the Professor of Sculpture at the Royal College of Art.

Outside the College her two closest friends were her brother Harry and Keir Hardie. Her time in London led to a closer friendship with Keir Hardie, whom she had first met at the age of thirteen when her father had stood for the Independent Labour Party at Gorton. Even after her father's death Hardie visited the family in Manchester, which led to gossip that he was having an affair with Mrs Pankhurst. For Sylvia, Keir Hardie became more than a father substitute, and their love affair appears to have begun soon after her arrival in London, and was to continue until 1912. They went out socially with Sylvia gaining acceptance as an old family friend.

By the end of her first academic year at the Royal College of Art it became apparent that a high number of scholarships for continuation of study at the college, and college prizes were awarded to male students. In the August, Keir Hardie put down a question on this issue in the House of Commons, which was answered with the information that sixteen scholarships were awarded with three female recipients. No change to this system was envisaged. The question must have caused considerable annoyance to the Principal of the College who was running the institution under the authority of the Board of Education. To find students getting questions asked in the House seemed intolerable, and the connection was made between Keir Hardie and Sylvia. The start of the autumn term cannot have been easy for either student or Principal.

The General Election of 1906 resulted in the Labour party having twenty-nine members returned to Parliament, including Keir Hardie. Sylvia was elated by this news, although she did not know if any of the other students shared her joy.[9]

In February 1905 her mother had arrived in London, thereby interrupting Sylvia's quiet life in Park Walk. There were no more Saturday afternoon painting sessions. Gradually Sylvia became drawn into her mother's activities for the Women's Social and Political Union, and began to neglect her work at college. It was Sylvia who founded the first London branch of the WSPU, consisting of Annie Kenney, an organiser in London, her aunt Mary Clark, and her landlady Mrs Roe, with herself as honorary secretary. In February, with Keir Hardie's assistance, Sylvia hired Caxton Hall where a meeting was held, and began to draw attention to the cause of Votes for Women. Sylvia nominally ran the London WSPU office. She wrote requesting an interview with the Prime Minister, Sir Henry Campbell-Bannerman. The request was refused, so on 2 March 1906, a group of women visited 10 Downing Street. On this date the Prime Minister was ill, but the women had their photographs taken by the press. On 9 March thirty women went to Downing Street only to be refused entry, but a message was received that the Prime Minister would receive a deputation from the Women's Social and Political Union on 19 May. In the meantime, Keir Hardie put down a motion for 25 April, and once again there was an attempt to talk the Women's Suffrage Bill out of time. Sylvia was in the House of Commons to see the uproar, partly caused by the women in the Visitors' Gallery calling for a division. This resulted in much bad publicity for the WSPU. On 19 May the deputation was received by the Prime Minister. The meeting was followed by a rally of women in Trafalgar Square. At his meeting with the deputation, Campbell-Bannerman categorically stated that his government would not initiate legislation towards votes for women. This led the suffragette movement to take increasingly militant action.

In June 1906 Sylvia's sister Christabel graduated and moved to London. She held different political ideas from Sylvia, and moved the WSPU away from the working class. Sylvia felt pushed out of Park Walk. She was in the last month of her scholarship at the College and hoped for some words of encouragement from her mother. Her landlady Mrs Roe wanted to know how Sylvia would pay her rent in the future. Sylvia resigned her position as secretary and left Park Cottage at the end of her course. She found new unfurnished rooms in Cheyne Walk.

Although in their first year at college students were too occupied with work and financial survival to think about the future, the worry about what would happen to them when they had to leave gradually increased as time went on. The main career prospect was teaching, and Sylvia realised that the women were handicapped as the best teaching posts would go to male students, even if they were less qualified. Other graduates produced commercial work for very little money. Sylvia noted that she personally knew of five cases of insanity in students who were at the College or who had recently left.

During her time at college she had become increasingly concerned with politics, as we have seen, and this must have distracted her attention from her studies. However, the quality of her work was seen as excellent and she was considered the strongest student during her second year. Professor Moira of the Painting School encouraged her to apply for a scholarship to continue her studies. The award of a further one year scholarship was not, however, made. Fellow students had told Sylvia there was considerable discrimination against women students in the awarding of prizes and scholarships at the College: also, the final decision of College awards lay with the Principal, Augustus Spencer, with whom Sylvia had clashed. Certainly, though there was a high proportion of women students at the College, comparatively few gained prizes or continuation scholarships. Sylvia considered the reason to be exclusion on the grounds of gender, leading to Keir Hardie asking a question in the House of Commons. The parliamentary answer, as we have seen, gave a ratio of just over 1 to 5, a number which did not reflect the proportion of women students at the College nor the quality of their work. It also seemed to be the usual practice for just one woman painting student in each year to receive a college scholarship. Questions about the Royal College of Art in the House of Commons displeased Spencer who in due course found out that Sylvia was responsible.

Life outside college work was hard. Henry Cadness, her tutor at Manchester, wrote telling her not to lose hope. At the end of the summer term Keir Hardie suggested she should sell sketches to the *Pall Mall Gazette* along with an article based on her recent prison experiences as a suffragette. Editors who agreed to see her thought she would want to write exclusively on votes for women. Sylvia made illustrations for Richard Jeffries' book *The Open Air*, and she approached the publisher, Bodley Head, but the book was not yet out of copyright and she abandoned the project. Sylvia survived by writing articles for the *Westminster Review*, work found for her by Keir Hardie.

She also did design work for the WSPU. Her work included a banner of woman as 'mother and worker', which was unveiled at the Portland Rooms in 1908, and a cartoon for the WSPU stall at the Hungarian Exhibition at Earl's Court – also in 1908. But she continued to be torn between the need to be an artist and the needs of society. By the autumn of 1906 she had become a militant suffragette. When Parliament reassembled on 23 October 1906, the WSPU went to lobby the House of Commons, and there was a scuffle. Court cases ensued.

Some of the WSPU women were placed on trial and sentenced without a full or fair hearing. Sylvia protested to the judge, who was by then hearing another case. She was ordered out of the court, but continued to speak from outside the courtroom. This led to her arrest for obstruction and use of abusive language, with a sentence of fourteen days in prison, with no visitors. She used this time to write poems to Hardie and on release publicised not the WSPU aims, but the terrible prison conditions, and used sketches to do so.

Hardie's close connection with the women's movement did not gain him favour with his colleagues in the Independent Labour Party, and in the spring of 1907 he resigned his chairmanship of the parliamentary group due to illness.

Sylvia continued with both her suffrage and her artistic activities: she designed a series of life-size studies for the Women's Exhibition, a publicity and fund-raising event held at the Princes's Skating Rink, Knightsbridge, in 1909. Her work included hangings 150 feet wide and 250 feet long which covered walls of the hall. The theme was 'Those who sow in tears shall reap in joy'. She sketched the designs which were then completed by students from the nearby Royal College of Art.

Between May and November 1910 over 4,000 demonstrations were held in favour of women's suffrage. In November 1911 it was announced that an Electoral Reform Bill would be introduced, but women's suffrage was not on its agenda. Sylvia suffered numerous prison terms and endured forced feeding. In the May of 1911 her first book, *The Suffragette: The History of the Women's Militant Suffrage Movement 1905–1910*, was published with some success, and that spring she visited the United States of America. Despite all this, she was also heavily involved in the problems of the Royal College of Art.

In 1909 the Board of Education had begun an enquiry into the College. The Board of Education took evidence about its organisation from staff and other educationalists as well as industrialists. What is remarkable is that when a group of past students requested that they might give evidence, their request was accepted. This evidence provides a clear and detailed account of the students' experience at the College, and helps to explain why Sylvia had not gained her Diploma.

In the April of 1911 John S. Currie,[10] a past student and a contemporary of Sylvia's, wrote to Mr Cartlidge, the Chief Inspector for

Schools of Art, with a request for a deputation of past students to give evidence to the departmental committee considering the Royal College of Art. Following a meeting with Cartlidge, and Sedgwick, the Secretary of the Board of Education's Departmental Committee, John Currie sent a memorandum of the points the past students wished to make:

1. That the Course of Architecture rigidly imposed by the Principal was extremely discouraging and detrimental to many students who had neither desire nor inclination for this particular course. We wish to state how students, to whom this course is uncongenial, are dealt with, and the depressing waste of time it entails.

2. That the attitude of the Principal in making the literary course also compulsory is strongly resented by the majority of students, not that there is any objection to a literary course, but it is generally felt that the lectures on subjects dealt with should be delivered by competent experts. At the present time the course is felt to be valueless both from a literary and artistic point of view.

3. That the instruction given at the evening life classes is of no practical value to serious draughtsmen.

4. That there is no instruction given in pen, or other forms of black and white drawing for illustrative purposes, though a large proportion of the students are eventually obliged to earn their living by this means.

5. That the manner in which recommendations for scholarships and diplomas are given is entirely unjust, and has no relation to the artistic capacity of the students.

6. That seeing it is generally felt that the organisation of the Royal College is unsatisfactory, and that we, the students, found the Principal to be neither an artist nor a sympathetic organizer we respectfully wish to ask, since we have suffered by the system – in what way does he merit the position he now holds as head of the Nation's School of Design.[11]

Currie added that the deputation would comprise students selected from among the number who held these grievances. The list of students who were willing to attend the deputation were Miss Dorothy Salmon (a fee-paying student 1903–5 and a Senior Art Scholar 1905–06); Miss Hornes (Local Exhibitioner 1903–4, fee-paying 1904–

7 and 1908); Miss Sylvia Pankhurst (National Scholar 1904–6); Mr Austin O. Spare (1902–5); Mr Edward English (National Scholar 1901–3, Royal College of Art Scholar 1903–6); and Mr John S. Currie (National Scholar 1904–6).

On Monday 15 May 1911, at 11.30 a.m., the Departmental Committee met to hear the students' evidence. The committee comprised Mr Chambers (Chairman), Sir Kenneth Anderson, Mr Cockerell, Mr Ricardo, Mr Warner and Mr Sedgwick (Secretary). In the afternoon they were joined by Professor Brown. The student deputation had been narrowed down to Mr Currie, Miss Pankhurst and Mr Spare.

The first point considered was the course of architecture, a course which had been introduced following the guidelines of an Advisory Council of Art in 1900. This established the rule that all students should spend the first six months of their course in the architectural school, with only the evenings free for life drawing (no painting being allowed in the evenings). The course had been implemented in 1904 (Spare having entered in the previous year, escaped the six months in the Architecture School). The situation was made worse in that the students entering the College in 1904 were unaware, until their arrival, of any change in the curriculum. The majority of students disliked the regulation, but they could not avoid a seemingly unnecessary study as they were nearly all scholarship students, and the Royal College of Art was the only college to which they could go. Further, most of the students had already passed some kind of architectural examination before going to the College, and although architectural knowledge was not compulsory, Royal Exhibitioner scholarship holders were obliged to have passed an architectural examination. There had been an exemption from the architectural course granted to students who were already qualified, but that rule had been abolished in 1902.

Personally, Sylvia felt angry that out of her two-year scholarship a quarter of her time should be spent in an activity which was not relevant to her study. The course on architecture began with lectures on the various styles, after which the students were set work which was later marked. In practice, however, they were not taught all the various styles, being obliged instead to measure woodwork and stonework, while the designing aspect was minimal. When the panel suggested that a practical exercise in architecture would be set to emphasise what a lecturer had said, Sylvia Pankhurst responded:

I wonder whether you have ever seen the lectures; they did not deal with the work we were doing so much; they told us a great many things which were most interesting, but most technical, such as the kind of concrete which was used in buildings and so on. There was a great deal of building construction in it, which of course was very interesting, but which did not really bear on the styles of architecture at all, or on such things as a painter requires. If we had not had any training in historical styles of architecture before we came up, we should have been quite at sea. We started with Georgian and Renaissance and went on to Gothic and then we finished up with an artist's cottage.[12]

The subject was taught as if the students were at the start of an architect's training, rather than as a course showing the relationship of architecture to the arts. She reiterated that if architecture had been taught hand-in-hand with another area it would have been much more valuable.

The students considered that the special importance placed on architecture did not help them to develop, and the emphasis of the final Diploma on the work done in the Architectural School seemed unfair, especially as there was no demand for monumental painters. The College's attitude towards the course on architecture seemed out of touch with what was happening in the art world. Furthermore, the six months away from their main area of study led to a decline in the skills which they were at the College to develop. John Currie pointed out that as a painting student he had no experience of designing or construction, and it was ironic that on leaving it was only he and Sylvia Pankhurst who designed work suitable for decoration of public buildings. Currie also stated that when he arrived at the College, he was not asked what work he wanted to specialise in, but merely told to go to Architectural School. After a time there was an option to do other work, but as the Painting School was overcrowded and there was usually more room in the Design School, students were encouraged to go there. As far as Currie knew, the situation was the same for all the other students in his year.

During the six months of special architectural study the evening drawing sessions were not enough to compensate, and the students were left virtually to teach themselves, as Sylvia explained:

After all, one must take into consideration something of the feelings of the students; there was an absolute rebellion against it, and it caused a great deal of depression and misery. The students came up from the country full of energy and enthusiasm; they worked very hard for their scholarships and are generally rather poor. 25s a week is not a very princely income on which to maintain oneself in London, and their parents have very often had to make sacrifices to let them come up. It is a tremendous set back to them that at the beginning when they come up here for work they have to take this architecture class. In the evenings one begins by drawing from the antique at the College, which is very good, of course, but students have a feeling that they have gone through that, and it does not depend on their ability as to how soon they are put on life drawing, but it depends on the rules. That reduces them to a fearful state of depression and misery, coupled with the architecture class. I wish that you could go into the school. It applies absolutely to the majority. I do not know of a single student in my year who did not rebel and complain.[13]

It is clear that Sylvia did not object to architecture being part of the education, but rather to having to take it at the expense of her other work.

The chairman then turned to the second point on the student's memorandum: the history of art and literary course. This was a course introduced in 1903 in an attempt to improve the literacy of students, as the graduates of the College were too frequently inefficient teachers because of their poor English. A lecturer in the history of art was appointed to teach languages and supervise the reading of students who needed help. The attendance of students was poor, and John Currie pointed out to the committee that, as with the course in architecture, the subject of history of art seemed to have too strong a place in the College work. As the lecturer was not a producer of any art or design, the students had no faith in his expertise. The subject matter of the lectures appears to have been art history presented in a very dry manner, although the students considered the accompanying slides interesting. Further, Sylvia explained that the lectures were given on Wednesday afternoons, and were repeated the following morning from 8.30 am till 9.30 am when notes on the lectures were dictated. The dictation was very detailed, including all punctuation, which the students considered insulting to their intelligence. This dictation was the nearest thing to English teaching at the College. The students were also expected to do homework. They considered that this course should have been optional, with the lectures given by artists and experts on the subjects. Sylvia voiced her concerns:

I do not think there is any pretence that the gentleman who teaches it is an artist, and therefore the students are prejudiced against him from the start. Personally, I do not think he knows anything about art. I do not want to say anything against him personally, but I do not think he knows anything about it; I really do not.[14]

The lecturer, Beckwith Spencer, was the Principal's brother. He was the subject of ridicule and his comments on artists were considered nonsense by Sylvia's contemporaries and later students of the College. Sylvia also admitted that:

in my own case I failed to attend to take all those lecture notes because I am a fast writer and I had already taken all the notes which were necessary or useful to me, and I did not see the advantage of getting up there at half-past eight in the morning to do such a useless kind of thing; therefore I frequently neglected those classes. For that I was hauled up and told that if I did that again I should not have my scholarship, and I was given to understand that it was practically a certainty that I should not have it. I do not think that that is at all the way in which students should be treated.[15]

Sylvia added that she did not wish to make her comments too personal but she had been told by one of her tutors that her work was considered the best in the end-of-year show. She hoped the Committee would not ask for the tutor's name, and added that Sir William Richmond (one of the College Visitors) had told her when he went round the College that he liked her work and considered she should get a scholarship. She also knew that her fellow students were of the same opinion. Great stress was laid on this point; for Sylvia, the reason why she was not awarded a scholarship was not her suffragette activities, but her neglect of the history of art course.

The committee questioned whether some of the books studied in the literary classes helped the intending teachers. The main influence seems to have been on the subject-matter of the student's paintings, and even a series of compositions had been set by the literature lecturer.

Sylvia also stated that the French classes were considered by those who were French conversationalists 'exceedingly bad' and this comment also applied to the Italian. Although it was important for students who were to travel to speak languages this was not the main teaching purpose of the College. She emphasised to the committee that lectures by specialists on anatomy, styles of architecture, and on the different processes and media used in art would be of real use, and that there were no specialist lecturers during her time at the College. This was seen as a lost opportunity, and indeed some of the students (including Sylvia) went to study at Chelsea Polytechnic from 7 till 9 in the evenings. Here they listened to lectures on life drawing and acquired good technical skills, at an institution where the teachers could really teach.

Austin Spare suggested that lectures on chemistry and colours would have been of use to the majority of students, and John Currie pointed out that at the Slade School criticisms by the opinions of the teachers was respected, notably Professors Tonks and Brown, as they were artists themselves. But the Committee had been informed in previous evidence given by Professor Brown that there was difficulty in getting students to attend lectures. Sylvia pointed out that it depended on the temperament of the student, and Spare suggested that painting students were glad of a break from their studio work.

This discussion led to the third point on the memorandum, that the evening life classes were of no practical value. Anatomy lectures were given as part of the evening drawing classes by a Mr Hayward. To many students it seemed that he had no understanding of art, and his lectures were of no use to the students, being highly anatomical, for example demonstrating particular muscles. During Sylvia's time at the College the lectures were held from 5 p.m. till 7 p.m. but were changed to 4 p.m. till 6 p.m. According to Sylvia 'We got no instruction as to the building up of a figure, and what real good drawing is I never learnt at the College; but I have learnt it since. Therefore, the training I had was of very little value to me.'[16] As all the 200 students of the College attended, the room was both overcrowded and stuffy. Haywood was in sole charge, but was assisted by trainee teachers who would teach on two evenings and draw on the other three evenings. Occasionally the Principal, Augustus Spencer, would call into the classes. The students commented that it was impossible for one person to teach so many students from all the schools in the College, and the most the lecturer could do was to walk round and make comments, with no time for detailed criticism. Cockerell was greatly surprised to discover that all the students attended with only one member of staff in charge.

The fourth point on the student memorandum was the lack of instruction in illustration techniques which would enable students to gain employment after leaving college. Sylvia agreed there was a need for lectures on techniques, but her complaint was about the quality of the teaching. Spare noted that most of his work since leaving college had been in black and white drawing, though this skill was not taught at the College. It was pointed out that there was an etching school, but the students replied that the etching class was always full (as the Professor of Etching, Frank Short, was highly respected), and that printmaking was a very different technique from drawing. Sylvia noted that the vast majority of students who did not enter teaching became illustrators, and therefore a knowledge of commercial reprographic techniques was of importance. Absence of this seemed contrary to the aim of the Royal College of Art which had been 'founded to produce industrial artists'.

As a National Scholar she had a right to attend the craft classes available in etching and embroidery, but they were full, and the subjects were only taught on Saturday mornings or one evening a week. Halsey Ricardo of the committee agreed that the craft classes were inadequate, but asserted that the need was for better accommodation so that there was room for the students to attend the classes. Also the committee knew of no demand for any special topic, though Sylvia emphasised the need for craft classes in general:

The object of the College, as I think you agreed in the beginning, is to train industrial artists, people who do things not so much for our manufacturers but in other directions. I think the courses in the College ought to offer a wide field for people who want to earn their own living, and after all, that is the trouble that artists have; they cannot earn their living easily, and there ought to be more opportunities for students who want to take up crafts ... I think students who are going to be craftsmen should have, in the last year of their course an opportunity of giving time to the necessary subjects. It is most necessary where they are going to earn their living. You cannot earn your living by painting pictures unless you are very clever; and some people have an aptitude for crafts. The style of the College is a big decorative style so far as it has any merit at all.[17]

Sylvia strongly emphasized the need for increased craft teaching to enable students to earn a living, especially with regard to the female students:

> the trouble is that when you leave College you have a certain amount of knowledge but you are not very expert in any direction, and you have not enough technical knowledge to go and offer yourself as an expert in anything. Assuming that students drift off into other kinds of employment, they are in a difficulty. Of course if they take up teaching they do not need all that expert knowledge for that. They will have art masters in the school, so it is a very distressing outlook for women who desire to go in for being teachers; and besides the market is overcrowded already.[18]

It should be remembered that Full Associateship Diploma of the Royal College of Art qualified graduates to hold the post of headmaster or headmistress. However, at this time only unmarried women could hold a teaching post and preference was given to male candidates as they were expected to be supporting a family.

The committee understood that a great many of the College's students were intending to become teachers, and John Currie in his evidence considered that all the students had been encouraged to enter teaching. Yet the inquiry had been told that the National Scholar students, who often came from industry, might be expected to return to practise some 'art industry' and that a shorter time away from industry would be beneficial. Indeed, complaints had been received that the National Scholars were diverted at the College into teaching because they were kept too long with scholarships. Sylvia pointed out that a shorter time spent at the College would have no effect as often such students stayed in London and became teachers because they wanted something better than their previous career. Sylvia was then asked why a teacher was better than a producer and replied:

> I think a producer is better than a teacher if the producer is a good producer. I think the opportunities for being a producer in this country, however skilled one may be, are not great. Most of the National Scholars have been in factory work, as for instance, Mr Currie, who was in the Potteries.[19]

John Currie pointed out that of those students who came from the Potteries he knew of only one who had returned. Sylvia emphasised that students returned to industry wanting to be producers, but they went into teaching because it was the only work they could get. This illustrates one of the continuing problems which faced the Board of Education; that there was a need to improve standards of design within industry, but industry was not willing to employ designers trained externally when the training was not, or perceived as not, relevant.

The fifth point of the discussion was the manner in which the recommendations for scholarships and diplomas were awarded. The students did not have confidence in the way the scholarships were given, considering that the system was entirely unjust and had no relation to the artistic capabilities of the students. None of the three students giving evidence was given a further award to enable them to complete their course at the College, which meant that their complaint could be seen as personal. But they were clear in explaining their own situations and how their cases were representative. John Currie did not complete his Associateship at the College because he was not given a scholarship for a further year, probably because he also had a prize from the British Institution which the Principal Spencer might have considered could be used to fund a further year at the College. He had not left on good terms with the Principal and therefore was unable to have any written recommendation from Spencer. Austin Spare did not receive a Diploma from the College, although Spencer had promised him one after only six months at the College, and Sylvia was not awarded a scholarship for a further year in order to get her Diploma. Sylvia commented that the recommendations for scholarships were in the hands of the Principal, who was not a competent judge:

> Anyone who had been to the College knows that the scholarships are not given so much on the question of merit, but on the question of conduct and general friendship with the principal. For instance there was one student who was told that she would have her Junior Royal College of Art Scholarship given to her because she had written a good paper in the literature class . . . . We are told that conduct is to have something to do with it. Now that is a very vague term and I do not think anybody misconducts themselves there. Of course misconduct is one thing, but I do not think that if

one arrives a minute late or forgets to put one's name down it ought to act against one's Scholarship.[20]

It was thought that even the best-behaved students did not get scholarships. Currie commented that the College did not seem to aim to teach but make the student more gentlemanly: 'Even in the life classes I have had keen exhortations to become more gentlemenly, and talk of that description is extremely depressing.'[21]

During Sylvia's time at the College, she considered probably the best painting student was a Miss Browning, who did not receive any kind of award. Sylvia also referred to the best woman student during her time having been trained previously at the Royal Academy school, attending the Royal College of Art solely to maintain her work. If this student is one and the same it would explain why an award was not made, the student already having had an extensive art education.

Students who studied in the Design School were considered to have a better opportunity to win a scholarship, and even women students in design were given awards for work in craft subjects such as embroidery, even when they were not particularly competent. Sylvia did not consider this fair, especially as women in the Painting School found it very difficult to gain scholarships. The one women student in the Painting School who did obtain an award during Sylvia's time at the college was training for teaching:

> and was on exceptional terms with the Principal. By this, I am not of course suggesting anything objectionable; she was frequently seeing him, and was a member of the Christian Union and that kind of thing. I do not think the Principal intends to be unjust, but I think that what guides him in what he does, is the student's character, and that he is not competent to judge who should have the awards. In my opinion, if the visitors, like Sir William Richmond, were allowed to give scholarships, it would be a much fairer way of doing it.[22]

It was apparent that scholarships at the College were given by the Principal, generally after discussion with the Professor of the School, and that the College Visitors came to judge the work only with regard to diplomas and travelling scholarships. The emphasis on the opinion of the Principal was considered by the students as unfair, especially when compared to institutions such as the Manchester

Muncipal School of Art, where each teacher had a vote in the award-ing of prizes.

Sylvia was aware that the group was laying itself open to criticism, and added that she was exceedingly sorry that there was not a successful student giving evidence. But it was a delicate issue, for as the Chairman of the inquiry stated:

It is one thing to say that the scholarships are not awarded on quite the considerations which you think ought to be taken into account, and it is quite another thing to say that in those circumstances the awards are not fairly made.[23]

It was difficult for Sylvia to give details, but she considered there were several cases where students felt they had a grievance, which would have been obviated if the Students' Union had been able to make complaints to the Board of Education. Her words reflect not so much a feeling of injustice for women students, as of the need for justice and equality:

The feeling that there is injustice is rife in the School, and I do not think it would be so if they felt they could appeal to the Board . . . . It seems unkind to mention the names of students but I know of one student, who everyone thought was not entitled to a scholar-ship, and she was given a Royal College of Art Scholarship while her local scholarship was still running.[24]

In all, it was felt that the scholarships should be granted by two or three independent judges and not by one person. Sir Kenneth Anderson asked if the injustice was unconscious? Sylvia responded that the students did not consider the diplomas to be given on the right grounds. John Currie added that when he was working with Sir William Richmond, he was told about the awarding of the trav-elling scholarship to one Lancelot Crane. Richmond considered this student's work to be the best, but he had great difficulty in getting the Principal to agree, as the latter wanted to give the award to a student named Woolway. (Sylvia noted that for the Diploma show the following year Woolway was allowed to put up two years' work, a thing that other students were not permitted to do.)

John Currie had learnt from students then at the College that the problem still continued. He pointed out that the National Exhibition scholarship was for three years, and was good because it allowed students to get their diplomas. Sylvia added that it would be better if the scholarships were awarded for the whole of the Diploma course, even if fewer scholarships had to be given. She suggested an award for five years, or a scholarship for the final three years, which would end the students' constant anxiety as to what they were to do if their scholarships were not continued.

The students had been told that there was no right of appeal to the Board of Education. When Sylvia was at the College there was a deputation, not started by her, to ask that the students should be allowed to make representations to the Board. They were told by the Secretary to the Board that they had the right to make a representation if the matter dealt only with social affairs and not with the curriculum. Even then students were told that they had to apply though the Principal, which would have been difficult if it was on an issue to which he did not agree, and also since the students had heard it said that he did not pass on requests. Sylvia spoke on this point:

> I went to the College to work; I did not go there to mix up with these things; but I do know that when there were certain things about which the students wanted to appeal, they were definitely told that the recommendations would not be passed on because the Principal did not agree with them. If evidence is wanted, the Secretary of the Students' Union would have to speak with regard to it because it was she who was told, and not I. [25]

Sylvia commented that the Students' Union was useless apart from social functions. Students joined on a voluntary basis, therefore it was not representative.

Halsey Ricardo stated that it was a pity that there was not a student in the deputation who had gone through the regular course, to which Sylvia agreed, stating that she felt she should have been given more time to write round and get students to come. Ricardo replied: 'You are not quite normal students, are you?' Sylvia responded:

> I do not think we are abnormal; I was there two years. I agree it is a pity that you have no others here, but there are three reasons which are keeping people away. One is that there has not been much time in which to attempt to get any students.

Currie joined in: 'Those students who hold teaching positions in London do not think it is in their interest to come, and a great many are in the provinces and cannot come.' Sylvia continued: 'We know one who would have come this morning except that he thought it might endanger his position. Of course we are exceptionally placed in that regard.'

This line of discussion seems to have been halted by the chairman asking what they had to say on the last point of their memorandum, the need for change at the College. Sylvia said:

> One feels in criticising these people and giving names, that one is liable to be unkind to the individuals. Students when they are promoted to the Upper School are not able to work there because there is no room. I do not know whether that remark applies to the men students.[26]

Certainly the accommodation for the women students was limited, notably in the Painting School, where the women could only attend the life class if there was room for them. The chairman of the committee noted that the Principal himself had made a complaint regarding the overcrowding, and indeed in the committee's report the main recommendation was regarding the need for better accommodation. The Painting School was criticised for the teaching bias towards mural and decorative work, but the Royal Academy was seen as the place to study fine art, and that institution was not open to Board of Education scholarship holders. There were capable teachers: Sylvia named Mr Alston, the assistant in the Painting School, though Currie only remembered Professor Moira seeing him twice during his eighteen months at the College. The chairman was surprised as he thought Moira did all the teaching in the Upper School. It was clear the students were discontented, and although the teaching methods might have been satisfactory for those students entering teaching as a career, for the rest the administration was not in sympathy towards talent. Currie pointed out that few students were able to live in London without working, and a little teaching helped many survive, especially as the press only used known illustrators.

The chairman then asked 'Do you think you have brought out all the points which you wished to make?' and Currie answered: 'I think we have covered all the ground.' Then Mr Cockerell broke in to ask about the need for student hostels. Sylvia answered by explaining that she had just returned from America where there was a system of college halls or recommended cheap and comfortable lodgings. The students preferred the halls. These formed part of the college, and the students had to obey the rules. Such a hall of residence would be very welcome for students at the College. She explained:

> At the Royal College of Art, I know that a great many students do not eat enough. It is not very easy to live on the little money that they get, and they do not look after themselves properly in many instances.[27]

She explained to the Committee that if a student was ill in lodgings there was no machinery by which enquiries would be made as to what had happened, and a letter would have to be sent to the College. Also there was no system of recommended lodgings, although Sylvia remembered the Matron recommending a few people on a casual basis. A proper College hostel would be more comfortable and would reduce illness among the students, often caused through not having enough to eat. Also ill health was in part due to poor ventilation. She concluded:

> There is a general depressing feeling in the College. I never was in a place where one felt that so keenly. The students are very miserable about their future . . . . I think the depression is keener in the Painting School.[28]

Cockerell noted that there had been rather different evidence about the Design School and about the Sculpture School. Sylvia pointed out that the Professor of Sculpture, Lanteri, and his assistant, Mr Clements, were very popular, with a building that was better as it was airier and lighter. Mr Ricardo was surprised, for the Sculpture Schools was housed in tin sheds, which would have been expected to be worse than the Victoria and Albert Museum building used by the Painting School. Sylvia commented: 'I was never so tired as I was at Kensington. By the time the evening class began, one did not want to do any work.' This, she considered, was due to the poor ventilation, as she had worked longer hours before going to the College. She added:

> But there is a great deal of discontent with the executive and a great deal of depression throughout the School. The executive management is unpopular with all the students with whom I ever came into contact. It has passed over our heads now, of course,

and it does not matter to us so there is no reason why we should trouble about it.[29]

The meeting was adjourned. What is clear is that the committee was aware of the need for better accommodation for the College, and that they used the students' evidence to assess the need for hostel accommodation.

In the afternoon sitting, the committee agreed that as the evidence taken in the morning contained some criticism of the Principal and the staff, printed copies of it should be sent to them to give them an opportunity to comment. Notes of comment were received from Professor Pite who was in charge of the course of architecture. He was forthright in denying the students' complaints and considered those on the Principal libellous. Mr George Haywood, who ran the evening classes, noted that his teaching of anatomy was artistic and not surgical, while Mr Beckwith Spencer, who taught history of art, commented that it was impossible for students to take notes in the lecture because the theatre was darkened for the use of a 'magic lantern', so that the students took notes in two groups the following morning. The Wednesday lectures, he noted, were treated from the aesthetic point of view, while those on Thursdays dealt with the historical outline. He ended: 'I have never known a student who, on entering the College could converse in French, nor one who, before coming to the College had any knowledge of Italian'.[30]

Together with these comments, a paper was drawn up by Sedgwick, the committee's secretary. It opens with the comment:

It would be futile to discuss such evidence as that of Miss Pankhurst which is almost all hearsay, or the opinions of students who possess so little knowledge of the work of the College . . .[31]

Sylvia had certainly annoyed the Board, but were the students so out of touch with the working of the College? The rest of Sedgwick's comments seem to refute their claims, but in a very defensive manner:

I would like to make the following observations on the matters of fact.
Firstly, as regards the general charge of injustice in the awarding of Scholarships: recommendations for Scholarships have always been made after a consultation between the Professors and myself.

Students upon entering the College are invariably asked what particular branch of study they desire to specialise in.

There has always been an exemption from the Preliminary Architectural course granted to students who are already qualified.

Students who have drawn from the Life, previous to entering the College, are allowed to join the Life class but if they are not found sufficiently advanced, they are put back to the antique.

All students do not study from the Life on any evening.

The decorative side of Black and White is taught in the School of Design and is further dealt with in the Etching Class.

Miss Harvey-George had visited Italy and was a very keen student of Art History. She had written exceptionally good papers which were far ahead of those of any other student in the College, and as there was some difficulty in deciding whether a Scholarship would be given to her or to another student of the Painting School this was allowed to count in her favour. But that she deserved the scholarship on purely artistic grounds is proved by the fact that she is one of the few women students who have taken the Full Diploma.

That Prof. Moira only came to Mr Currie twice in 18 months is of course untrue.

In conclusion I would ask if the evidence of these students is published, that it should be published as it stands without omissions.[32]

Transcripts of the evidence were sent to the witnesses for correction. Austin Spare required no corrections, John Currie returned his proof copy with corrections, and Sylvia Pankhurst sent both corrections and a supplementary letter which she requested to be added to her evidence. Most of her corrections are minor, but she notes that when the Chairman asked for their comments on the need for change at the College the transcript of Sylvia's answer read: 'One feels in criticising these people and giving names, that one is liable to be unkind to the individuals.' The transcript continues saying she went both to Rome and Paris. Sylvia commented in the margin of the transcript:

There is something left out here but not this, for I did not say this. It is not the fact. I want to speak specially for the women students.[33]

Her annotated corrections did not appear in the final printed version held by the Department of Education and Science, and her letter has not been found. Did the Board conveniently forget to add in the students's corrections? Perhaps it did not matter too much as the transcript of the proceedings remained confidential, only the Report being published.

The departmental committee was finally to report that it:

recognised the weight of some of the criticisms made which were supported by other evidence received by them and by their own investigations . . . At the same time they felt that many of the criticisms especially those of a more personal kind were such that it was impossible for the Committee either to investigage them satisfactorily or to arrive at any conclusion about them. They desired, therefore, to be absolved from pursuing these matters any further.[34]

But perhaps the students' evidence did have some effect. That same year the exemption for the course in architecture was reintroduced for qualified students, though whether as a direct result of the Committee's findings is unclear. All students entering the College continued to take one term's architectural study until 1922 when a system was introduced of one day's study each week during a student's first year. This did not change until after reorganisation in 1948.

The literary course declined and in about 1916 the Board of Education cut Beckwith Spencer's pay, advising that he was free to find other work. His brother complained, and in 1918 the post of lecturer was combined with that of part-time registrar, until Spencer finally left in 1923. He was not replaced and the historical content of the lectures on the architecture course was increased. Until 1948 when Robin Darwin arrived as Principal there was no history of art course. The Department of General Studies (Cultural History) was set up in 1958. It is ironic to note that as a student the painter David Hockney, like Sylvia Pankhurst, clashed with the College authorities over the emphasis on lectures which took him away from his painting, and only gained his degree after much discussion concerning his failure to fulfil the requirements of the subsidiary study.[35] The evening life classes, and Saturday etching and craft classes also continued until after the Second World War, and the School of Graphic Design eventually evolved out of a School of Typography and Design for publicity set up in 1948, finally enabling the College to produce designers aware of commercial needs. The system for the recommendation of awards continued, but the emphasis on the personal opinion of the Principal shifted to that of the Professor of each School in the College.

Augustus Spencer as Principal might, on his appointment to the post in 1901, have been perceived as someone who could introduce educational reform, but he was handicapped by the demands of the Board of Education and a severe lack of funding from the Treasury. Also, although an educationalist, he appeared to be out of touch with the rapid growth of 'industrial art'. He was succeeded in 1920 by William Rothenstein who encouraged new young artists and designers to teach at the College, but who faced the same restrictions of finance and government intervention as Spencer. The College finally received its Royal Charter as a wholly postgraduate university in 1967.

The evidence concerning the cramped accommodation shocked at least one member of the committee, and the final Report emphasised the urgent need for a new building in which to house the College. Sadly this did not come about, despite lengthy discussions over site and building design, due to the outbreak of the First World War. The College continued to use a variety of buildings, and although a special block was constructed in the 1960s the problem of inadequate accommodation continued. Even the Sculpture School buildings which Sylvia and her fellow students considered light and airy, but which the departmental committee considered temporary, remained in use until the late 1980s.

For Sylvia, giving evidence to the committee indicates her strong affinity with Art. At one point in the proceedings the chairman asked her: 'What is a knowledge of art, in your opinion?' She replied: 'To draw and paint.' [36] Although she entered the College with the aim of becoming a full-time artist, the work of the WSPU altered her career focus. If she had attended the history of art lectures she might have gained a scholarship which would have enabled her to take her full Diploma of Associateship. But her outspoken attitude had not benefited her career, and no doubt Spencer was annoyed that questions about the College were asked in the House of Commons.

Sylvia remained highly concerned with art throughout her life, and continued to use her knowledge and skills in a practical manner. In 1914 she opened a toy factory at the rear of the Women's Hall on Old Ford Road, London. Sylvia was helped in the design of the toys by an old friend from the College. Walter Crane donated prints of his drawings for children's books and ideas for jigsaw puzzles to the factory, which produced wooden toys and stuffed dolls which were sold to Selfridges and elsewhere. The factory was later made into a co-operative.

As for Sylvia's own work her early period reflects a study of historical styles, with her watercolours of Venice showing a more modern concern for colour, used in blocks and with bold brushwork. Her skills are evident in the confident and striking portraits of Keir Hardie. Although she devoted her life to politics, a continued concern and love for art is apparent, and her experiences at the Royal College of Art encouraged an independence of spirit.

NOTES

1. The Manchester Art Museum was furnished by the designers W.A. Benson and William Morris who fitted out a sitting room and bedroom, whose designs were considered suitable for copying by ordinary workers. This had been instituted by a wealthy Mancunian, Thomas Horsfall, whose idea was, in part, to dissuade working people from buying furniture of an unsuitable type, and to encourage them to make their own. This ethic brought him into conflict with the furniture trade, which criticised the quality of Morris's furniture in their journal. See T. Horsfall, *Suggestions for a Guide Book to Life* (Manchester: J. Heywood, 1886).
2. Liberty's was opened in 1875 by Arthur Lasenby Liberty (1843–1917). The shop specialised in Japanese objects which came into vogue following the showing of Japanese ware at the 1862 Exhibition in London. Japan had only recently been opened to the West, and the goods presented a new alternative to Chinese and Indian objects.
3. E. Sylvia Pankhurst, *The Suffragette Movement* (London: Virago, London 1977) p.105.
4. Walter Crane had been closely associated with the Manchester Municipal School of Art since 1883, when he had been made a tentative offer of the headmastership. In 1888 he was the guest speaker at the January prize-giving though it was not until September 1893 that he was appointed visiting director, a post he held until July 1896. He was paid £600 per annum for teaching one week in every month. This encouraged the development of design teaching at the school. In 1896 he was briefly Art Director of Reading University College, and in 1898–9 became the Principal at the Royal College of Art for one year. He designed textiles and wallpaper and was well respected as an illustrator. See W. Crane, *An Artist's Reminiscences* (London, 1907), and D. Jeremiah, *A Hundred Years and More* (Manchester Polytechnic, 1980).
5. This was an award instituted in 1848. See Jeremiah, op. cit p.36

6. The 1911 Report noted that for the year 1908–9 62 per cent were be-
    tween twenty and twenty-five years of age, 18 per cent over twenty-five
    years and 20 per cent were under twenty years of age. *The Departmental
    Committee on the Royal College of Art: 1911 Report* (London:
    H M S O, 1911) p.13.
7. Augustus Spencer was appointed in 1901 by the Board of Education,
    having already successfully reorganised the teaching of art in Leicester-
    shire, and the Board hoped for similar reforms in London. But his role
    was, however, one of administrator rather than teacher, involved in
    forming good relationships with schools, and manufacturers, and as-
    sisting students in obtaining employment at the end of their course. He
    also acted as Master of Method (teacher training) for those students
    who were intending to become teachers.
8. Richard Pankhurst, *Sylvia Pankhurst: Artist and Crusader* (London:
    Paddington Press, 1979) p.48
9. S. Pankhurst, op. cit., p.197.
10. The deputation was headed by John Currie (c. 1884–1915). Born at
    Newcastle-under-Lyme, he won a National Scholarship and a British
    Institution Scholarship which enabled him to study at the Royal College
    of Art in 1904–6. On leaving the College he obtained a post at Bristol
    School of Art, which he held for about eighteen months. At the same
    time he appears to have been appointed as an Occasional Inspector
    under the Department of Agriculture and Technical Instruction (Ire-
    land), but resigned in late 1909. He returned to London and studied
    part-time at the Slade, and became friendly with Mark Gertler and
    Augustus John. Currie tried to obtain a teaching post, and informed the
    Board that he could not attend an interview on one date due to teaching
    at Hoxton. He also worked as a portrait painter and commercial illus-
    trator. In 1911 he left his wife after four years of marriage, and in 1912
    was working in Newlyn. He began a relationship with a Miss Dolly
    Henry and they lived in Hampstead until October 1914 when he fatally
    shot her and himself. The Board of Education Papers noted 'He is an
    Irishman'.
11. Public Records Office : ED24/87, Letter to the Secretary of the Depart-
    mental Committee on the Royal College of Art, from John S. Currie 5th
    May 1911.
12. *The Departmental Committee on the Royal College of Art : 1911*, Proceedings
    of the Thirteenth Day, p. 2.
13. Ibid. p.5.
14. Ibid. p.6.
15. Ibid. p.6.
16. Ibid. p.9.
17. Ibid. p.11
18. Ibid. p.12.
19. Ibid. p.17.
20. Ibid. p.13. Sylvia could not remember the name at this time but later
    gave it as Miss Harvey-George.
21. Ibid. p.6.
22. Ibid. p.14

23. Ibid. p.15.
24. Ibid. p.15.
25. Ibid. p.18.
26. Ibid. p.19.
27. Ibid. p.19
28. Ibid. p.20.
29. Ibid. p.21.
30. Public Records Office : ED 24/86, Beckwith A. Spencer. Comments of College staff on the evidence of Mr Currie, Mr Spare and Miss Pankhurst.
31. Public Records Office : ED24/86, Sedgwick, Secretary to the Departmental Committee.
32. Ibid.
33. Public Records Office : ED24/87, 13 June, 1911.
34. *Final Report of the Departmental Committee on the Royal College of Art 1911* (London: H M S O, 1911).
35. C. Frayling, *The Royal College of Art* (London: Barrie and Jenkins, 1987) p.162.
36. *The Departmental Committee on the Royal College of Art : 1911*, Proceedings of the Thirteenth Day, p.8.

2

Sylvia Pankhurst as an Artist

JACKIE DUCKWORTH

As a child, Sylvia's first ambition was to become an artist. But for many other concerns in her life, she might have achieved this aim. As it was, she created her last drawings and designs at the age of twenty-nine; still in the infancy of her artistic career. In this short time she gave much as an artist and as a suffragette; wherever possible as both.

The artworks she produced are important not only for their competence – she evidently had skill as a draughtswoman and in portraying the warmth of her characters – but also for her choice of subject. Who she drew, what she drew, and where she drew were part of the significance of her work. The evidence shows that in her periods of practice as an artist she was prolific.[1] A number of drawings, paintings and sketchbooks still exist, together with a few photographs of her decorations and examples of postcards and other graphics. It is probable that there are many other paintings which have been lost or have not yet come to light. For example, she mentions selling paintings of Venice whilst working at her mother's shop in Manchester. This correlates with the fact that she spent almost a year in the Italian city, painting at a vigorous pace.

It is difficult to determine exactly how or why she became an artist. With both her parents very active outside the family circle, it is possible that loneliness, despite her sisters and brother, led to a devotion to painting and drawing. Her father enjoyed collecting pictures and her mother opened a shop selling textiles and objects to beautify the domestic interior. She grew up in an aesthetically-aware environment.

Sylvia would sometimes accompany her father to public meetings at which he was to speak. Later she reflected on this experience in the context of the decisions which had mainly influenced her life:

> The first, early made when I was still a young child, was to work as an artist in the service of popular movements, decorating halls, producing banners, cartoons, designs etc – whatever might serve to beautify and inspire the movements of the masses, the drab ugliness of which smote my soul with pity.[2]

In this respect it is important to be aware of the work Sylvia may have seen at this impressionable age. The work of the Arts and Crafts movement was prevalent in her home environment, and especially the work of Walter Crane, who is recognised as being chiefly responsible for revitalising the 'ideal' woman of Pre-Raphaelite imagery, adapting her to the iconography of socialism. This may have been an influence on Sylvia in the series of icons she later produced for the suffragette cause.

Around the time Sylvia was growing up, straitlaced Victorian moral value painting began to soften, giving way to the aesthetic values of the Edwardian years. A vogue for sentimental, anecdotal and problem pictures also developed. Whistler was influential at this time, and some of the French Impressionists had exhibited their work. The New English Art Club was formed in 1886 to exhibit more progressive works and British Impressionists in opposition to the complacent Royal Academy. However, in 1886 there was also a retrospective of the work of John Millais which fired a renewed interest in the revival of medievalism and the Pre-Raphaelites. The influence this style had on Sylvia is quite obvious in her designs for graphics, illuminated addresses, calendars and banners.

It is also important to place in perspective her ambition as a woman to be an artist. An article on 'Woman as Painters' in the London arts magazine, *The Dome* (April-July 1899), reported that the Society of Women Artists had just held its forty-fifth exhibition. The author of the article, C. J. Holmes, mentioned a number of now-familiar names of women artists. Even before 1900 large numbers of women trained and attempted careers as artists. Since the first half of the nineteenth century it had become an acceptable occupation for women and there were opportunities for women all over Europe, if, of course, they could afford to buy the time of master painters.

Many of these women did not place the importance of their work above marriage. In 1900 an elaborately-illustrated book on *Women*

Painters of the World from 1413 to the Present Day was published, which must have been available to Sylvia at the Royal College of Art. The editor, Walter C. Sparrow, had one answer to the criticism that women's painting was inferior to that of men's. 'Why compare the differing genius of woman and man!'

So it was not particularly unusual to practise as a woman artist. However, to achieve any level of success or recognition was a challenge equal to winning 'Votes for Women'. Sylvia's struggle for equality and fairness at the Royal College of Art has already been discussed in this book. Later she reflected this experience and her early career in the light of an awareness of social injustices which became particularly important to her in her late twenties and thirties.

> . . . whether it was worth while to fight one's individual struggle, as fight one must, and that strenously, to make one's way as an artist, to bring out of oneself the best possible, to induce the world to accept one's creations, and give one in return one's daily bread, when all the time the great social struggles to better the world for humanity demanded other service.[3]

But these choices still lay ahead of the young Sylvia. She had drawn regularly from an early age. She had illustrated the family journal and was complimented on the drawings she made at school. While the family was living in rural Cheshire, she spent time painting landscapes in the fields. The Pankhursts then returned to an urban environment, Victoria Park in Manchester, where Sylvia was given private painting lessons by Elias Bancroft, an eminent Manchester painter of the period. She was of course delighted by this opportunity and by what she was learning. Later she wrote:

> Charcoal, Whatman's drawing paper, stamps and rubbers of squeezed bread, came to my knowledge as a revelation. I felt a sense of power in seeing the founded shapes stand forth from my blank paper, and the rich chiaroscuro which charcoal could produce. I revelled in still life groups, and at home, arranging jars, bowls, and foilage to my own fancy, attempted to reproduce them in water-colours.[4]

During her first year at the Manchester School of Art her attendance was sporadic and she suffered from headaches, neuralgia and depression. But she did manage to complete a design for an illuminated address to be given to the Prince of Wales, the future George V. She attended half-time during her second year, working the other half at her mother's shop, newly opened at 60–62 Nelson Street, Manchester. It traded under the same name as the shop in London, Emerson & Co. Sylvia returned to full-time education for her third year: the family finances had been reduced by the loss of her father and only the Lady Whitworth Scholarship she was awarded enabled her to complete the course. Studying under Walter Crane, she won medals for Historic Ornament, Anatomy, Design and Plant Drawing. She was also awarded the Primrose Silver Medal for design, given to the best female student, and a National Silver Medal for designs in mosaic panels intended for a fountain.

But her most significant achievement was to be awarded the Proctor Travelling Scholarship, which enabled a graduating student to travel and study for a period of three months. She chose to study mosaics in Venice. She also intended to spend some time in Florence to study the frescoes, but found that there was not enough time to do both. She wrote poetically about her time in Venice.

A wondrous city of fairest carving, reflected in gleaming waters swirled to new patterning by every passing gondola. Venice in the brief, violet twilight; Venice in the mournful loveliness of pale marble palaces, rising in the velvet darkness of the night: the promised land of my sad young heart, craving for beauty, fleeing from the sorrowful ugliness of factory-ridden Lancashire, and the dull, aching poverty of its slums; Venice, O City of dreaming magic![5]

She extended her stay for six months, until the spring of 1903, when she received a letter from her sister asking her to return home to help in the shop while Christabel studied for her law exams.

My decision to return to Manchester was made without any hesitation. I was clearly aware that I was leaving a life of security, where I was happy and beloved, and which attracted me above all because therein I might study and improve in the art which was very precious to me . . . .

Soon after my return to Manchester I realised that so far as my mother's business was concerned my presence was not required. I competed for a scholarship to the Royal College of Art in London and won it.[6]

There are several pictures still in existence dating from her time in Venice. In *The Suffragette Movement* she mentions selling them at her mother's shop alongside designs for cotton print fabrics. Of the paintings still extant, there is one oil on canvas whilst the rest are a combination of gouache, watercolour, and coloured ink on paper. Two are studies of mosaics in St Mark's (11 ins by 19 ins approx.). Another is a copy of Carpaccio's *Triumph of St George* (10 ins by 9 ins).

Most of Sylvia's paintings were on a very small scale by today's standards, but this was dictated by the fact that she was travelling and her work needed to be easily portable. The three studies already mentioned were the standard fare of the art student as apprentice, learning the construction of traditional design and the use of pictorial space by studying and copying the Old Masters.

A further series of works concentrate on the everyday life of Venice and illustrate vegetable sellers and market stalls. The figures are drawn in pencil and delicately coloured in watercolour. The brushwork is controlled and the pictures lack depth; white paper frequently shows through and disjoints the image. The oil painting *A View of a canal in Venice* (14 ins by 10 ins) is a detailed perspective view of one of the canals receding into the distance and around a bend. The tall buildings of Venice's canalside apartments reach up from top to bottom of the sides of the picture. Sylvia appears to have used a very fine brush and the marks are fine and detailed, building up the painting through several sittings. The manner in which she worked seems to have been inhibited by the tiny scale and her style demands to be given more space, larger paper or canvas.

In response to her sister's letter she returned to Manchester and discovered that her mother had secured her a commission (one which gave her only three weeks to the deadline) and had also rented rooms above the shop as a studio for her. When she found she was not needed in the shop she would be able to continue painting.

The commission was exactly the type of work which as a child she had wished to produce, namely the large decorations for the ILP Hall built in memory of her father; a place where political discussion and debate would continue. She had her *Scheme of Decoration* printed onto a card alongside her studio address to promote herself as an artist and designer as well as to use in illustrating her designs. These were made available at the opening of the Hall at which she shared the stage with Walter Crane, giving a speech explaining the designs and the principles of the ornamentation. Her *Scheme* gives an idea of her artistic intentions

As this hall bears the name of a pioneer whose life was given for the ideal and for the future, emblems of the future and the ideal have been chosen with which to decorate it.
The Entrance Hall. The symbols are the peacock's feather, lily & rose, emblems of beauty, purity & love; with the motto: 'England arise!' and the name of the hall.
The Large Hall. Symbols: Roses, love, apple trees, knowledge, doves, peace, corn, plenty, lilies, purity, honesty, honesty, bees, industry, sunflowers and butterflies, hope.
The panels illustrate Shelley's line: 'Hope will make thee young, for Hope and Youth are children of one mother, even love.'[7]

After completing the commission, she returned to her role in the shop and her studio, before embarking on her two-year National Scholarship at the Royal College of Art.

There is little work available from her time at the Royal College, There is a postcard, requested by Keir Hardie, which began life as a design for a poster in support of the Unemployment Bill which he intended to have fly-posted throughout London overnight. The poster was never printed but the image joined the powerful ranks of political postcards. The design has the feel of a bold woodcut and a sense of realism, with the figures standing out of the picture holding high a placard pronouncing 'Workless and Hungry. Vote for the Bill'. The figures are thickset and dressed in workclothes. Strong in composition, it may have been an image remembered from her childhood days spent at rallies with her father. A man in the forefront wears a white shirt and brown trousers; a woman has on a red shawl and a white apron. Behind, a crowd is milling about against an orange and blue background.

Another ink drawing 'Feed My Lambs', produced as a postcard, reverts to a more whimsical style. It shows a protective female figure, her arm round a child, with the other hand lifting a drinking bowl to its mouth.

She also made two portraits of Keir Hardie during her time at the RCA. Both of these are now in the collection archives of the National Portrait Gallery in London. One is a drawing on buff-coloured Ingres Paper (22 $\frac{1}{4}$ ins by 16 $\frac{3}{4}$ ins) in red, white and black chalk. It has been drawn with a quick and lively hand; confident lines emphasise the shape and character of the face. Broad and directional marks sculpture and give depth to the drawing and she has used some of her earlier techniques of smudging and blending. The second picture is a watercolour, and much smaller (14 $^7/_8$ ins by 10 $^1/_2$ ins). It portrays Keir Hardie with a pipe in his mouth. She has used a fine brush and delicate strokes to define this head and shoulder portrait. The positioning of the character on the page and well-chosen lines indicate the whole of the seated body which the onlooker's eye creates. The head and face is painted in fine detail.

The Women's Social and Political Union absorbed some of Sylvia's time, not only in lobbying and administrative duties, but also in creating artwork and banners for the cause. In the early stages of the campaign, simple reproduction of the motto in large numbers was required and she found herself painting the phrase 'Votes for Women' and 'Will the Liberal Government give Women the Vote?' hundreds of times during her Christmas vacation in 1905.

When her two-year scholarship came to an end, she had given little thought to how she might make a living and to what she would do next. Much later, in *Myself When Young*, a compilation of autobiographies by famous women published in 1938, she explained her dilemma.

With my eager desire to work for the Golden Age, I could not be satisfied to win an existence by commercial art, and the deterrent thought at times stirred mockingly in my brain that who would live by the fine arts must do so at the pleasure of the rich, not in the cause of the People and the Poor.[8]

It was usual for students to complete a five-year diploma, and her tutors in the painting school advised her to apply. But it seems that her health was not good at this point. With this, and with the WSPU making increasing demands of her, she decided not to extend her studies. She found two unfurnished rooms in Cheyne Walk, and attempted to establish herself as a freelance artist and writer. This was, of course, not easy, and made even less so because her name was already associated with the suffragette movement. Newspaper editors assumed she would be writing about the 'Votes for Women' issue, and would not expect a fee. Keir Hardie gave her two commissions for illuminated addresses, and she found a slot in the *Westminster Review* writing on 'Women's Affairs' under the pen-name 'Ignota'.

She always remained conscious of the debate within her on how to spend her life.

the idea of giving up the artist's life, surrendering the study of colour and form, laying aside the beloved pigments and brushes, to wear out one's life on the platform and the chair at the street corner was a prospect too tragically grey and barren to endure.[9]

She was to become totally involved with the WSPU as an artist, finding a balance between what she believed in and the art which she wanted to create. She was asked to design the WSPU membership card, which she did in a similar style to the 'Workless and Hungry' poster designed for Keir Hardie. The image shows a group of women marching behind the leader carrying a banner declaring 'Votes, Votes, Votes' and coloured in browns and blues. The figures are strong and sturdy. Most of them wear clogs and carry children, pails of water, or baskets; a definitive portrayal of working-class women. It is perhaps ironical that as the WSPU progressed this group of women were not of particular interest to it.

Sylvia experienced her first imprisonment at the end of October 1906. The first eight days were spent as as 'Class Three' which allowed her access to drawing materials, paper, pens, ink and pencils. The sketches she then made were her first real works documenting actual events. After her release on 6 November, she held press interviews, and provided journalists with copies of her drawings. A series of four were redrawn by an engraver and published in the *Pall Mall Gazette*, January-June 1907.

The first picture, *Ready for Supper*, shows a woman in prison dress seated at a table with a large mug and bread. The background is a bare brick wall and small window, half barred, with the letter 'B' monogrammed onto it. *Scrubbing the Bed* shows a figure, with her back to the onlooker, on her knees scrubbing at a wooden bench or platform. *Dinner* portrays two prisoners, dressed in prison uniform – white bonnet and apron with black arrows and a dark dress with white arrows – carrying a large tray of meal containers between them. They seem to be struggling under its weight. In *The Bread Basket*, a solitary figure is holding a large rectangular tray of rolls. Her head is downcast.

Her next commission was for W.T. Stead, the celebrated campaigning journalist and one-time editor of the *Pall Mall Gazette*, who asked her to produce a poster. She began a work illustrating Broadicea riding into battle in a chariot, but another spell in prison interrupted its completion. This time she spent three weeks in Holloway, again producing drawings whenever possible. On her release she resumed the commission, but the brief had changed and Stead now requested black and white drawings for a penny pamphlet. There was a misunderstanding and the project was cancelled.

It was at this point, in the early summer 1907, that Sylvia created her most important works, both visual and literary. She began a series on working women, intending to publish a book entitled *Women's Trades*. This did not come to fruition, but a full-page article, illustrated by one of her paintings, appeared in *Votes For Women*, the WSPU newspaper, in August 1911.

This self-set project made it necessary for her to travel from place to place and consequently she was inhibited in what she could carry. Transport and travel were not easy. As in Venice, this dictated that she worked small, and that she worked predominantly in gouache. She also carried with her a small case of clothes and books. Presumably, she was in a state of excitement and filled with enthusiasm and ambition to expand on the freedom to study and draw what she wished, which she had relished in Venice. She recorded these women's lives as a valuable documentation for the future in a style of painting without too much sentimentality or emotion. She painted what she saw without attempting to beautify or romanticise the subjects for public consumption. They are true studies with much attention given to details of surfaces, the type of machinery used, the working environment, and the condition of the workers. She uses a roundness of style and a quality of fine brushwork.

Her first visit was to Cradley Heath, in the Black Country, where she stayed with a local woman who ran a sweet shop. She is probably the subject of the untitled full-length portrait of an old woman. She sits, foot on stool, relaxing by her hearth, reflecting on her long and hard life. It is an acute portrait. The picture shows good composition and a balance of patterned areas and blocks of flat colour. The woman's expression is dignified, and is skilfully painted in several subtle layers. The lace collar is particularly delicate. It is a small picture (12 $^{3}/_{4}$ ins by 20 ins) and the lace, wickerwork chair, and detail on the wrought iron grate is extremely fine and must have been applied with a minute brush. The folds and fullness of the dress have body and depth. Overall, the painting shows dexterity and good manipulation of the brush, as well as an accurate and trained eye. She also shows a willingness to use abstract marks where possible or necessary.

Unfortunately no other illustrations from the Black Country survive. Her interest was primarily in the women involved in making chains and nails, working at the dilapidated and dangerous forges, doing basic and ill-paid labour unprotected and unsupported by the unions.

Never have I seen so hideous a disregard of elementary decencies in housing and sanitation as in that area. Roads were too often but beaten tracks of litter-fouled earth; rubbish heaps abounded; jerry-built hovels crumbled in decay. The country was utterly blighted; there were none of the usual amenities of town life, only its grosser ugliness.[10]

She was summoned to Rutland briefly, to speak and demonstrate, after which she made her way to Leicester and rented a room there. Her next project concentrated on women shoemakers in a small producers' co-operative. She comments in her notes that on witnessing her painting, the women remarked on her skill and patience, which surprised her as she felt their work was equally detailed.

Two paintings from this series remain. One, *A close-up of a woman skiving off the edges* (13 $\frac{1}{2}$ ins by 17 $\frac{3}{8}$ ins), features skilful painting of the skiving machine. The machine appears to be in motion. The head of a woman is confidently positioned to look downwards, but her body seems less well-defined and the fabric unconvincing. The structure of the stool can be seen through her skirts, which may be faulty in terms of painting but shows us how Sylvia tackled that particular problem of placing the figure squarely onto the seat. The lines for the window frames and the edge of the bench have been drawn free-hand and many pencil marks have been applied over painted areas for definition.

Another untitled painting from this period, *Women working at benches* (10 $\frac{3}{4}$ ins by 16 ins), shows the high-ceilinged environment of the factory. She used many layers of fine pale watercolour washes to build up the large glass windows, giving an impression of a light, airy room. However, the blue/greys and grey/ochres give a more realistic cold feel. Vague textures of brickwork show through, indicating that the factory is in a densely built-up area. In some places, she has used a dry brush and gouache to highlight. The women are hard at work, concentrating with their heads bent downwards. The lack of colour conveys the true austerity of this working environment. There are, however, a couple of areas left unclear; a central leg of the table and one of the women workers in the background. Sylvia may have intended to repaint the picture at a later date to a larger format.

From Leicester, she travelled north to Lancashire to her next subject, the 'Pit Brow' girls, and the extremely hard physical work they were employed in. She noted

> their great muscular strength and power of endurance, which they possessed in abundant measure. They worked alongside the men and appeared almost stronger than the latter, splendidly made, lithe and graceful. Their rosy cheeks contrasted strangely with the wan, white faces of their sisters in the neighbouring cotton mills.[11]

Unfortunately, no paintings drawings or sketches are extant from this period. After a short period of suffrage activity in Bury St Edmunds, her next stop was Staffordshire to visit the Potteries. Gaining admission to one of the major firms, she uncovered the terrible and dangerous conditions in which the women worked. Yet again, in the Potteries, the role of the woman worker was subservient to that of men: both in terms of the meagre wages they received and the low type of work they were allowed to do. Again, this was endorsed by both Trade Unions and employers.

Eight drawings from this period remain, making it the largest collection of the series. *In a pot bank: scouring and stamping the maker's name on the biscuit china* (13 ins by 14 ³/₄ ins), shows four women hard at work at a bench, concentrating on mounds of pots requiring attention. The four figures are cleverly arranged, three at the same forward angle, with a fourth perched forwards over a pot to balance the composition. The boards of the workbench create lines which lead perspectively to the back of the picture, providing depth. The figures are sturdy and the folds in their clothing are defined by rubbed white chalk, charcoal and pencil lines.

Sylvia's ability to portray hands in motion seems questionable in this picture. The hands in the foregoing are quite sketchy and blurred. The women's expressions seem to be smiling and animated, as if caught in conversation. In contrast, the untitled picture *A red-headed girl working in a pottery* (10 ⅞ ins by 15 ins), shows a girl sitting in cramped isolation, in a dark picture – possibly done by the light of a late autumn afternoon. She has managed to depict the bleaker side of factory work, reminding us of child labour (particularly for girls), limited access to education, and most of all poverty: the child has bare feet.

The third picture, *In a pot bank, finishing off the edges of the unbaked pots on a whirler* (10 $\frac{1}{2}$ ins by 17 ins), has a lighter atmosphere and colour is present. The work the woman is doing seems relatively skilled. The row of tools hung above her head are clearly identifiable. It is obvious much concentration has been focussed on the detail of this picture; how the light falls on the metal pail, and the metal of the tools. *Old-fashioned pottery, transferring the pattern onto the biscuit* (14 ins by 20 ins), is a well-balanced composition. The problem of depth and the scale of the figures has been well achieved. Another example of Sylvia's difficulty with hand movements can be seen in the young woman working a sponge or rubbing the plate. The soup tureen, exquisitely painted in the foreground, is very lively and glows with its patterned glazed finished in the factory light. In the far left corner of the picture a man stands with his apron on, working some kind of press, but his face looks towards the working women and he seems to be checking their progress. Meanwhile, their expressions seem to be of deep concentration.

Dipping and Drying on the Mangle (12 $\frac{1}{2}$ ins by 16 $\frac{1}{2}$ ins), shows two figures, rather stiffly drawn, presenting racks of blanks to the glaze. *In the Dipping House, scraping off the glaze* (11 ins by 13 $\frac{1}{2}$ ins) would be the subsequent stage of the process in the previous picture; a lone female stands in a deeply-folded dress, carrying out her repetitive and dangerous task. *In a pot bank: an apprentice thrower and his baller at work* (18 $\frac{1}{2}$ ins by 13 $\frac{1}{2}$ ins) is a lively drawing. Sylvia has used bold chiaroscuro effects to exaggerate the bleak room. The two figures are positioned in such a way as to show the hierarchy between their positions of employment. This occurs again in the painting *An old-fashioned pottery, turning Jasper ware* (13 ins by 18 ins). She has used a very narrow range of muted colours; the whiteness in the paint reflects the clay dust that was prevalent. She has captured the concentrated expression and hunched position of the male worker. The woman appears to be looking to the far distance, whilst working the wheel that drives the lathe. The many surfaces in the room have been well portrayed. There is a definite textural difference between the whitewashed rough walls, the fabric of the clothes, the metal of the machinery and the wood of the bench worktops, which Sylvia achieved by varying the use of her brush.

From Staffordshire, she travelled to Scarborough and the community of Scottish fisherwomen working in the East Coast herring industry. She considered them to be 'beautified by their outdoor life', and remarked on how they chatted, like a shoal of birds. Two gouache and watercolour paintings survive. One, *Scotch fisher lassie cutting herrings* (10 ins by 11 ins), a very small, circular picture, succeeds in portraying a difficult pose with the 'lassie' leaning forward over a crate. Sylvia has expressed the variety of surfaces in a competent manner. It is a dark green-grey picture, but the woman wears a startling bright orange headscarf. Her face is white, her arms look raw and chapped, and in contrast to Sylvia's comments, conditions appear hard. Again, many layers of watercolour and fine brushwork have been applied to build up the picture in a limited palette of reds and greys. The second picture is similar in content and shows two women, this time working over a barrel, one figure facing and the other with her back to the viewer, entitled *Two old folk packing herrings* (7 $\frac{1}{2}$ ins by 11 ins). The darkness of the picture suggests cold and dank conditions.

The next group of women workers she visited were the agricultural workers in Berwickshire. She described them as being neat, well-spoken and dressed in old world peasant costume, in their black hats and pink cotton handkerchief underneath, pinned together under the chin and on the breast. She also noted the kind of work they performed, stacking or stooking the sheafs together in a precise fashion and the piling of corn onto the cart and off again. On wet days they worked in the barns, plaiting straw ropes for thatching, threshing corn and bruising oats.

Four paintings still exist from the studies she made here, one of which she later gave to Haile Selassie's daughter. Of the three other paintings, one (*untitled*: 10 $\frac{1}{2}$ ins by 5 ins) represents the women loading produce onto a cart. It is very small painting and she has adopted a slightly different style; a very loose, almost impressionistic watercolour, with less detail applied. It is an atmospheric picture with moody autumnal skies and the bright pink of the women's scarves stands out boldly. *Berwickshire farmhands threshing* (12 $\frac{1}{2}$ ins by 9 ins), a slightly larger picture, returns to her more structured style. The threshing cart, seen in action, is well portrayed, but the two figures look a little stiff, and again, the pink scarf lifts colour into the picture and lightens the purple of the dress. The third picture, in her more lucid style and colour, illustrates a group of sturdy figures in the hayloft, some with their backs to the picture. The room is dull, as might be expected on a wet day, and they appear to be occupied in plaiting.

To Elsa Gye

On behalf of all women who will win freedom by the bondage which you have endured for their sake, and dignity by the humiliation which you have gladly suffered for the uplifting of our sex, We, the Members of the Women's Social and Political Union, herewith express our deep sense of admiration for your courage in enduring a long period of privation and solitary confinement in prison for the Votes for Women Cause, also our thanks to you for the great service that you have thereby rendered to the Woman's Movement. Inspired by your passion for freedom and right may we and the women who come after us be ever ready to follow your example of self-forgetfulness and self-conquest, ever ready to obey the call of duty and to answer to the appeal of the oppressed.

Signed on behalf of the Women's Social and Political Union.

Emmeline Pankhurst

7. *Illuminated address for WSPU prisoners.*

8. *WSPU membership card.*

The final visit she made was to Glasgow. By day she painted the women at work in a cotton mill near Bridgton and in the evening, she spoke at women's suffrage meetings or wrote about the conditions she found in the factories; about the intolerable heat and claustrophobia. There are two paintings that illustrate these observations: *In a Glasgow cotton mill, mending a pair of fine frames* (11 ins by 17 ins), and *Changing a yarn package* (11 ins by 16 $^3/_4$ ins). The latter picture shows a woman in bare feet and an inappropriately full, gathered skirt, re-threading the machine. In the foreground an elongated perspective presents the full width of the machine and distant walls and windows of the factory. The expression of the subject is rather sad, distant and introverted. She looks away from her work.

The second painting takes a different angle, with three spinning machines in a row, carefully represented. A small grey-haired woman perches on the edge of a wicker basket and looks out of the picture. She is quite pale, her eyes tired. The painting is well finished in great detail and the texture of the baskets has been carefully painted. Sylvia has also managed to convincingly portray the spinning machine in action.

On completing her project, she returned to London and immersed herself in work for the WSPU. She spent several months as an unpaid organiser of meetings, as well as speaking at them. A tradition was evolving in the suffrage movement, following that of the trade unions, of furthering the cause through peaceful but colourful demonstrations. In June 1908, Sylvia observed one such gathering organised by the National Union of Women's Suffrage Societies, the Independent Labour Party, the Women's Liberal Association, and the Fabian Society.

On 21st June, the WSPU held a similar rally, and Sylvia prepared heraldic designs and border decorations for the banners, to be mass-produced by a commercial company. The role of artist for the WSPU embraced designs for Christmas cards, badges, banners and illuminated addresses, the memorabilia being sold through *Votes for Women*. For example, an advertisement dated 10 December 1908 offered a penny Xmas card of a 'pretty design', and on 8 October 1909, a new coloured button 'of a special design in suffragette colours' was available, also for a penny. For some of the design work she would be paid a modest fee, whilst if funds were low, she would not be paid, for as she noted 'the creation of a Michael Angelo would have ranked low in the eyes of the W.S.P.U. members beside a term served in Holloway'.[12]

Sylvia developed at this time her most popular and well-used motif, that of the female angel standing on her toes, and blowing a curved trumpet. There are two variations of the design, one facing left and the other right. They were to become the icon for the WSPU. The motifs adorned the *Votes for Women* binder, were embossed into its hardcover exhibition programmes and illuminated addresses. The left-facing angel holds her trumpet in one arm and behind her wings there is a pole with a flying banner bearing the inscription 'Freedom'. This figure is set within a circular motif, and there is a border with four links of broken chain to the right and left and flowers in the bottom segment. The inner circle and background is a grid of prison bars with the letters WSPU emblazoned across it.

This angel and motif is also found on the suffragette tea service, made by Williamson and Sons in the Bridge Pottery, Longton, about 1910. She is also seen as the centrepiece to the banner of the West Ham Branch of the WSPU, but without the border details. The banner is created from grey-green chintz cotton, with purple and green velvet. The right-facing version can be seen on the cover of the programme for the Women's Exhibition in the Princes Skating Rink, in May 1909, for which Sylvia created the whole decoration, a series of massive banners. Influence for her 'angel' could have stemmed from images she saw in Venice, together with the role of the female icon in Pre-Raphaelitism.

This image of the trumpeting angel was further expanded. The wings were removed and the face turned to look out of the page. She is breaking out of prison gates; broken chains lie on the floor and a banner flows behind her bearing the slogan 'Votes for Women'. Accompanying her through the gates is a flock of doves, presumably of peace. It was issued as a Christmas card and in 1914 Constance Lytton used it to adorn the cover of her book, *Prison and Prisoners*.

Another in the series shows the female as 'sower'. The maiden sowing the seeds walks from left to right sowing the seeds of emancipation and throws the seed from her right hand. This motif is contained within a circle again, and has a border stating 'Votes for Women' and 'Women's Social and Political Union'. It was used on greetings cards and handbills for mass meetings. This 'muse' also became the central figure in the Ice Rink decorations and was used as a character in the cartoon in *Votes for Women*, 14 July 1911.

A further design is on the WSPU calendar of 1910, again showing a winged angel, this time carrying a candle and guiding a woman in prison dress. She holds a folded banner announcing 'Votes for Women' and marches through a hilly landscape. Once more, this motif is set in a circle which is itself placed on a rectangular background of bunches of grapes and vine leaves which interwine around the lettering 'A Votes For Women Calendar, 1910, WSPU'. The pattern is reminiscent of Arts and Crafts influences and may give us an insight into the type of work she produced for textile designs when she was a student.

Sylvia also designed banners, one of which seems more than influenced by her drawings of working women. It shows a woman in poor working clothes holding a child. There are four other banners recorded. One in the Museum of London is that of the Bradford Union. It bears the city's coat of arms and the motto, 'Grant the Womanhood the justice England should be proud to give'. A second design is entwined with wreaths of flowers and proclaims that 'Human Emancipation must precede Social Regeneration'. This is on a green ground with a deep purple border and is written in gold lettering. The third is in the same colouring and depicts a pelican feeding its young from its own breast – the traditional emblem of religious sacrifice – and has the motto 'strong souls live like fire-hearted suns to spend their strength'.

The fourth banner has 'Rebellion to Tyrants is obedience to God' in gold letters on a violet ground with roses, thistles and shamrocks decorating it. It can be seen in the background of a photograph showing Christabel Pankhurst and Mrs. Pethick-Lawrence on the occasion of the unfurling of the banners on 17 June 1908 in the Queen's Hall for a special press preview. All these banners are relatively large for carrying, eight feet by nine feet, and cost 14 guineas each, which was very expensive for a Suffragette banner. Fabric was sold by the WSPU for eight shillings and six pence a banner-sized piece [42 $\frac{1}{2}$ p] or ready-made with appliqué lettering at sixteen shillings [80p]. The Artists' Suffrage League, which had produced many of the banners for the parade which Sylvia had seen in June, spent between 15s [75p] and £2 on them.

More women were arrested as the WSPU encouraged direct action. In order to recognise their dedication the organisation commissioned an illuminated address to be presented to each prisoner, together with a badge of honour. The latter became a symbol of the prison: a portcullis with five tooth-like projections, containing within it a broad arrow in three segments, purple, white and green. Attached to the back is a pin and from the two top corners silver chains hang down. The illuminated address has a background of intertwined roses with three symbols set within it. To the right, a prison arrow is surrounded by a wreath of berries. To the left, prison bars have the sun rising from behind entwined branches of thorns. At the bottom is a heart.

In the top third of the design a much larger circle enclosed three figures. Two are trumpeting angels and the third faces frontwards and holds out a banner declaring 'Freedom'. At their feet are wild flowers. The landscape rises to a hill and a stylised rainbow arches across. The lower two-thirds of the design is taken up with the WSPU address dedicated to the prisoner.

In February 1909, Mrs Pethick-Lawrence asked Sylvia if she would design and make the decorations for the Princes' Skating Rink Great Women's Exhibition to be held that May. The hall was 250 feet long and 150 feet wide. Each section of canvas banners was to be at least twenty feet high. Although it seemed an impossible task for the deadline, she accepted it. Like the ILP hall in Manchester, it was work she wished to do. To help her she enrolled the assistance of a few contemporaries from the Royal College of Art. Amy Browning and two other women were paid thirty shillings [£1.50] a week. (The highest-paid chainmakers had earned five shillings [25p] in 1907.) She also employed four male ex-students at the rate of 10d [about 4p] an hour.

The first and major problem was finding premises large enough to accommodate the making of banners on this scale. Sylvia rented Avenue Studios in Fulham, where the quarter-size cartoons were made, and another room above a stable where the canvas could be laid out on the floor and designs subsequently enlarged. Stencil techniques were used, with the suffragette colours – purple, green and white – to repeat the vine leaf and rose pattern designs. Only the central banners at either end of the hall were to be painted by hand. The total running surface area of the banners was 420 feet in length, with a twenty-foot drop.

The first stage was to cover it all with cream paint. Four designs were made, one for each side of the main panel at either end of the hall. They were also integrated within the decorations for the longer side walls. Two of the women enlarged the tree designs, vine leaf and grape arches and pillasters to scale. These were painted black in outline and carefully cut into stencils by the men, after which they used them in the three colours on the prepared cream ground.

Meanwhile, Sylvia and Amy tackled the major figures. A thirteen-foot female sower carried a sheaf of grain, on either side of which they drew blossoming almond trees with crocuses – the promise of spring – at her feet. Accompanying this was a text from the Psalms: 'They that sow in tears shall reap in joy. He that goeth forth and weepeth, bearing precious seed shall doubtles come again with rejoicing bringing his sheaves with him.' Overhead the sun radiated out to the arches and in the background thistles, symbolising adversity, flourished. This whole design was set within an archway of vines, grapes, bramble roses and laden with fruit and flowers. At the other entrance to the hall an equally large version of her sower, sowing the grain this time, stood with wild flowers at her feet, whilst above her three doves carry an olive branch and an ivy pattern made up the archway. The project was only just finished in time, Sylvia working for two whole nights prior to the opening to make sure it would be ready. The exhibition ran from 13 to 26 May 1909. These banners were re-used in 1911 and reproduced in publications for several years.

Sylvia took a short break in the summer of 1909 in Kent, returning briefly for some militant activity, and then back to Cinder Hill to spend time on her painting and writing independent of the movement. It is possible that two rather nondescript landscapes in oils were produced here. One, again small (10 ins by 14 ins), a light-coloured picture, showing a rough country road meandering through low hills to the sea in the far distance, is painted much more heavily than her usual style, giving a very textural surface, and is rather block-like and impressionistic. The other painting is of a sunlit road overhung with trees; two figures hover in the background, and it is not an especially interesting picture. Another painting possibly made at this time is a study in watercolour and pencil of a young girl in a kitchen. In some ways, the picture symbolises the confusion of the period of decision-making she must have been going through. The young girl stands between two open doors at the front and back of the picture. She looks a little unsure of approaching either. However, it is a light and bright painting in bold pinks and mauves, with a lot of white in the paint generally. Bright sunlight casts the shadow of the window into the rooms, and there is a feeling of optimism.

Sylvia returned to London and nursed her sick brother for four months until his death. During this time the doctor commissioned her to make a picture on the theme of 'Affection' for his wife. However, he could not have been satisfied with her drawings and it finally came to nothing. She moved on to Notting Hill Gate and set up her studio there. She began a whole new series of larger drawings, similar in some ways to the much earlier drawing of Keir Hardie, in red, black and white in neutral coloured Ingres paper. One is a self-portrait (26 ins by 20 ins). Her mouth is slightly open in a bright and youthful expression. It is a head and shoulder portrait, and the coat she is wearing is less complete then her face and bonnet. She was still experimenting with the width and shape of her shoulder. The background is heavily blacked with charcoal and outlines the brightness of her face. This drawing is more heavily coloured than the rest, and boldly drawn.

Another drawing which may also be a self-portrait has the same white bonnet or peasant cap, and has been described as a portrait of a farm girl. The arms are raised upwards, but neither hands nor any object is drawn. She could be swinging a scythe or holding up a banner. The energy of the drawing has more the feel of a revolutionary heroine marching to victory. She wears a white bodice and a delicate pattern of floral lace is painted white on white. Another two untitled and un-named portraits of young women (18 $^3/_4$ ins by 24 ins, 16 $^1/_4$ ins by 22 ins) belong to this series. Their faces are drawn in detail and their dresses and bonnets are confidently sketched.

In the early summer of 1910, Sylvia travelled to Austria and southern Germany with Annie Kenney and Mrs Pethwick-Lawrence. She took a sketchbook which has been preserved, and together with two loose pages it makes twenty pages, mostly in watercolour and pencil. Many were illustrations of actors in the Oberammergau Play, which they had attended, or of children in Tyrolean costumes playing in the village square.

Another sketchbook was begun in Parten Kirchen. It features working people and in particular a watercolour of a young woman painting decorations onto wooden ornamental plaques (10 ins by 7 ins). It is a distinguished picture. She has found the opportunity to use bright and primary colour in bold, decorative shapes. The picture is inspiring; Sylvia was obviously impressed by the skill of this young woman, working as she was on commercial objects. The freer and more relaxed style, confident and bright could be a consequence of being abroad and on holiday, not having to dedicate time to the suffragette cause. It may give us a rare opportunity to summise how her work might have progressed had she continued practising purely as an artist. In many ways the picture reflects back to her earlier studies of working women, though the freer and healthier environment contrasts with the shabby urban conditions of her British counterparts. She had matured immensely through the varied projects and commissions since the women workers series to the more competent and confident artist creating this picture. Equally, the work in her sketchbook of 'The Crucifixion' – a bare-footed youth and a potter at work – show a similar competence and character.

Sylvia was invited to America to lecture and she spent a few months there, lecturing, travelling, visiting several jails and encountering bitter racism in certain states. On her return to Britain, she resumed her own work, having earned enough money lec-   turing to finance herself for a short time. She proposed a large oil painting on the subject of a group of girls dancing against a dense background of trees. Several preparatory sketches still exist: studies of the figure, and the body in various positions of movement, particularly lower legs, ankles and feet. In some cases the girls have bells around their ankles. There are also several life-drawing studies, two of trees and flowers, and two of small children. She did not, however, begin the actual painting itself and it seems that these sketches were her last activities as an artist. Although it is difficult to imagine exactly how the final image might have looked, we could see it in two ways: either a semi-pagan celebration of womanhood in the tradition of maypole dancing, or as an extension of her social documentary studies. The figures as sketched are in country working dress, though their buckled and bowed shoes look like those of professional dancers.

The painting's progress was interrupted by a request from the WSPU for help in adapting her Queen's Skating Rink banners. The new site was the Portman Rooms in Baker Street. The roof sloped down at either side and Sylvia felt the best way to use this problem was to hang the banners away from the sides and construct aisles at the sides, the banners thus becoming soft walls. Sylvia exaggerated this feature by designing columns and bases for the bazaar fitters to cast. The stallholders were dressed in eighteenth-century costume as a variety of characters, gentlewomen, fisherwomen, fortune-tellers, etc. Their costumes were paid for by their wearers and were made up by volunteers of the Artists' Suffrage League in the studio of Georgina and Marie Brackenbury.

Sylvia's final project for the WSPU was for a meeting and gathering in Hyde Park on 14 July 1912. She worked night and day prepar-

ing for this event, recreating the French Revoluntionary scarlet caps
of liberty as well as replicas of the flags, banners and mottoes used
at the Radical Peterloo meeting in Manchester of 1819. In *The Suffragette Movement* Sylvia describes the scene:

> The blaze of colour in the Park. The scarlet caps, gorgeously flam-
> ing red on their long poles. The wide banners, floating above the
> concourse, like boat sails floating in concentric circles, gaily
> emblazoned as for some huge regatta, with all the colours of the
> comrades, for every organisation had its colours now: purple,
> white and green, often repeated for the W.S.P.U.; orange and
> green for the Irish; strong, almost startling bars of black and white
> for the Writers; green and gold with red dragon of Wales; the
> sombre black and brown for the Tax Resisters . . . . . . brilliant red
> and white for Labour . . . .[13]

It was soon after this, however, that she decided to abandon her
ambition to become an artist. She notes in *Myself When Young* that 'I
had planned with the newly-appointed Governor of a Women's
prison to decorate the Assembly Hall and to train females to assist'.[14]
Later, she explained:

> The fourth decision, which was the climax and coping stone to the
> rest, was to abandon my artistic work once and for all and to live
> in the East End of London to build up a Suffrage Movement
> amongst the poor women there.
> Again, I consulted no-one; I had regret but no doubt. This deci-
> sion I made when I had earned enough money by lecturing in
> America to do some large decorations which I had long wished to
> produce.
> The decision entailed not merely the abondonment of artistic
> work but the building up of a movement independent in method
> and ideas from that in which my mother and sister were en-
> gaged.[15]

The only recorded artistic work she produced after this date was
the festive cover for the *New Times and Ethiopia News*. Her character
was one of complete dedication. If she committed herself to something it was wholly and completely. Considering the lack of opportunities for women – as artists in particular – her achievement,
though partly perhaps attained through family contact (which is not

to underrate her skill) is impressive. Although in general the work she produced was not particularly avant-garde in technique, it can be argued that her series on working women was an original concept, that of documentary painting. These pictures are certainly her most interesting works. With her choice made to concentrate on helping to improve the conditions of the poor women in the East End of London, we lost the artist capable of and dedicated to visually recording these conditions for future generations. In retrospect then we can regret that the artist within her did not win that persistent debate on '. . . whether . . . to induce the world to accept one's creations, and to give one in return one's daily bread when all the time the great social struggles to better the world for humanity demanded other service'. Sylvia might have been able to allow herself to become a very skilled artist and to have contributed in a greater way to the art and design history of Great Britain.

NOTES

1. Many of the pictures and other artworks referred to in this essay are illustrated in Richard Pankhurst, *Sylvia Pankhurst, Artist and Crusader* (Paddington Press, 1979).
2. E. Sylvia Pankhurst to the Dutch *Women's Yearbook*, 10 December 1930, E. Sylvia Pankhurst Papers (hereafter ESPP), 10, International Institute of Social History, Amsterdam.
3. Margot Oxford, The Countess of Oxford and Asquith, (ed.) *Myself When Young; By Famous Women of To-day* (Frederick Muller, 1938) p. 284.
4. E. Sylvia Pankhurst, *The Suffragette Movement. An Intimate Account of Persons and Ideals* (Longmans, Green & Co., 1932) p.146
5. Ibid., p.161.
6. E. Sylvia Pankhurst to the Dutch *Women's Yearbook*, 10 December 1930, ESPP 10.
7. Richard Pankhurst, 1979, p. 39.
8. Margot Oxford, 1938, pp. 284–5.
9. Ibid., p. 285.
10. E. Sylvia Pankhurst, 1932, p. 261.
11. E. Sylvia Pankhurst, 'Pit Brow Women', *Votes for Women*, 11 August 1911, p. 730.
12. E. Sylvia Pankhurst, 1932, p. 284.
13. E. Sylvia Pankhurst, 1932, p. 394.
14. Margot Oxford, 1938, p. 300.
15. E. Sylvia Pankhurst to the Dutch *Women's Yearbook*, 10 December 1930, ESPP 10.

3

Suffragism and Socialism: Sylvia Pankhurst 1903–1914

LES GARNER

In the early twentieth century Sylvia Pankhurst fought for socialism, feminism and votes for women. An evaluation of her life in this period can enrich our understanding of all three. Surprisingly perhaps, though her activity in these years has been adequately recorded, principally by herself in *The Suffragette Movement – An Intimate Account of Persons and Ideals*,[1] it has often been misunderstood and undervalued. In particular Sylvia had much to contribute to the still unresolved debates surrounding class and sex and to the battle to integrate socialism and feminism, preventing them becoming exclusive terms and ideologies. Sylvia also played an important part in creating a political climate that made votes for women more rather than less likely, arguably more so than her renowned sister Christabel. An understanding of this can perhaps further develop the re-evaluation of the importance of the WSPU to the suffrage campaign. However, this chapter will not re-tell the suffragette story, nor give a narrative account of Sylvia's role in it except when recent misconceptions make it necessary to do so. Instead, through Sylvia it intends to analyse the thorny dilemmas and complex struggles which socialists, feminists and suffragists like her faced.

To appreciate Sylvia's contribution in these areas several questions about her individual political development need to be briefly raised. Why did Sylvia become involved in suffragism and socialism? How and why did she retain her loyalty to the latter while Christabel and their mother Emmeline moved to the right? Why did she pursue an independent path yet remain within the WPSU for so long? How far was her independence driven by envy of Christabel on the one hand and a desperate need to seek her mother's attention on the other? Was her socialism and her shadowy relationship with

Keir Hardie solely due to the influence of her father Richard and her lifelong mourning for him? In other words, how far did the family legacy explain and determine Sylvia's political position throughout this period?

Patricia Romero in her recent biography, *Sylvia Pankhurst – Portrait of a Radical,* [2] tends to cite the Pankhurst clan and the complex relationships within it, as the most influential factor in shaping Sylvia's life and work. Romero describes an 'internal consistency' within Sylvia which was centred around her attitudes to Christabel, Emmeline and most important of all, her father Richard. From Dr Pankhurst she 'inherited his enthusiasm and need for causes' while his death left 'a permanent emotional scar from which she never really recovered'.[3] Indeed, it was this that played such as important part in the development of her affair with Hardie, described as 'a substitute for her dead father'.[4] Other crucial episodes of her life in this period are explained in a similar way. Thus the vital break with the WSPU in 1914 was in part due to sisterly rivalry for maternal attention while the horrors of the hunger strike and forced feeding were endured partly because of 'the need to top Christabel in her mother's affections'.[5]

Though it is undoubtedly true that the influence of Sylvia's family was strong (and it was clearly acknowledged by Sylvia herself) it must not be exaggerated to the point whereby it becomes deterministic, preventing individual autonomy and the ability to make political choices. Moreover, as a method of historical enquiry the biographical approach clearly has many pitfalls. For example, if the biographer dislikes her subject – in this case variously described as 'self-centered, opinionated, immature, obsessive . . . not subtle – radicals rarely are'[6] – it obviously compounds the effect of bias. Secondly, and more importantly, by concentrating on the individual, biography can downgrade or ignore the context in which she operated. People certainly do make history, to paraphrase Marx, but not in circumstances of their own choosing. The role of the historian is to balance, relate, understand and explain both.[7]

The circumstances in which socialists, feminists and suffragists operated in the 1900s were rich in potential but they were also turbulent, complex, fluid and above all, divided. On a general level, the suffrage battle, the constitutional crises over the Lords and Home Rule for Ireland, and the growth of a militant class struggle after 1910 hardly presents a picture of relaxed Edwardian tranquillity. For women, political circumstances pushed and pulled them in conflicting ways. The sad litany of oppression – the law, unequal wages, economic dependence and so on – that fuelled the suffragist and feminist movements were opposed by contemporary forces that emphasised their domestic and maternal role. The rise in male unemployment, the fall in the birth rate, the fear over the nation's health and foreign competition created strong opposition to suffragism and feminism alike. As Lord Cromer, the leader of the Anti-Suffragists, argued in the *Anti-Suffrage Review* in 1910 'How can we hope to compete with such a nation as this [Germany] if we war against nature, and invert the natural roles of the sexes?'[8]

Yet the response of what loosely might be called 'The Women's Movement' to this complex situation was not united. Indeed, as Rowbotham argues, there had been broadly two feminisms since the early nineteenth century, 'one seeking acceptance in the bourgeois world, the other seeking another world altogether'.[9] Feminists were divided too in their arguments, some accepting the 'natural differences' between the sexes, others realising such differences were socially defined. These divisions understandably crossed over to the suffrage movement. Though apparently united in demanding votes for women, suffragists faced inter- and intra-organisational conflict and were ultimately divided by style, tactics and political allegiance. Confronted by a political scene at Westminster that hindered rather than enhanced their chances of success and facing a crowded and controversial legislative agenda, the suffragists certainly faced an uphill task.[10]

The Labour movement was also divided, though by 1900 it had made significant gains, principally in the Trade Unions and in the development of independent political representation in the Commons. Yet it too was divided along reformist and revolutionary lines, with the latter becoming increasingly significant in the period 1910 to 1914. This was fuelled by the growth of syndicalism and by a growing disillusionment with Labour at Westminster, perceived as it was to be the lap-dog of the Liberal Government. But it was also divided over feminism and an hostility developed among some that easily crossed the gradualist/revolutionary divide. Belfort Bax,[11] of the Social Democratic Federation, was openly hostile, while others, like Bruce Glasier and Philip Snowden, of the ILP, were at best lukewarm. There was a socialist feminist current in the left in the 1900s but it too faced momentous difficulties in achieving its goals.[12]

Many of the divisions outlined above surfaced around the key issue of the vote. The franchise in the 1900s was linked to property qualification and many men (possibly a third) could not vote.[13] Thus the classic suffragist demand of votes for women on the same terms as men would result in a limited reform likely only to enfranchise bourgeois women. For a socialist, the only logical demand therefore was for adult suffrage. For many feminists this made votes for women even less likely as it would guarantee opposition from those hostile to, and fearful of, universal suffrage.[14] But above all, for the socialist feminist the dilemma was agonisingly acute. She was torn between loyalty to her class and loyalty to her sex. For many it was not an easy cross to bear or a problem with an easy and simple solution.

For the ILP and the Labour Party in Parliament votes for women was also a tricky issue in a tricky and dangerous world. For both, a commitment to universal suffrage was unavoidable. Yet how far this included a commitment to include women as a priority was less clear. According to Sylvia, many socialist men seemed to think that women's interests could be safeguarded and promoted by men; votes for women were not therefore necessary.[15] In any case as the adult suffragist Margaret McMillan put it, 'The ILP was not formed to champion women. It took that battle in its stride and might drop it in its ardour. It was born to make war on capitalism and competition'.[16] Moreover, Labour in Parliament, though tied by its dependence on the Liberals after 1906, had its own priorities essential to its supporters and, in the case of the Osborne judgment of 1909, which threatened to starve the party of funds, its very survival. Under such circumstances it is surely understandable that many in the Labour Movement saw a limited measure of votes for women as a political risk not worth taking. It was not necessarily a principled stance but within its own terms it was logical. The way forward lay firstly, in convincing Labour supporters that such a measure would not harm its prospects and secondly in working for a political climate where the party in power (the Liberals from 1906) would agree.

Sylvia had of course been made aware of many of these complex and awkward issues during her childhood and adolescence. The various Pankhurst households appeared to act like a magnet to the British and European Left. Visitors included Malatesta, Kropotkin, Annie Besant, William Morris, Tom Mann, Louise Michel, a gaggle of Fabians and perhaps most crucially of all in Sylvia's case, Keir

Hardie. The Pankhurst family shared Dr Pankhurst's concerns, which clearly included socialism and feminism. Though calling for universal suffrage for men and women in his election address in the Gorton election in 1895 when he stood for the ILP, he left a legacy that would have supported a limited measure provided a campaign for such a demand remained firmly rooted in socialist and Labour movements. Had he lived to see it, Richard Pankhurst, like Keir Hardie, would have enthusiastically supported the birth of the Women's Social and Political Union. It is interesting to speculate how far that support would have dwindled as the Union moved away from its political roots.[17]

The WSPU in its early years was clearly located in local Labour and suffrage circles. Mrs Pankhurst originally wanted to call it the Women's Labour Representation Committee and saw the Union as 'a new organisation which would carry on political and social work on behalf of working class women'.[18] It was keen to recruit working class women like Hannah Mitchell and the Oldham cotton worker Annie Kenney[19] and all the founding members, including Sylvia, were in the ILP (she joined at the earliest opportunity when she was sixteen). From 1903 to 1905 the Union was in fact dependent upon the ILP for publicity, lecture platforms and audiences.[20]

The main objective of the WSPU was, as always, to campaign for 'the vote as it is or may be granted to men'. However, in the early days a primary strategy was to convince the trades unions, the ILP and the Labour Representation Committee that they could actively support this without harming their own interests. Consequently, the Union made much of an ILP poll (inspired by Keir Hardie) which purported to show that if the classic suffragist demand was granted, the vast majority (82 per cent) would be working-class women. Though statistically useless – it was for example based on a questionnaire only sent to ILP branches and only fifty out of 300 replied – it was eagerly seized on by the Union. Whether it was valid or not, it showed where the priorities of the WSPU lay.

Sylvia felt comfortable with the political philosophy and strategy of the Union. Like Hardie, she uncritically accepted the ILP survey which clearly showed it 'could press for the enfranchisement of women on the same terms as men without handing an advantage to the propertied classes'.[21] Providing a campaign for a limited measure was based on working-class women and was linked to the ultimate goal of adult suffrage, Sylvia could give it her wholehearted support.

Her position at this time was reflected in a debate she organised for the Fulham ILP which she joined in 1904 after moving to London to begin her two-year course at the Royal College of Art. Isabella Ford, the veteran socialist and suffragist, spoke for a limited measure, Margaret Bondfield, a union organiser and future Labour MP, for adult suffrage. Bondfield argued that industrial organisation was more important than votes for women but if the franchise was to be extended only adult suffrage would do. In any case, votes for women was 'the hobby of disappointed old maids who no one wanted to marry'. 'My heart' Sylvia added 'was in adult suffrage, but this sort of argument was destructive of any sort of enfranchisement'.[22]

Sylvia's view was further reflected in an illuminating row she had with Keir Hardie, with whom she had begun a secretive affair in 1904. As it also illustrates further the dilemma socialists and feminists faced over women's suffrage it is worth considering in some detail. Hardie, as a keen supporter of votes for women, doggedly campaigned to get the ILP and the Labour Party to support a limited bill. At the Labour Conference in Belfast in January 1907 he failed, with an adult suffrage amendment being easily carried. Hardie was so upset that he threatened to resign and a crisis ensued. A compromise within the Labour Party was reached, yet Hardie appeared to change his position in the following March. At a WSPU meeting he declared that if a Women's Suffrage Bill had not been passed within two years a movement would develop that would accept nothing less than adult suffrage. By this time adult suffrage was anathema to the WSPU, who in any case demanded votes in the current parliamentary session. More importantly, to Sylvia it seemed Hardie had abandoned his support to women's suffrage in order to preserve Labour unity. Sylvia felt so outraged that she warned Hardie 'that my friendship with him might even become a competitor with my loyalty to the suffrage cause'. His reply came as they continued their discussion while walking the Thames Embankment. Pointing to a group of unemployed, homeless men Hardie asked 'Do you ask me to desert these?'[23]

By 1908, the WSPU had certainly deserted its working-class and northern origins, and in spite of her argument with Hardie, Sylvia's loyalty to the family organisation became increasingly ambivalent. For two years the Pankhursts, with Sylvia on the left and Christabel and Emmeline on the right, had been taking different paths which were ultimately to lead to the fissure of 1914. The contrast in their journeys and the motives for taking them can further develop our understanding of Sylvia Pankhurst and her concerns.

The WSPU, under Christabel and Emmeline Pankhurst's leadership, changed its original character in several interconnected ways. It moved away from its northern ILP roots described above and developed tactics that made the mass involvement of working-class women unlikely and indeed, unwanted. The original loose commitment to a democratic constitution for the Union was also jettisoned and an autocracy developed. And perhaps most importantly of all, the Union, under the guidance of its autocrats, became openly hostile to Labour.

This hostility can perhaps be traced back to 1903 when Christabel voiced her suspicion about the ILP's true commitment to votes for women. Possibly with leaders like Glasier and Snowden in mind, she wrote in the *ILP News* of August 1903 that socialists were generally silent on the position of women and if not antagonistic, not really concerned: 'Some day when they are in power, and have nothing better to do, they will give women votes as a finishing touch to their arrangements'. She added 'Why are women expected to have such confidence in the men of the Labour Party? Working men are as unjust to women as are those of other classes'. Though this may have seemed harsh to some of her readers, it was not a totally unfair criticism and it was made within the context of a debate inside the ILP. Moreover, Christabel continued to talk on ILP platforms in terms of the benefits women's suffrage would bring to working women.[24]

But by 1906, Christabel clearly no longer wished to pursue women's suffrage through the Labour movement. She insisted on the need for independence for the WSPU and initiated a new policy which stated the Union and its members would not support any party until votes for women were granted. This radical change emerged at the Cockermouth by-election in August 1906 and caused great consternation to many women who were members of the WSPU and the ILP. Though these women were critical of Labour, they still saw votes for women as a class issue. Christabel and Emmeline disagreed and within a year both had resigned from the ILP. They now wanted the Union to appeal to women of all classes – a change which partly explains the move to London in 1906 and Christabel's insistence that Sylvia's work with East End working women should cease. 'The House of Commons, even its Labour members, were more impressed by the demonstrations of the feminine bourgeoisie than the feminine proleteriat', Christabel later argued. 'My democratic principles and instincts made me want a movement based on no class distinctions, and including not mainly the working class but women of all classes'.[25]

Christabel, unlike the radical suffragists of Lancashire described by Liddington and Norris in their excellent *One Hand Tied Behind Us*,[26] no longer wished to face the hard slog of turning Labour wholeheartedly to the women's cause, nor did she seek to keep the issue within a socialist framework. Instead, she preferred direct harassment of the Liberals through the new militant tactics which began after the infamous Free Trade Hall incident of 1905. After the arrest of Christabel and Annie Kenney, the most important result of the fracas was that it created widespread, national publicity for the WSPU. In the early days of militancy this attention led to increased membership and funds, thus further enabling the Union to sever its links with the ILP.

Yet as the Union's militant tactics grew, it became increasingly evident that the campaign relied on individual rather than mass action. In comparison to the industrial struggles of 1910 to 1914 or the Ulster Unionists rebellion against Home Rule, its threat was minimal. In any case, individual illegal acts could and were treated as a law and order issue. Moreover, the spiral effect of militancy – where to be newsworthy each act had to be more provocative than the last – carried with it the increasing danger that it would alienate as many people as the Union hoped to attract or influence. The other problem with such a strategy was that it necessitated (or to the leaders, justified) autocracy. This created the ironic situation whereby the WSPU, alone among the major suffrage societies, became an autocratic organisation fighting for a democratic reform. Not surprisingly, many members, fighting for votes and independence, could not accept this situation. As Teresa Billington-Greig argued 'if we are fighting against the subjection of women to men, we cannot honestly submit to the subjection of women to women'.[27]

Teresa, who became a leading feminist critic of the WSPU,[28] was writing in 1907 just before the first major split which led to the formation of the Women's Freedom League. Though partly fuelled by personality clashes between, on the one side, herself and Charlotte Despard, and on the other Christabel and Emmeline Pankhurst, the crisis clearly indicated unease about the WSPU's new direction. Apart from demanding a democratic constitution, Billington-Greig and Despard in particular had a long commitment to socialist and radical politics. (She became the Labour candidate for Battersea in 1918 and was a fervent supporter of Irish and Spanish republicanism.[29]) Though the League was also committed to a limited measure and independence from any political party, its development under Despard's leadership clearly placed it on the left within the suffrage movement as a whole. It emphasised the needs of working-class women, worked with them, encouraging them to unionise as well as join the League. And, though still critical of the Labour Party's commitment to women's suffrage, the WFL increasingly associated itself with the wider goals and aspirations of the Labour movement. In doing so, the League, while remaining loyal to the early days of 1903, stood in marked contrast to the WSPU's subsequent development.[30]

Once the dictatorship of Christabel and Emmeline had been established, the Union rapidly developed along its new lines. It constantly emphasised its classless appeal and dropped any pretence of being a working-class organisation. As early as October 1907, new recruits were encouraged to leave 'any class feeling behind you when you come into the movement. For the Women in our ranks know no barriers of class distinction'.[31] Furthermore, apart from the odd, short-lived lapse, the Union actively discouraged the participation of working-class women. As Emmeline Pankhurst argued, the battle was best fought by 'the fortunate ones . . . the happy women, the women who have drawn prizes in the lucky bag of life'.[32]

The denial of the importance of class went hand in hand with the Union's monomania about the vote. The struggle now was solely for the vote, and any benefits that accrued to working women would be just part of the general reforms that would inevitably follow the enfranchisement of women or rather, as Rosen argues 'once one woman in seven could vote, as such would have been the result of extending the existing franchise to women, the measure so doggedly advocated by the WSPU'.[33] Women workers did not even need trade unions for, according to Christabel 'the men employers . . . will think that, as women are citizens, they ought to have better treatment'[34] while her mother argued that the miners won an eight-hour day purely because 'the miner has a vote. You see what the vote will do. You see what political power will do'.[35]

The inherent logic of this argument – that class differences were irrelevant and only the possession of the vote gave access to political power – drove the WSPU to the inevitable conclusion that power lay with one sex, men. It was their unwillingness to share power – and their fears of the new chaste sexual morality that voting women would bring – that lay behind the opposition to women's suffrage, an argument ultimately developed by Christabel's *The Great Scourge and How to End It*, published in 1913.[36] By now, the Union refused to work with men (possibly a factor in Fred Pethick-Lawrence's departure with his wife, Emmeline, in 1912) or to share platforms with them. In the latter years of the Union's campaign, it was a development that took the WSPU outside the boundaries of mainstream suffragism and indeed, the old battle between limited and adult suffrage. In the old days of 1903, that had been a tactical debate that recognised the importance of sex *and* class in the oppression of women. By dropping the latter, the WSPU increasingly stood alone.

The path the Union took under Christabel and Emmeline Pankhurst's direction clearly moved them towards the right. In any case, and in spite of their allegedly 'revolutionary' tactics, they did not want to smash the parliamentary club but to join it, to enter the political establishment rather than breaking it down. The Union's strategy, again in contrast to the rest of the suffrage movement, also pushed it towards the right. The policy of attacking all government candidates after 1907 could only aid the Tories, while there is some evidence Christabel hoped for a Tory victory in the general election of January 1910.[37] By 1914, her intentions were clear, for the election of a Tory government was 'the keen desire of the WSPU'.[38] Yet the whole policy, without a clear pledge from the Conservatives was, as Billington-Greig remarked, 'suicidal':[39] such a pledge was never made. And finally, this strategy has to be seen in the context of the Union's outright hostility to the Labour Party (officially opposed in 1912) and the Labour movement in general. The Union had come a long way politically since 1903: Sylvia Pankhurst's journey can only be understood against this background.

On the surface, and indeed in public, Sylvia appeared to remain a loyal member of the WSPU up to and during the split of 1914. She was active in the early campaigns in London and became the first secretary of the Central London committee in 1906. In the same year she suffered her first imprisonment in Holloway and throughout the early days was busy with her mother in lobbying Parliament and gathering support for private members' bills which promoted women's suffrage. At Mrs Pankhurst's bidding, Sylvia frequently and loyally returned from her artistic tours of 1907 to help the Union in by-elections. She also devoted her considerable artistic talents to designing and producing propaganda material for the WSPU. Finally, Sylvia wrote in *Votes for Women* a series of bland and uncritical accounts of the Union's history which were included in her first book,*The Suffragette*, in 1911. This tepid work was prefaced with fulsome praise for the 'four who form the inner heart of the organisation, Mrs Pankhurst, with her magnetic personality, Christabel, the daring political genius and organiser of tactics'[40] and the Pethick-Lawrences, destined to leave one year later in October 1912.

But Sylvia was a loyal Pankhurst first, and a member of the WSPU second. In spite of her acquiescent support for the suffragette campaign, she privately expressed growing concern while increasingly making her own independent political decisions and commitments. Though many of the criticisms were voiced by Sylvia in her *Suffragette Movement*, her life throughout the Union's history – her art, her relationship with Hardie, her tours in England, Scotland and the USA and her commitment to socialism – was almost one long protest against the direction the WSPU was taking. In family terms Sylvia faced a choice between the calls of Christabel and their mother, Emmeline, and the radical legacy of her father, Richard. Ultimately it was the latter, so strong during the Union's birth in 1903, that won through. In that sense, Sylvia was the most loyal Pankhurst of them all.

Though hindsight makes it easier to discern a logical pattern to Sylvia's political development from 1903 to 1914 and beyond, such a pattern was clearly there. Her commitment to votes for women as a sex and a class issue was evident from the beginning, as was her belief in how the battle, with its ultimate goal of adult suffrage, would be won. Her response to Christabel's orders, expressed by Annie Kenney, to rouse London, was typical. With Hardie and Lansbury's help, and that of the socialist Dora Montefiore who had been working in the area for some time, she gathered and organised over 300 working women from the East End to march on Parliament. Though Romero argues their involvement was stage-managed, many of these women had already been involved in unemployment marches in 1905.[41] Even if the accusation was valid, the significance of Sylvia's action remains the same – they again showed where her political sympathies remained. In contrast, on her arrival in London in the spring of 1906, Christabel ordered that the involvement of the working women from the East End had to stop. This was undoubtedly a reason behind Sylvia's resignation from the secretaryship of the Central Committee, and marked the first public and political breach with her sister and her direction of the WSPU.

Sylvia had by this time begun her relationship with Keir Hardie. The details of the affair need not concern us here, yet a relationship between the two clearly existed.[42] Sylvia had known him since childhood and even after the affair ended she retained a lifelong respect for his work and political commitment. Her love for him strengthened her own commitment to socialism and thus again helped to distance her from the WSPU. The affair also reflected the difficulties socialist supporters of a limited measure of votes for women faced. We have already seen how the debate over limited versus adult suffrage strained their relationship in 1907 but for Hardie the situation was particularly difficult. On the one hand he was faced with hostility from orthodox adult suffragists in his own party, on the other, with growing criticism from the WSPU. This increased after Christabel's decision to oppose Labour officially in October 1912 and her tactics included heckling of his meetings. For Hardie, a keen supporter of the WSPU in the early days and a defender of the suffragettes throughout, this must have been particularly galling. But, like Sylvia, he would not renege on his loyalty to his class or to working women – their relationship stands as a testimony to the commitment.

Sylvia's own commitment to her sex and to socialism, and the difficulties this created were, as we have seen, evident throughout 1907. This was shown in her tour of the north of England and Scotland which was undertaken to reveal the reality of working women's lives in the fields, the factories, the mines, the potteries and elsewhere. Sylvia recorded her experiences in *Votes for Women*, sketches and, much later, in *The Suffragette Movement*. As Christabel and Emmeline courted the 'feminine bourgeoisie', Sylvia trudged around the country attempting to portray the oppression of their less fortunate sisters. From the 'poor, miserable creatures, clad in vile, nameless rags'[43] of the potato pickers in Berwick-on-Tweed to the haggard women of the Potteries, prone to miscarriage and still-birth due to lead poisoning, there was ample evidence to record.

However, Sylvia's tour did more than merely confirm to her the plight of working women. It illustrated again the difficulties socialists and feminists like her faced. She noted for example the failure of trade unions to protect these workers or to end discriminatory practices. Writing of a scene in the Black Country, she recalled that she was wounded '. . . to see a mother, or sometimes an old grandmother, blowing the bellows at a paltry wage, for a lad in his 'teens, already doing skilled work, and occupying an industrial status to which his mother could never attain'.[44] Yet this did not degenerate into the simplistic sex war analysis of Christabel's campaigns in 1913 to 1914. Sylvia condemned the conditions workers of both sexes faced, seeing, for example, that women in the Potteries who worked with men were but 'slaves of slaves', all maimed by lead and the greed of their employers.[45] Sylvia clearly refused to ignore the specific oppression women faced but she also refused to ignore the importance of class: the struggle for votes needed to recognise both.

Sylvia's unease about the WSPU's move away from this position continually resurfaced during and after 1907. She suffered a less than sisterly rebuke from Christabel for proclaiming her commitment to socialism on a WSPU platform[46] and was unhappy with the events that led to the formation of the WFL. She urged her mother not 'to fear the democratic institution' but as she recalled later 'I might as well have urged the wind to cease from blowing!'[47] Sylvia was also concerned with the new election policy which she felt often benefitted the Tories at the expense of Labour. Yet Sylvia remained in the WSPU and some of her criticisms were not expressed till much later. *The Suffragette*, for example, dismisses the WFL split in just over one page, and the new election policy attracted no criticism at all.[48] In spite of the bias and hindsight of *The Suffragette Movement* however, Sylvia's political direction was clear. Her loyalty to her family, her unwillingness to harm the cause, perhaps even the hope the Union would return to its original route and her lack of self-confidence all kept Sylvia quiet for the time being and out of the limelight. She was not yet ready to go it alone and desert the family clan but how long would it be before the chains were broken and the silence ended?

A key tipping of the balance, as Barbara Winslow argues, was Sylvia's two visits to the USA in 1911 and 1912.[49] Made to raise money for the WSPU and to see if she could earn some income for herself as a journalist, they were crucial to her political and personal development. Firstly, as she travelled the length and breadth of the States they confirmed and widened her commitment to socialism. She became involved in strikes in New York, meeting Elizabeth Gurley Flynn of the Industrial Workers of the World; crossed paths with socialist feminist Margaret Sanger, Crystal Eastman and others; and worked with several suffragist groups. In Fargo, North Dakota for example, she helped to set up the Women's League of North Dakota, interestingly arguing that men should be admitted as associate but not voting members.[50] And, possibly for the first time, she became aware of the pernicious effects of racism, creating a media outcry, for example, when she spoke to a Black college in Tennessee.[51]

Sylvia's visits to Milwaukee, which boasted a Socialist administration, were particularly significant. Though welcoming its efforts, Sylvia was critical, arguing that few radical changes had been made and that local workers needed to be more involved. She felt the city government meetings should be open to all and that employees should help to run their own departments. Sylvia was particularly keen to emphasise the involvement of women for 'even under socialism it would not be satisfactory to women to leave everything to be managed by men'.[52] Sylvia was beginning to show her distaste for reformism or socialism imposed by managers and benevolent intellectuals. Her comments on the Milwaukee administration, on the contrary, reflected her growing belief in socialism from below, created by, and in the interests of, working men and women. It was a belief she was soon to develop in the East End.

The trips to America was also important in developing Sylvia's ability to break out on her own after her return in 1912. For the first time perhaps, America made her feel independent of her family (though the Pankhurst name was obviously a crowd puller) and aware of her own political abilities. No longer on the sidelines or in the background, Sylvia was out in the public eye addressing workers, public meetings, even State legislatures. Moreover, press coverage was generally warm and complimentary. For the first time, it placed Sylvia not Christabel or Emmeline in the limelight. Though this had its drawbacks (Sylvia later complained of faked photographs for example that portrayed her in an unfavourable light), she realised she could cope with the attention. The visit to America, a land of 'great wealth, luxury . . . and squalid poverty',[53] not only enhanced her socialist convictions but significantly increased her feelings of self-worth and independence. This finally enabled Sylvia to act independently on the basis of her own political judgement and concerns: the parting of the Pankhurst ways was now inevitable.

Sylvia's commitment to feminism, socialism and a suffrage campaign based on the working class was crystallized by her renewed involvement in the East End following her return from the USA in early 1912. It was a critical time for the WSPU with Mrs Pankhurst and the Pethick-Lawrences awaiting trial, increasing government repression and Christabel in self-imposed (and comfortable) exile in

Paris. Though there was an appearance of a political or leaderless vacuum at the WSPU's head, it is not enough, as Romero argues, to claim that Sylvia was purely motivated by a desire to fill it.[54] The differences by now were too great and her motives clear:

> Our cue was to fan the flame of popular enthusiasm and to broaden our movement to take in even greater numbers and new sections .... It was necessary, above all, to arouse the poor women of London, the downtrodden mothers whose lot is one dull grind of hardship in order that they may go in their thousands to demonstrate before the seats of the Almighty.[55]

In many ways, as Sylvia realised, the East End was an ideal place to build such a movement. Apart from being familiar to her, it had a long tradition of struggle and was, if Parliament could be so described, near to the seats of the Almighty. She hoped her campaign in 'that great abyss of poverty' in the capital 'would be a rallying cry to the rise of similar movements in all parts of the country'[56] yet the difficulties were immense. However, by 1912 Sylvia was clearly convinced that an autonomous mass movement of working-class men and women was not only necessary to win votes, but to create a society based on their interests. 'Not by the secret militancy of a few enthusiasts, but by the rousing of the masses, could the gage be taken up which not merely some Cabinet Ministers, but history itself had flung us'.[57] In every respect – working with men, attempting to create a democratic mass movement, associating with the wider goals and aspirations of the Labour Movement and socialism – Sylvia stood outside the limited, elitist and ultimately conservative outlook of her sister Christabel and their mother. By 1914, she was forced to resolve her own personal tug-of-war between her commitment to socialism and feminism on the one side and on the other, her loyalty to her family and the WSPU. The result of the competition again reveals much about both.

In spite of early obstacles, including the suspicion of local middle-class reformers and suffragettes fighting merely for 'Votes for Ladies', Sylvia with her friend, the rich American socialist Zelie Emerson, quickly established themselves in the East End, opening WSPU shops in Bethnal Green, Poplar, Limehouse and Bow. Sylvia received some help from the wealthier London branches of the Union, yet HQ was, as we have seen, unconcerned with organising working-class districts. This changed when the limelight fell on the East End during

Lansbury's by-election in Bow and Bromley in November 1912. As Lansbury was fighting on a women's suffrage platform that accepted the WSPU's request that Labour MPs should vote against the government at every opportunity until women were enfranchised, the Union headquarters gave him some support. Lansbury though was defeated – a result in part due to the friction between Labour workers and the organiser sent from the WSPU headquarters at Clements Inn – and the WSPU interest in campaigning in working-class districts evaporated. Sylvia however was 'determined the East End work must go on'.[58]

By May 1913, Sylvia had united branches at Bow, Bromley, Stepney and Hackney (followed later by Canning Town) into the East London Federation of the WSPU. This was governed by a council which was composed of elected delegates from each branch and four honorary secretaries, including Sylvia and the treasurer, Norah Smyth. In its democratic structure, the Federation clearly moved away from the autocracy of the national WSPU and Sylvia obviously regarded this as essential to building members' confidence and autonomy. 'We must get members to work for themselves' she wrote in 1914 'and let them feel they are working for their own emancipation.'[59] The Federation trained members to organise and speak for themselves and held afternoon and evening meetings so all women could attend. It also organised talks and debates on a whole range of issues including sex education, trade unionism, the law and housing.[60] In so doing, it became an organisation that was concerned with more than the vote and one which was interested in raising women's political consciousness around issues that directly affected their lives. However, irksome though Sylvia's independent line may have been, 'Queen Christabel' tolerated it, and even allowed her younger sister to record her activities in articles in *The Suffragette* throughout 1913. The issue that led to the breach was the public association of the WSPU with socialism and within a year, Sylvia was on her own.

Throughout 1913, Sylvia remained committed to the vote and as a 'mouse' under the infamous 'Cat and Mouse' Act, suffered imprisonment and force feeding several times. In this, she was no different from the countless suffragettes who risked jail in Christabel's desperate campaign. The difference was not only that she wanted such a campaign to be democratic and broadly-based but also that women's suffrage should also be seen as a class issue. Throughout 1913, once early apprehensions had been assuaged, the Federation developed a warm relationship with local socialist and Labour movements. This was evident in several demonstrations – for example the May Day march in 1913 where Federation members mingled with trade unionists and socialists – but was cemented in the struggle over free speech.

The Home Secretary, Reginald McKenna, who was responsible for the Cat and Mouse Act, banned suffragette meetings and censored *The Suffragette* as the WSPU's militant campaign reached new heights. Government repression only made the suffragettes more determined but brought in sections of the Left who though lukewarm or even hostile to the WSPU, were willing to act against restrictions on civil liberties. Demonstrations and protests by the Federation against the state or local council's repression of free speech were not only violent but marked by the involvement of socialists and trade unionists. When famous leaders like George Lansbury and John Scurr were imprisoned for their part in the struggle this involvement significantly increased.

The battle over free speech further turned the women's suffrage issue into a class question. At the Trafalgar Square demonstration of August 1913 for example, trade unionists, socialists and feminists, including Keir Hardie, Will Thorne, John Scurr, Dora Montefiore and Sylvia, addressed the crowd of over 20 000. Speeches condemned the government and, in spite of the absence of the WSPU on the platform, extended its sympathy to the suffragettes. But most significantly of all, speakers attempted to make connections between the suffragette and Labour movements, claiming that they were both a part of the same struggle. Sylvia welcomed this but stirred the crowd further by repeating the WSPU's famous motto 'Deeds not Words'. Yet instead of burning empty houses or pouring acid on golf greens, she significantly added 'it is the argument of sticks and stones from the East End women that is going to win freedom for women'.[61] A battle in Downing Street ensued.

Sylvia, though based in the East End, hoped her campaign would spread nationally. Writing in 1915 she claimed that her work in 1913 and 1914 did 'a tremendous amount of good work all over the country, for following the cue of East London, working people from Land's End to John O'Groats were beginning, more than they had ever done before, to feel that votes for women was their question'.[62] This is an exaggeration perhaps and does not credit the work of the radical suffragists in the north, but if only partially true, it constituted a threat, if only a potential threat, of far greater significance than that of the WSPU, whose militant campaign by this time could be dismissed as a law and order issue. A movement that brought together socialism and feminism, even hinted at bringing them together, was far more dangerous. Oddly enough perhaps, it was the same combination that led to the final split in late 1913.

This followed Sylvia's appearance at a meeting in the Albert Hall called by the Herald League, a socialist grouping around George Lansbury's *Daily Herald*, to protest against the lockout of Dublin workers and the imprisonment of James Larkin. On the platform with Sylvia were Lansbury, Charlotte Despard and the Irish revolutionary, James Connolly. While Connolly denounced the domination of nation over nation, sex over sex and class over class, Sylvia spoke 'to show solidarity with the Dublin workers and to keep the Women's side to the front'.[63] The Daily Herald, a keen supporter of Connolly and Larkin's Irish Transport and General Workers Union, gleefully reported that 'One great result of the militant Suffrage Movement has been to convince many people that the vote is not the best way of getting what one wants ... every day the industrial rebels and the suffrage rebels march nearer together'.[64]

Christabel was livid. She angrily denied that 'the WSPU is marching nearer to any other movement or political party', especially the Herald League, as it was 'a class organisation' and the vote would only be won through all classes of women.[65] Sylvia, who had known that a row would ensue as Christabel had ordered that the WSPU was not to be represented at the meeting, argued two months later that the WSPU leaders' 'view of the difference ... was that we had more faith in what could be done by stirring up working women ... while they had most faith in what could be done by people of means and affluence'. She added in a memorable phrase that 'they said a deputation to the Labour Party was all very well for us, but one for the King was better for them'.[66] Summoned to Paris, Sylvia later recorded in an undated manuscript *'The Women's Movement of Today and Tomorrow'*, held in the Pankhurst Papers in Amsterdam, that she was 'told to inform our members that, owing to our democratic constitution, and because of our proletarian character, we must be put outside the parent body'. Sylvia finally left the fold and the independent East London Federation of the Suffragettes (ELFS) was formed in January 1914.

Though autocrats are threatened by democracy, it was Sylvia's socialism that finally drove her out of the WSPU. Her belief in class action, her commitment to the ultimate goal of adult suffrage described by the ELFS in 1914 as 'the only possible demand of a working-class',[67] her refusal to attack Labour, alongside her continued willingness to work with men, hardly fitted in to current WSPU thinking. On the contrary, as Sylvia realised, 'my relatives were moving to the right and I and our Federation to the left'.[68] Sylvia's attempts to keep in the Union – she sent a circular to WSPU branches days after the Herald meeting – were doomed to failure for, as Christabel truthfully argued 'conflicting views and divided counsels in the WSPU there can not be'.[69] Perhaps the most surprising feature of the split was that it took so long to happen.

Though the Federation was expelled from the Union, it was the WSPU which stood in isolation from the women's suffrage movement as a whole. In many ways, Lansbury's comments about the closeness of the industrial and suffrage rebels was not without foundation. As Beatrice Webb wrote in *The New Statesman* in 1914 'the whole of the women's movement finds itself side-stepping almost unintentionally, into Labour and Socialist politics'.[70] This was due to the political situation at Westminster and the changed position of the Labour Party. The political impasse described earlier still seemed formidable, yet it was clear that parliamentary bills that only offered a limited extension of the electoral register were doomed to failure. If women's suffrage was to come at all, it would only be as part of a wider measure of franchise reform. And though Asquith and the Liberals could exist without the support of the Labour Party, how long could they ignore the next general election, scheduled for 1915? Equally significant was the Labour Party's resolution of the old conflict between limited and adult suffragists at its Annual Conference of 1912. Though still committed to the latter, it decided to oppose any franchise bill that did not include women. This still did not appease Christabel but as Liddington and Norris argue, 'Labour and Suffrage were reunited after a separation of seven or eight years'.[71]

These developments had an effect on the rest of the Women's Suffrage movement. The Women's Freedom League under Charlotte Despard was already sympathetic to Labour, but the largest and most influential organisation, the National Union of Women's Suffrage Societies, had always campaigned for the vote on non-party lines. This changed in May 1912 when it decided to support any party which included women's suffrage in its programme.[72] As its President, the lifelong Liberal Millicent Fawcett, later admitted, 'our change of policy was in effect a declaration of war against the official Liberal Party and of support of Labour'.[73] An election fighting fund employing over sixty organisers sympathetic to Labour was set up to aid the party in by-elections and it met with some success, four Liberals narrowly losing their seats in by-elections where the new policy was in operation in 1914.[74]

By 1912, the NUWSS, the WFL and Sylvia were pushing suffragism and Labour closer together, and emphasising votes for women as a class issue. 'All Women's Suffrage Societies now fully realise' the longstanding suffragist Isabella O. Ford wrote in 1913 'that the unjust position of working women is at the very root of our demand ... I can speak with the utmost intimate knowledge of the National Union at this point, for I have always been a member. Our demand has never been for the propertied'.[75] Asquith could not fail to note this message or ignore its threat. As Margaret Robertson, a member of the NUWSS delegation to the Prime Minister in the same year, put it:

> working men have come to regard this not as a sex question but as a democratic one. They think their class should have more representation and have begun to identify Anti Suffragism with the war of capital against labour ... The Trades Unions ... believe that opposition to [votes for women] comes from capitalists who want women cheap ... the Unions are increasingly determined that the woman must be enfranchised.[76]

It is in the context of Liberal Party concerns, the scheduled general election of 1915, the coming-together of mainstream suffragism and Labour (alongside perhaps, the threat of ever-increasing class struggle) that the significance of Asquith's response to the famous East End deputation in June 1914 should be considered. That it met at all was a tribute to Sylvia's strength and astounding courage, for Asquith had consistently and repeatedly refused to see her. In spite of her efforts and those of suffragists elsewhere, he was now hiding behind the hostility created by WSPU militancy, and also claiming that the demand for the vote only came from a few women. Asquith refused to see Sylvia even though she threatened to mount a permanent hunger and a thirst strike in or out of prison until he gave in. Arrested on 10 June, imprisoned till the 18th, Sylvia left the East End for the Commons determined to carry out her threat even though, as she plainly realised, it could end in her death. 'Is She to Die?', the *Woman's Dreadnought* (the ELFS weekly paper) asked; was Sylvia about to pay the ultimate price in her struggle, as she lay against Cromwell's statue by the Houses of Parliament?[77]

It may have been dramatic, Sylvia may even have been sublimi-
nally trying to attract her mother's attention and approval, but above
all it was brave and it worked. Sylvia would have fasted to death
and an exasperated Prime Minister, perhaps remembering the recent
death of Emily Wilding Davison, gave in. 'I don't want, if I can help
it, to secure her the martyr's crown', he desperately wrote to a
friend, Venetia Stanley, 'but *que faire?*'[78] After further pressure from
a worried Hardie, Asquith agreed to see six working women, but not
Sylvia, on 20 June – it was left to them to emphasise again the
growing working class support for women's enfranchisement.
Though Sylvia helped in preparing their statements to Asquith, it
was appropriate she herself did not go. 'Let these working mothers
speak for themselves' she argued, 'it was for this I had struggled.'[79]

Though wary of the six and keen to repeat his condemnation of
the 'criminal methods of the WSPU', Asquith did appear to change
his tune. Moreover, if votes for women were to become a reality, he
appeared to support a wide rather than a limited measure. 'If the
change has to come' he told them 'we must face it boldly and make
it thorough going and democratic in its basis.'[80] Asquith gave no
details or firm commitment to promoting this change, but his remarks were interpreted as significant and as a sign that suffragists at
the least had grounds for renewed optimism. 'Mr Asquith Begins to
Take Notice',[81] the NUWSS declared, while *The Labour Leader* argued
that 'Beneath his words there seemed to be a recognition that the
enfranchisement of women cannot long be delayed'.[82] As Emmeline
Pethick-Lawrence later argued, it was perhaps 'the first sign that he
was beginning to change his attitude of hostility to women's
suffrage'.[83]

One swallow may not make a summer, and one deputation of six
working-class women does not change a Prime Minister's mind. It
was what Julia Scarr, Elsie Watkins, Mrs Parsons, Jessie Payne, Mrs
Savoy and Mrs Bird represented that lay behind his apparent change
of heart. As further evidence of the merging of women's suffrage
with Labour and with a general election only a year away, the
deputation and the forces behind it constituted a threat to the Prime
Minister's position and party. Anti-suffragist though Asquith was,
he was not stupid and 'if the change had to come', it had to be faced,
from his point of view sooner rather than later. The deputation did
not single-handedly secure votes for women but neither, as Romero
implies, was it insignificant in the long struggle for votes for women.
Labour had already changed its position and what was now re-

quired was to show the Liberals that it was in their interests to do likewise. It is impossible to state what would have happened if the war had not intervened but the tide was perhaps at last turning in the suffragists' favour: Sylvia and her Federation played an important part in this process.

What then does Sylvia's life in this period illustrate about socialism, feminism and the women's suffrage movement? What does it show about Sylvia herself? Firstly, it again reflects the tremendous potential of suffragism to raise the political and feminist consciousness of countless women. As the socialist and radical suffragist Ada Nield Chew put it in 1912, 'If there is, lying dormant, one spark of latent freedom for growth, you have some ground to work on, some hope of results'.[84] The spark was the obvious insult of being denied a vote and the result was a fire potentially more damaging than any arson campaign organised by the WSPU. Moreover, as the revolutionary socialist MP Victor Grayson argued three years earlier, 'the right of women to the vote must be discussed on another basis than the value of the franchise. Their claim is to be recognised as intelligent human beings'.[85] Yet if the suffrage movement exposed obvious inequality between the sexes and politicised many women, it was deeply divided in aims, strategy and political aspirations, unable, like other single-issue campaigns, to conceal fundamental differences between its members.

The Pankhurstian breach of 1914 reflected two irreconcilable political positions at opposite ends of the suffragist scale, which no vague appeal to the mythical spirit of 'Woman' could heal. For Sylvia, as for increasing numbers of suffragists in the NUWSS and WFL, the campaign for votes for women was a sex *and* a class issue and it was this that drove her political development and shaped her strategic thinking. Of course, as we have seen in the case of adult suffrage, this position was not without its problems, not always successfully resolved. As a socialist, Sylvia wanted to maintain and expand the links with working-class movements but, as a feminist, without ignoring the specific oppression of women. Yet the struggle had to be by and for working-class women and based on the notion that *the vote was not enough.* Sylvia Pankhurst had no intention of packing her political bags once the vote was won. 'I am a Socialist' she wrote in 1913 'and want to see the conditions under which our people live entirely revolutionised.'[86] To achieve this required more than access to the parliamentary franchise and an analysis that explained political power in terms beyond mere possession of the vote.

In contrast, the WSPU leadership denied the importance of class and actively discouraged the involvement of working-class women in its campaign. Though paying lip service to other goals, it suffered from increasing monomania, as if votes for women was a panacea for all ills. The suffragettes, it seemed, could pack *their* bags once the battle was over, for there was little wrong with fundamental economic and class structures, only women's lack of the vote. Quite clearly, as Teresa Billington-Greig observed in 1911, 'The leaders of the militant movement do not want a revolution; we were mistaken who believed that they did; they would be afraid of one'.[87] Moving to the right and into splendid isolation, and locating men, all men, as the primary cause and agents of women's oppression, the WSPU adopted a political position that ignored the crucial importance of class. Sylvia may not have been successful in developing an ideology that could combine sex and class within a socialist feminist framework, but Christabel and Emmeline's position was not only a betrayal of the Union's roots but anathema to her and increasing numbers of suffragists and suffragettes. It was this rather than familial tensions that led to the split of 1914. To claim otherwise is to misunderstand the fundamental differences and conflicts within English suffragism.

Without straying too much onto ground covered by other contributors to this volume, the journeys Sylvia, Christabel and Emmeline took after 1914 surely confirm this explanation. During the war the WSPU became exceptionally nationalistic and xenophobic. 'Its chauvinism', Sylvia wrote, 'unexampled amongst all Women's Societies'.[88] The interests of women were submerged beneath the interests of the nation, and the once-despised Lloyd George became the new hero. The rights of workers – men and women – no longer mattered either, for that 'old delusion, class war, is exploded. The interests of the Nation are one and indivisable. The true, the natural and the divinely intended human grouping is according to nations'.[89]

Their rigorous anti-pacifism (Hardie, for example, was portrayed in a cartoon in *The Suffragette* receiving the Nobel Peace Prize from the Kaiser with a caption that read 'Also the Nobel Prize (tho Tardy), I now confer on Keir Von Hardie'[90] was only matched by an equally virulent opposition to socialism, and later, to the Russian Revolution of October 1917. Of course the threats of Germany and revolutionary opposition to the war were linked in Christabel's mind for had not 'Bolshevikism' been invented by a German, Karl Marx?[91] The extreme right-wing philosophy of what remained of the WSPU (there were two further breakaways during the war) culminated in the programme of the Women's Party, which replaced the Union in November 1917. Though making some reference to women, it had little to offer to them or to a working class ravaged by war. Violently anti-socialist, it was a monument to the direction Emmeline and Christabel had taken since 1905. Not surprisingly, Christabel stood for Parliament as the 'Patriotic Candidate and Supporter of the Prime Minister and Coalition' at Smethwick in 1918, her mother for the Conservatives, at Whitechapel ten years later. Neither make easy or comfortable heroines for radical feminists to claim.

On the other hand, Sylvia's commitment to socialism and a feminism, located in working-class communities, continued to develop and grow throughout the war and the immediate years after it. Barbara Winslow and Ian Bullock discuss this in subsequent chapters, yet it can be seen that the seeds of Sylvia's political progress were sown during her 'suffrage period' up to 1914. What is especially significant is how her campaigns and analyses, though never rigorous in their theoretical construction, began to take her beyond the political boundaries of suffragism, to the point at which she rejected its basic tenets. Her emphasis on class encouraged a view that demanded more than mere access to, or participation in, the existing political, economic and social structure – rather, it called for a new one altogether. The glaring inequality of wartime sacrifice and the events in Russia in 1917-18, ultimately convinced Sylvia that votes for women and the subsequent reforms which might ensue were not enough.

Clearly, Sylvia began to reject the limits of liberal or bourgeois political democracy. At the general election of 1918 for example, she hoped 'for nothing . . . saving that it might serve to spur the workers to abolish Parliament, the product and the instrument of the capitalist system'[92] and she was fiercely critical of those in the Labour and socialist movements who still wanted to play the parliamentary game. Ironically, given her pre-war battles and campaigns, the fact that women (over thirty) could vote in the election was of little importance, for power rested elsewhere. Sylvia came to this political position not simply through sororial conflict or familial tensions within the Pankhurstian clan but through her own actions and her commitment to socialism and the needs of the working class. Her feminism remained rooted in the working class too, though it is debatable how far she constructed a clear ideological and practical framework for socialist feminism. Would the specific oppression of women be simply washed away by the great revolutionary tide emanating from Russia and sweeping across Europe? Nonetheless, and in spite of some contemporary critics on the Left today,[93] Sylvia Pankhurst proudly belongs to an English socialist feminist tradition, and her life to 1914 provides the student of suffragism with another outstanding example of its rich and radical potential.

Notes

1. E. Sylvia Pankhurst, *The Suffragette Movement – An Intimate Account of Persons and Ideals* (London: Longmans, 1931). Though written several years after the events described took place and in spite of the problem of hindsight and an occasional tendency to exaggerate, Sylvia's book is still crucial to an understanding of her life and work.
2. P. Romero, *E. Sylvia Pankhurst – Portrait of a Radical* (London: Yale University Press, 1987).
3. Ibid., p 18, 20.
4. Ibid., p. 34.
5. Ibid., p. 79.
6. Ibid., p. xii.
7. A biographical approach is certainly useful and has proved to be extremely popular for this period. Recent work, for example, has included E. Linklater, *A Unhusbanded Life – Charlotte Despard: Suffragette, Socialist and Sinn Feiner* (London: Hutchinson, 1980), D. Nield Chew, *The Life and Writings of Ada Nield Chew* (London: Virago, 1982), J. Liddington, *The Life and Times of a Respectable Rebel* (London: Virago, 1984) and L. Garner, *A Brave and Beautiful Spirit – Dora Marsden 1882-1960* (London: Avebury, 1990).
8. *Anti-Suffrage Review*, 1910. Quoted in L. Garner, *Stepping Stones to Women's Liberty – Feminist Ideas in the Women's Suffrage Movement 1900-1918* (London: originally Heinemann, now Gower Press, 1984), p. 9. See ch. 1, 'Feminism and the 1900s' for a further discussion of this theme.
9. S. Rowbotham, *Women, Resistance and Revolution* (Harmondsworth, Penguin, 1974), p. 50.
10. For a further discussion of the parliamentary obstacles suffragists faced see D. Morgan, *Suffragists and Liberals: The Politics of Women's Suffrage in Britain* (Oxford: Blackwell, 1975) and M. Pugh, *Electoral Reform in War and Peace 1906-1918* (London: Routledge and Kegan Paul, 1978).
11. E. B. Bax, *The Fraud of Feminism* (London: Grant Richards, 1913).
12. See, for example, S. Rowbotham, *Hidden from History: 300 Years of Women's Oppression and the Fight Against It* (London: Pluto Press, 1977).
13. For a further discussion of party political attitudes to the franchise and its importance to conflict over the constitution see N. Blewitt, *The Peers, The Parties and The People: The General Election of 1910* (London: Macmillan,

1972).

14. The connection between an anti-women's suffrage position and opposition to universal suffrage is discussed throughout B. Harrison, *Separate Spheres: The Opposition to Women's Suffrage* (London: Croom Helm, 1978).
15. *The Suffragette Movement*, p. 167.
16. M. Macmillan, *The Life of Rachel Macmillan* (London: Dent, 1927) p. 75. Quoted in J. Liddington and J. Norris, *One Hand Tied Behind Us – The Rise of the Women's Suffrage Movement* p. 131.
17. *The Suffragette Movement*, pp. 1–146.
18. A. Rosen, *Rise Up Women! The Militant Campaign of the Women's Social and Political Union 1903 –1914* (London: Routledge and Kegan Paul, 1974) p. 30.
19. A fascinating contrast of experience of working-class members of the WSPU is provided by the autobiographies of Mitchell and Kenney: A. Kenney, *Memories of a Militant* (London: Edward Arnold, 1924), H. Mitchell, *The Hard Way Up: An Autobiography of Hannah Mitchell, Suffragette and Rebel* (London: Faber and Faber, 1968).
20. Rosen, pp. 24–48.
21. *The Suffragette Movement*, p. 169.
22. Ibid, p. 178.
23. Ibid, p. 249.
24. For example, Christabel spoke on 2 July 1905 to the West Salford ILP on 'What the Labour Party Would Do For Children'. Rosen, p. 47.
25. C. Pankhurst, *Unshackled: Or How We Won The Vote* (London: Hutchinson, 1959), p. 67.
26. Radical suffragists – like Selina Cooper and Ada Nield Chew – were northern working-class women who were involved in the Labour movement and fought for the vote and a wide social programme including equal pay, the right to work, birth control and child allowances.
27. 2nd Annual Conference Report of the WSPU, 1907.
28. See T. Billington-Greig, *The Militant Suffrage Movement – Emancipation in A Hurry* (London: F. Palmer, 1911). In this she complained that 'the movement has lost status as a serious rebellion and become a mere emotional obsession, a conventional campaign for a limited measure of legislation, with militancy as its instrument of publicity and the expression of its hurry', p. 113.
29. For further information on this fascinating woman see Linklater, *An Unhusbanded Life*.
30. There is as yet no thorough work on the history of the Women's Freedom League. For the suffrage period, see Garner, *Stepping Stones*, pp. 28–43; for a brief review of its long history see S. Newsome, *The Women's Freedom League 1907–1957* (London: WFL, 1957).
31. *Votes for Women*, October 1907, p. 6.
32. E. Pankhurst, *Why We Are Militant* (London: WSPU, 1913), p. 7. WSPU pamphlet.
33. Rosen, p.183.
34. C. Pankhurst, *Some Questions Answered* (London: WSPU c.1911) WSPU leaflet.
35. E. Pankhurst, *The Importance of the Vote* (London: WSPU 1914). WSPU

pamphlet, p. 9.

36. C. Pankhurst, *The Great Scourge and How To End It* (London: WSPU, 1913).
37. Morgan, *Suffragists and Liberals*, p. 64.
38. *The Suffragette*, 6 March 1914, p. 459.
39. Billington-Greig, *The Militant Suffrage Movement*, p. 57.
40. E. S. Pankhurst, *The Suffragette* (London: Gay and Hancock, 1911) p. iv.
41. Romero, *E. Sylvia Pankhurst*, p. 43, where she argues that Hardie put Sylvia in touch with Lansbury 'for help in filling the hall mostly with poor women from Bow and Bromley who attended more for the refreshments than the political message'. For a different and more balanced view see Rosen, *Rise Up Women!* pp. 58–61. In any case, it is hardly surprising that fares were paid or light refreshments laid on.
42. Hardie, a married man and respected political leader, left no evidence of the affair. The material left by Sylvia that relates to their relationship is often ambiguous and undated while *The Suffragette Movement* is hardly explicit. However, a close relationship between the two was established and was, as Romero and others have argued, probably sexual.
43. 'The Potato Pickers', *Votes for Women* 1908, p. 294.
44. *The Suffragette Movement*, p. 262.
45. The Countess of Oxford and Asquith (ed.) *Myself When Young by Famous Women of Today* (London: F Muller, 1938), p. 289–90.
46. *The Suffragette Movement*, p. 270.
47. Ibid., p. 264.
48. E. S. Pankhurst, *The Suffragette. The history of the women's militant suffrage movement 1905–1910* (New York: Sturgis and Walton, 1911) p. 173–4.
49. B. Winslow, 'Sylvia Pankhurst (1905–24), Suffragette and Communist', Ph. D thesis for Washington University, pp. 69-80. (Sylvia's own account of her visits to North America is briefly sketched in *The Suffrage Movement* pp. 347–50.)
50. Ibid., p. 74.
51. *The Suffragette Movement*, p. 348.
52. Sylvia Pankhurst, unpublished manuscript on her trip to America, International Institute Social History, Amsterdam, E. Sylvia Pankhurst Papers [ESPP] 117, p. 62.
53. *The Suffragette Movement*, p. 349. Clearly impressed by the USA, she added that 'some day I might become an American citizen', p. 350.
54. Romero, *E. Sylvia Pankhurst*, p. 62 argues that 'Sylvia saw Christabel's absence as her opportunity to head the movement'.
55. Sylvia Pankhurst, 'The Woman Movement of Today and Tomorrow' ESPP 131.
56. *The Suffragette Movement*, p. 416.
57. Ibid.
58. *Women's Dreadnought*, 8 March 1914, p. 1.
59. ELFS Executive Committee Minutes, 25 February 1914, ESPP 206.
60. *East London Observer*, 27 December 1913.
61. *The Suffragette*, 15 August 1914.
62. *Women's Dreadnought*, 2 January 1915.
63. Sylvia Pankhurst, *The Suffragette Movement*, p. 502.

64. Quoted in *The Suffragette*, 14 November 1913, p. 95.
65. Ibid.
66. ELFS Executive Committee Minutes, 27 January 1914, ESPP 206.
67. ELFS Executive Committee Minutes, 30 November 1914, ESPP 206.
68. S. Pankhurst, 'The Woman Movement of Today and Tomorrow', ESPP 131.
69. Christabel to Sylvia Pankhurst, 27 November 1913, ESPP 193.
70. *New Statesman*, 14 February 1914, quoted in Pugh, *Electoral Reform*, p. 17.
71. Liddington and Norris, *One Hand Tied Behind Us*, p. 247. The TUC adopted a similar policy the following year.
72. Special Council Meeting of the NUWSS, 14/15 May 1912, Fawcett Library.
73. Quoted in Liddington and Norris, *One Hand Tied Behind Us*, p. 247.
74. Pugh, *Electoral Reform* p. 22. See also J. V. Newberry 'Anti-War Suffragists' History 62, 206.
75. *Common Cause*, 3 January 1913, p. 671.
76. *Common Cause*, 15 August 1913, p. 319.
77. See Sylvia Pankhurst, *The Suffragette Movement*, pp. 563–77, *Woman's Dreadnought*, 20 June and 27 June 1914.
78. H. H. Asquith, *Letters to Venetia Stanley*, (edited by M. and E. Brock) (Oxford: Oxford University Press, 1982).
79. *The Suffragette Movement* p. 572.
80. *Woman's Dreadnought*, 27 June 1914, p. 57.
81. *Common Cause*, 26 June 1914, p. 243.
82. Quoted in *Woman's Dreadnought*, 4 July 1914, p. 65.
83. E. Pethick-Lawrence, *My Part In A Changing World* (London: Gollanz, 1938), pp. 304–5.
84. *The Free Woman*, 18 April 1912, p. 435.
85. *The Problem of Parliament – a Criticism and a Remedy* (London: New Age Press, 1909).
86. Sylvia Pankhurst to Captain White c. 1913, ESPP 197.
87. *The Militant Suffragette Movement*, p. 113.
88. *The Suffragette Movement*, p. 593.
89. *The Suffragette*, 17 September 1915, p. 325.
90. *The Suffragette*, 30 July 1915, front page.
91. *The Britannia*, 22 March 1918. Later, in *The Britannia*, 30 August 1918, Christabel argued that all socialist books should be burned by 'the public hangman'. *The Suffragette* had become the more patriotic *Britannia* in October 1915.
92. *The Workers' Dreadnought* 14 December 1918, p. 1152. Significantly, *The Woman's Dreadnought* changed to this title in July 1917. Indeed, the change from East London Federation of Suffragettes to Workers' Suffrage Federation (February 1916) to Workers' Socialist Federation (June 1918) tells its own story.
93. See Tony Cliff, *Class Struggle and Women's Liberation 1640 to the Present Day* (London: Bookmarks, 1984) pp. 125–32. Though excellent on the limitations of reformism, Cliff underestimates the consciousness raising potential of movements like the battle for Women's Suffrage and misunderstands in particular Sylvia's 'collaboration with bourgeois feminists' (p. 131).

4

Sylvia Pankhurst and the Great War

BARBARA WINSLOW

When war broke out in August 1914, Sylvia Pankhurst, who had been a long-time supporter of Home Rule and Irish independence, was in Dublin compiling a firsthand report on Irish events for her newspaper, *The Woman's Dreadnought*. British troops had fired on a crowd of innocent civilians, and the incident became known as the Bachelors's Walk Massacre. Devastated by the declaration of war, Pankhurst 'could not realise its full horror.'[1] She had known that war was imminent; her mentor and lover, Keir Hardie, had warned her, but she had been so embroiled in the struggle for votes for women that thoughts about war – or, more important, about antiwar organising – were pushed to the side. Knowing that it was coming, however, in no way softened the blow. She took the first boat back across the Irish sea and quickly returned to London. On board, surrounded by young drunken men in khaki, she spent a sleepless night agonizing over the future:

> Vainly I tried to shut out the noise of that sad wassailing, tormented by the visions of those drunken faces at the station, seared by the thought that men were going to die, without heed to the beauty and purpose of life . . . going like cattle to be slaughtered, mere pawns in the hands of those whose very identity was unknown to them. I thought of armies marching along the thoroughfares of Europe; bringing destruction to peaceful homes: of all the multitudes called up to fight, each one leaving behind him the desolate grief of women . . . . [T]he scenes, peoples, the movement I had visited . . . bitterly would they suffer . . . . Throughout Europe would be a vast widowhood, the cries of fatherless children, the groans of injured men . . . [A] triumph sadly immense for

the annihilating power of violence maintained by the great stores of wealth, drawn up from any and every source, and ultimately from the great toil and hard privations of the people, beneath a great hunger, 'till famine prove the victor'.[2]

The First World War brought tremendous changes to the life of Sylvia Pankhurst. Since 1903, she had been totally involved, with her mother and sister, in the Women's Social and Political Union (WSPU), the organization that represented the militant wing of the woman's suffrage movement. As the suffrage agitation escalated, Sylvia found herself more at odds with her mother Emmeline and her sister Christabel, who had broken their relationship with the labour and socialist movement. In 1912, Sylvia went into the East End of London to organise working class women to fight for the vote, women's emancipation and socialism. In 1913, Christabel expelled her sister from the WSPU, and Sylvia continued to build her own organisation, the East London Federation of the Suffragettes [ELFS] and its newspaper, *The Woman's Dreadnought*.

The women's suffrage movement, of which Sylvia was a participant, collapsed with the onslaught of war, and women who had been involved in the struggle for the vote were now equally divided amongst themselves on the issue of supporting or opposing the war.

The socialist movement, in which Pankhurst was also involved, both in England and internationally, was thrown into confusion. The movement had long condemned wars as a means by which ruling classes solved their internal domestic problems at the expense of the working class. Prior to 1914, socialists, radical trade unionists, and most feminists shared Pankhurst's pacifism. The Second International, an international organization of Socialist parties, had resolved that, if war broke out, it was the duty of socialists not to support their government's belligerency; it called for workers of all involved countries to go out on strike against war. However, when fighting did break out, many abandoned their principles of 'sisterhood' and 'international working class solidarity' to support their own national ruling class against workers and 'sisters' of other nations.

This chapter traces the social crisis that revolutionised Pankhurst and her organisation. The European conflagration presented Sylvia Pankhurst with the issues of socialism and feminism, which were never fully resolved due to wartime contradictions. The wartime experience was a crucial transition in the life of Pankhurst. In 1914, she was a socialist suffragette, pacifist, and sympathiser with the

Independent Labour Party (ILP) and the Labour Party. By the time of the signing of the Armistice in 1918, Pankhurst was an International Socialist and revolutionary feminist.

Between 1914 and 1917, the ELFS made a shift of which Pankhurst was not fully aware. It changed from a political organisation that mobilised women to fight for political demands for themselves, to a feminist social-welfare organisation that attempted to provide the same relief that the government should have provided to alleviate the misery caused by the war. The organisation's demand for suffrage also changed from votes for women to universal suffrage. An indication of this change of emphasis is that, in March 1916, the ELFS was renamed the Workers' Suffrage Federation.

By the end of the war, however, Pankhurst's experiences of fighting against the horrors of the war and government repression even greater than in the days of suffrage militancy had led her to a revolutionary political position. She came to realise that her organisation should not be trying to provide resources for the East End, but rather should fight for a socialist and feminist restructuring of society. During the war years, Pankhurst emerged as one of Britain's leading revolutionary antiwar agitators. In 1918, the organisation's name and focus changed again; this time it became the Workers' Socialist Federation and was no longer an East End-based organisation, but a national federation with branches in England and Scotland.

ANTIWAR ORGANIZING

Given the widespread collapse of socialist and pacifist ideals once war had broken out, the first task facing Sylvia Pankhurst was to convince the ELFS that it must oppose the war. Upon her return from Dublin, she found that a number of the members and officers – Jessie Payne and Norah Smyth, two leading members, for example – supported England's cause. Pankhurst's fierce and uncompromising opposition to the war, and her determination to impose her position on the ELFS cost her dearly in terms of members.

The peak of the federation membership had been reached at the height of the suffragette campaign in the East End in 1914. With the general overwhelming patriotism at the beginning of the war, the ELFS lost many members and supporters, both middle- and working-class. Elvina Haverfeld, the Federation treasurer, resigned, although Norah Smyth and Jessie Payne changed their positions about the war and remained in the ELFS, and Dr Barbara Tchaykovsky was so repulsed by the fanatical belligerency of Christabel and Emmeline that she left the WSPU and became a devoted worker for the Federation.[3] As the East End began to feel wartime hardships, however, the original outburst of patriotism dissipated, and the ELFS/WSF won new recruits. Even so, there were no more than a few hundred people actively involved in the ELFS/WSF during wartime.[4]

The problems of membership were discussed at Federation meetings quite openly. East Londoners were faced with the disincentive of intolerable conditions brought on by war. For example, in October 1916 and again in September 1917, it was reported difficult to get people to meetings because of the bombing of the East End. Outdoor meetings were slightly more successful, as were indoor and outdoor meetings held in provincial towns.[5]

From 1914 to 1917, all sixteen of the executive committee members lived in the East End. By 1917, half had left the organisation. Only four remained on the executive committee until 1920, and many of the new recruits came from outside the East End. Men were admitted as members but, unlike women, had to be nominated and seconded by the branch committee (the executive committee of a local branch) and then approved by the executive committee.[6] They also served on the executive committee after 1918, but never dominated the proceedings.[7] In 1915, the ELFS set up an associate membership category for young people aged fourteen to eighteen who wanted to join.[8]

After 1914, the ELFS expanded outside the boundaries of the East End. Before war broke out, the ELFS had branches in the North London area of Hackney. By October 1915, there was a branch in Holborn, and by 1916, branches were organised in Hoxton, St Pancras, Holloway, and Islington. Some of the local branches set up their own offices with a bookstore.[9] By 1917, the WSF had thirty branches in many parts of England, South Wales, and Scotland. Many of the branches were in key industrial areas, and by the end of the war, the WSF had established links with other leading socialist and industrial militants. However, none of the branches outside London's East End had either the numbers or social influence of the original ELFS.

In the war years, the ELFS also attracted a remarkable group of women socialist organisers and agitators. Emma Boyce was a roving organiser for the ELFS/WSF. An early member of the ILP, she joined the WSF in the early years of the war. She had had twelve children of whom four had survived, and three of these fought in the war. She spent time organising in Newcastle and Glasgow. Being an organiser was dangerous work. I. Renson, a colleague, described a particular incident:

> When we were in Reading, me and my brother witnessed the breaking up of a 'Stop the War' meeting in the Market Place in about September 1918 by soldiers. The meeting was organised by the ILP and the chief speaker was Mrs Boyce of Hackney. Soon after this elderly lady got on to the platform, it was pushed over and she fell off backwards, but she appeared to have been caught by her friends who were behind her.[10]

In her fifties, when she worked with the WSF, Boyce was a tireless activist, speaking sometimes five times a week and travelling around the country. She was elected a Hackney Labour councillor in 1918, and after 1923, served as the governor of the London Maternity Hospital. She died in 1929.[11]

Another new member was Jessie Stephens, a Glaswegian who had been active in the militant suffragette movement as well as in the Socialist Sunday schools (organisations that borrowed the Sunday School form, but not the content) and the ILP.[12] When war broke out, she went to London, hoping to find a job, and met Pankhurst, who immediately asked her to work for the ELFS. Stephens, only twenty at the time, went back to Glasgow to think about Pankhurst's offer, finally deciding to take it. The Stephens family was very poor, and Jessie did not have the train fare to go back to London, but one night her mother defied her husband and secretly gave Jessie the fare.[13]

After the young woman had spent some time in London, Pankhurst sent her out to organise the provincial cities. Stephens later described her work:

> There were two of us, Mrs Boyce, a working woman who'd brought up a family of twelve kids and was going around the country, just like me. She gave me lots of hints as what to do. She says, 'always take with you a pound of candles because you'll find in some places no light, when you'll want to read in your bed and you can't . . .'
> When I was working for Sylvia I got thirty bob a week and it wasn't enough sometimes to pay my digs when I was travelling

through the country. But I used to go to the ILP branches as well – freelance, of course, because none of us were on salary – we had to depend on the branches to pay us what they could . . . . You couldn't buy new clothes on that. In fact, I went to Burnley market once and bought a remnant there for 6d to make myself a blouse. My first stop on the WSF tour was Sheffield where I was lucky enough to find lodgings with Mrs Manion. The friendly atmosphere helped me enormously in this first provincial venture.[14]

Stephens was also successful as a fund raiser for the ELFS/WSF. She stayed on until the spring of 1917, when she became an ILP organiser for Bermondsey. Stephens enjoyed working with and respected Pankhurst, who she said 'could charm when she liked, but at the core was inclined to be as autocratic as her mother and elder sister Christabel'.[15] Like so many others, Stephens continued her political activism after she left Pankhurst's organisation. She participated in the birth control movement and was the first woman president of the Bristol Trades Council. In 1975, when she was interviewed by *Spare Rib*, the English feminist magazine, Stephens was eighty-one and still active in the Trades Union Congress.[16]

Still another activist was Lillian Thring, a militant suffragette from London who in 1911 moved to Melbourne, Australia, where she came into contact with revolutionaries and joined the Industrial Workers of the World (IWW). She was famous for being a brilliant public speaker. Married in 1913, she lived briefly in the Sudan and then returned in 1915 to England, where she joined the ELFS/WSF. She was especially active in the 'Hands Off Russia' campaign and the Workers' Committee Movement. As an alumna of the WSF, Thring was active in the Communist Party, the ILP, and the antifascist and trade union movements in the 1930s, 1940s, and 1950s.[17]

Upon the outbreak of war, the ELFS had to rearrange its priorities. When its executive committee met to discuss the wartime emergency, it decided that it had three options: to continue suffragette activities as if nothing had happened; to try and alleviate suffering in the East End; and 'to make capital out of the situation', meaning to exploit the issue of the war in order to gain new members.[18] Suffrage work took a back seat to defending the East End: the executive committee voted for the second choice. However, given Pankhurst's passionate pacifism, the federation did all it could to make political capital out of the wartime catastrophe. Pankhurst was aware of her political isolation; she could 'not say much against the war at present as so many people have relations in it, that they will not listen yet'.[19] It was not until 1915, when antiwar sentiment was developing, that the WSF took a clear antiwar position.

During the first two years of the war, the ELFS/WSF was, for the most part, largely responsible for initiating what antiwar activity existed in London. Its tactics were similar to those used during the suffrage agitation. Meetings were usually held at the East India Dock Gates followed by a procession to Victoria Park. Even though most of the demonstrations were large, with numbers of soldiers and sailors participating, they were smaller than the suffragette demonstrations had been, and they were met with greater hostility than before.[20] Melvina Walker, who lived in Poplar two doors away from the recruiting office on East India Dock Road, wrote that Dock Road was an extremely good spot to have chosen for that office, for it was a 'parade ground for the unemployed'.[21] The dock gates, once the sacred ground of socialist agitators, became a platform for recruiters. Pankhurst travelled to Glasgow in October 1914, where, at a well-attended meeting sponsored by the ILP, she said that peace must be made by the people and not by the diplomats, thus becoming one of the first suffragettes to speak out against the war.[22] In December, along with a hundred other prominent English women, she signed an open Christmas letter, published in *Jus Suffragi*, an international women's suffrage publication, from the 'British Women to the Women of Germany and Austria', which said, 'We are with you in this sisterhood of sorrow'.[23]

The war began with a volunteer army – in keeping with Liberal ideas of individual freedom. But by 1915, the realities of trench warfare led not only to an increased need for new recruits, but also to a need to discipline the civilian population. Early in 1915 there were strikes of engineering workers in Glasgow and dockers in Liverpool as workers decided they had a right to share in the increased profits that their extra war work was creating. The government passed draconian legislation, designed to get more recruits into the armed forces and to better discipline the workers in defence-related industries. The Defence of the Realm Act (DORA), passed in August 1914, was continually amended. Under the DORA it was illegal to spread information 'likely to cause disaffection or alarm' to anyone in the military or among the civilian population. Suspects could be arrested without a warrant. Power was given to search anyone's premises at any time or place and to seize documents or anything the government deemed suspect. Furthermore, persons arrested under the DORA could be tried by military court-martial as if the individual were a soldier on active duty.[24] It was under this act that individual antiwar agitators like the Scot John Maclean were imprisoned.

In May 1915, the government also passed the Munitions Act, which regulated the lives of all workers employed by the munitions industry. Finally, after 1915, the government began to pass a long series of acts designed to 'soften up' the British public and to get it ready for 'Prussian' type conscription in 1916, then full conscription in 1918. Pankhurst and a growing number of socialists campaigned against military conscription for men and industrial conscription for women; they also objected to the fact that only labouring people – workers and the military – were being conscripted, not capital, essential services, and supplies.[25]

Pankhurst was particularly appalled by section 40d of the Defence of the Realm Act. This made it compulsory for women suspected of being prostitutes to be inspected for venereal diseases. It was against the law to have sexual intercourse with a member of H M Forces if one had such a disease. Pankhurst argued that this laid innocent women open to blackmail and false imprisonment; it punished women and led men to believe that, since they were automatically absolved from any guilt in transmitting venereal diseases, prostitution was right and necessary.[26] Yet feminists who had earlier campaigned against the Contagious Diseases Act – with the exception of the Women's Freedom League – remained silent about this and other new versions of repressive legislation.

The government also rushed through the National Register Act, which made it compulsory for all citizens to supply the government with detailed particulars of their lives and their trade or profession. Penalties would be imposed on anyone who did not register or falsely claimed to have registered.[27] Pankhurst, the ELFS, and other trade union and radical groups opposed the Act because they saw it as the first step toward conscription.

In July 1915, the ELFS announced it would march through London protesting against the Registration Act and the conditions of sweated labour. Pankhurst had written to Lloyd George asking him to meet this deputation, whose objective was to call attention not just to the registration of workers, but also to the high cost of food and coal and to the low level of women's wages: it would also demand equal pay for equal work. For this march Pankhurst had no support from official representatives of organised labour or from working women's groups such as the Women's Trade Union League, the Women's Cooperative Guild, or the Women's Labour League. Unable to get Trafalgar Square, she settled for an indoor meeting in a small meeting room.[28] *The Daily Herald*, a sympathetic Socialist newspaper edited by George Lansbury, tried to paint a rosy picture of a demonstration which was clearly hurt by bad weather and poor attendance:

> Neither thunderstorms nor rain are capable of dampening the courage and endurance of Sylvia Pankhurst and her East End friends and comrades. A few men joined with them last Sunday to march for nearly three hours over the London roads from East to West, but only after much talk and misgivings, for when the time to start had arrived thunder was still in the air and rain had scarcely ceased; but although mere men had declared it foolish to start, Miss N. Smyth and S. Pankhurst were both cheery and hopeful, and what is more, the young women and others who brought their banners and collecting boxes were determined, rain or no rain, to start off, and so . . . to the sounds of the *Marseillaise* we started off.[29]

In August 1915, the ELFS also staged a demonstration opposing registration which won support from a large number of prominent individuals and organisations such as the Suffragette Crusaders, the United Suffragists, the Amalgamated Society of Toolmakers, Engineers and Machinists, the British Socialist Party (BSP), and the National Union of Gasworkers. The speakers at the rally were Charlotte Despard, suffragette and Irish nationalist; George Lansbury, East End Socialist, friend and supporter of Pankhurst and the ELFS; Bessie Ward of the London section of the Shop Assistants' Union; Julia Scurr, Sylvia Pankhurst, Charlotte Drake, and Edith Sharpe of the ELFS; W. I. Appleton of the General Federation of Trade Unions; Margaretta Hicks of the National Women's Council; and Miss L. Rothwell of the Women's Trade Union League.[30] This demonstration was large and well received.

Pankhurst, speaking for the ELFS, said that the register had been initiated 'solely for the purpose of exploiting the workers and [would] be used for that object'. She went on to denounce war profiteering and women's sweated labour, finally saying that she would refuse to sign the register, for she, like millions of Englishwomen, still did not have the vote.[31]

However, the demonstration had no effect on the government, which later that year passed a bill that called upon men to 'attest' that they would undertake military service if and when they were called upon to do so. Known as the Derby scheme, this was the last attempt to keep recruitment on a voluntary basis. Conscription for single men was introduced in January 1916, and universal manhood conscription in May 1916.

The ELFS/WSF continued its opposition to conscription. In December 1915 the ELFS, represented by Charlotte Drake, Emma Boyce, and Eugenia Bouvier, participated in a 'No Conscription Conference' held under the auspices of the Poplar and Hackney Trades Councils.[32] This meeting led to a major 'No Conscription' demonstration, on 9 January 1916, with 2,000 people attending. Speaking for the federation were Drake, Walker, and Bouvier.[33] This rally, however, was far smaller than the earlier 'No Conscription Conference'. In the same month, the ELFS/WSF began to lobby Parliament in the vain hope of convincing MPs not to vote for conscription.

Because of the imminence of conscription, other radical and socialist groups began for the first time to work with the ELFS/WSF in antiwar, antirepression activities. In February 1916, the ELFS/WSF, the ILP, and the newly formed No-Conscription Fellowship held a meeting attended by 500 people. Melvina Walker spoke for the Federation, and according to the *East London Observer*:

> She dealt with the evils of conscription from the working woman's point of view and suggested that if they did not actively oppose it now it would not be very long before the women of England were conscripted and sent to make bombs by which other mothers' sons would be slaughtered.[34]

On 1 March, at another meeting sponsored jointly with the Forest Gate and District branch of the No Conscription Fellowship, Emma Boyce, who had three sons in uniform, spoke out for the Federation against conscription. She argued that, if military conscription was introduced, industrial conscription and the crushing of the workers would be next.[35] Also that week, Nellie Best, a woman unknown to Pankhurst, was imprisoned for violation of the DORA. Hundreds of women organized by the ELFS/WSF demonstrated against her imprisonment.[36]

During the second week of March, the newly renamed Workers' Suffrage Federation organised a demonstration in Trafalgar Square which demanded 'human suffrage' and repeal of the DORA, the Munitions Act, and conscription. New provisions under the DORA enabled the Army Council or the Admiralty to occupy factories that employed vital workers and to requisition and to regulate their output. The Munitions Act, passed in May, was supposed to come into force in July 1915. In making provision for the settlement of labour disputes in munitions works, the act proscribed strikes. In order to prevent wages from increasing when workers moved from plant to plant, workers were forbidden to leave their place of work. The Act also provided for limitations on profits and established Munitions Tribunals to deal with offences committed under the act. As the government took over more and more industries and services, the scope of the act was further extended.

The focus of the Trafalgar Square march, held on 8 April, 1916, was to oppose the full scope of the government's repressive legislation.[37] The WSF worked hard for it. Norah Smyth went to the Dockers' Union for support; similarly, Mrs Walts visited the Gasworkers. Miss Beamish approached the Canning Town ILP, the BSP, and the Shoreditch Trades Council.[38] On 12 March, Mrs Drake and twenty other members were arrested in the East London area of the Isle of Dogs for sticking publicity posters on walls. The posters said 'War is Murder' and 'The Soldiers in the Trenches are Longing for Peace'.[39]

This demonstration, numbering 20,000, was perhaps the largest of the antiwar protests to date. The WSF led a large contingent on the familiar six-mile route from Bow to Poplar to Trafalgar Square. On the platform were leading members and supporters of the WSF: Pankhurst, Charlotte Drake, Melvina Walker, Dr Tchaykovsky, and Eva Gore-Booth, suffragist, Irish nationalist, feminist and poet. Also speaking was a Glasgow city councillor, Mr Taylor, who reported on the engineers' strike that was sweeping the Clydeside and about the situation of workers who had been arrested under the DORA.[40] Despite the presence of a large number of hostile soldiers and sailors who threw red dye and physically assaulted some of the speakers, the demonstration was an indication of growing opposition to war and wartime conditions.

In May, the ELFS issued a leaflet which was distributed to women in the East End. It warned:

In a few days conscription will be the law of the land. Can the mothers realise what this means? Do they realise that henceforth every boy born of an English mother will be branded with the mark of Cain? For let nobody be deceived by this lying tale of conscription for the operation of the war. It has come to stay. Are we going to strike a blow for freedom and right. If so that blow must be struck at once. Now is the time to act. Now is the time to work. The work of the Workers' Suffrage Federation is to waken up the people to a sense of their obligation and of their rights.[41]

True to its promise, the WSF continued antiwar agitation throughout 1916. In June, it called a Woman's Convention Against Conscription, where it was decided to ask Prime Minister Asquith to receive a deputation of working women – consisting of most of the women who had met him about woman's suffrage in 1914 – who would explain why they opposed conscription.[42]

This time Asquith did not agree to the demands made by the WSF. Conscription and DORA was far too important to the success of the war effort. In all probability, Asquith knew that even though the WSF could organise demonstrations, it was not as powerful as in the prewar suffragette days. Furthermore, he was aware that the East End, like the rest of the country, was divided on the issue of the war and that most working people would support the government rather than the WSF.[43]

In December, the WSF held a well-attended open-air peace rally at the East India Dock Gates that ended with several arrests. A young man named Attlee (not the future Prime Minister) was speaking against the war when a group of angry men began asking why he was not in uniform. The men tried to throw Attlee off the stage. The police, who had done nothing to protect the speakers, ordered the meeting to end. Pankhurst, Walker, and Charlotte Drake began to speak. The police then arrested them as well as Minnie and Edgar Lansbury (the daughter-in-law and son of George Lansbury) claiming that it was for their own good. The crowds were very hostile, explained a sergeant named Loftus, and they wanted to throw Pankhurst in the river.[44] The charges were later dropped.

With the inevitable passage of conscription, the WSF turned to the peace campaign, which had already been initiated by Helen Crawfurd and Agnes Dollan, ILP women in Glasgow. They thought about bringing working women from the provinces to march upon Parliament, but it proved too expensive.[45] The organisation also sent its members on a 'peace canvass' in the East End, which unfortunately

met with little success. The *Dreadnought* explained why the canvass-
ers' arguments fell on hostile and bitter ears:

> It was pathetic to find poorly clad women with pinched white
> faces and backs bent with excessive toil, excitedly cry out,
> 'We want peace on our own terms.' It is strange that past experi-
> ence has not taught them that they will be given no voice in the
> terms of settlement and that their interests will not even be
> considered . . . . [S]ome said, 'we want our sons to have their
> revenge,' and others cried, 'Our sons are dead; your talk of peace
> can never bring them back'.[46]

Nevertheless, the WSF continued its dogged antiwar agitation. It
continued to hold open-air and antiwar meetings in the East End,
especially by the dock gates. More and more, the WSF found itself in
demonstrations with socialist organisations such as the BSP and the
ILP. It picketed the 1917 Labour party conference, where a number
of delegates shouted abuse at the women.[47] The treatment the WSF
members received at the hands of the Labour Party convinced Sylvia
that the party no longer represented the interests of working people,
thus helping to shape her strong antiparliamentary convictions.

Pankhurst also attended the 1918 Labour Party Conference, where
she moved the British Socialist Party's resolution that the Labour
party withdraw from the government because of Liberal-Tory support for the war. Again, she was rudely treated, and her motion was
lost.[48] It was these wartime experiences with the Labour Party which
convinced her of its bankruptcy and of the futility of working with
it.

Pankhurst's antiwar activity was not solely confined to the East
End; she also worked with women from the earlier suffrage campaign. Contrary to popular belief – which Pankhurst herself helped
create in *The Home Front*, a highly personal account of her experiences during the First World War – not all women in the suffrage
movement supported the war. In fact, half of them opposed it, and
many who had been involved in the Women's Congress, an international organisation of feminists, formed the British section of the
Women's International League in late April 1915.[49] Pankhurst attended a preliminary meeting in London, was elected to the executive committee, and moved that the title be changed to the Women's
International Peace League and that women who were not British
citizens be allowed to join. The resolution was defeated.[50]

She was very critical of the WIL; some of her feelings, no doubt, were due to the fact that many of its leaders had been involved in the nonmilitant National Union of Women's Suffrage Societies, and Pankhurst considered them politically timid. For its part, the WIL was cautious and did not wish to be associated with radicals.[51]

The monthly WIL meetings lasted from 10 am to 6 pm, and she would return to the East End exhausted. In October 1915, there was a discussion as to whether the ELFS should formally affiliate with the WIL. Despite her criticisms of it, Pankhurst argued that the league was 'the best and most ambitious interpretation of the women's movement today', pointing out that the ELFS was 'more advanced than most of the others [women's groups] who belong to the League and our mission is to lead them'. She further suggested an East End branch of the WIL. Charlotte Drake argued that affiliation would be too great a drain on the Federation, but Pankhurst's motion was carried.[52] The debate became academic two months later when it turned out that the WSF had too few members; 5,000 were required for affiliation.[53] Pankhurst resigned from the WIL in 1917, when it refused to support one of its own members: Emily Hobhouse had been strip-searched and called a traitor by the British government after travelling to Belgium to report on the truth of British stories about German atrocities.[54]

Pankhurst's relationship with the WIL shows that she did not want herself or the ELFS to be 'insular', as she argued at the October 1915 executive committee meeting – even if this meant working with middle-class women and former opponents within the suffrage movement.[55] She had her differences and impatience with the WIL: for example, it had refused to support the demonstration protesting against Nellie Best's sentence for violating the DORA (Mrs Swanwick, who chaired the meeting, told Pankhurst that she 'didn't think the sentence was severe . . . . [I]t might have been death').[56] Yet Pankhurst was uncharacteristically charitable about its work. 'It carried no fiery cross; but tried in a quiet way, sincerely, if at times haltingly, to understand the causes of war, and to advance the cause of peace by negotiation, and the enfranchisement of women.'[57]

During the war, Pankhurst emerged as one of the leading socialist anti-war agitators. In September 1915, she spoke at an anti-war, anticonscription rally of 600 or 700 people in Bristol.[58] In July 1915, when miners in South Wales successfully struck in defiance of the Munitions Act, Pankhurst took up their cause. She spoke at meetings in South Wales and later wrote regular articles for the *Rhondda*

Socialist. The ILP wanted to run Robert Smillie, the miners' leader, for Parliament in Keir Hardie's old district, and the ILP asked her if she would like to campaign for him. The general membership of the WSF voted unanimously that Pankhurst should do this, for Smillie was a suffragist, supported trade union rights, and opposed conscription. Another motivation for Sylvia to campaign for the miners' leader was that her mother and older sister actively opposed Smillie because of his opposition to the war and conscription.[59] In 1915, she also took a dangerous trip to speak in Belfast. Crossing the Irish Sea was risky during the war since German U-boats were always on patrol.[60]

In 1916, Pankhurst spoke at several meetings in Glasgow with George Lansbury and John Maclean, the pioneering Scottish Marxist and leading revolutionary on the 'red Clyde.' She praised and defended women who had successfully organized a rent strike. Speaking in opposition to her mother and sister's industrial campaign, she warned shop stewards to stand firm against conscription and profiteering; they should beware, she said, of the dilution of their jobs by unskilled workers, who would be forced to do their work for a fraction of their proper wages. She also urged strike action when necessary, even though it was illegal.[61] In May 1917, school children in Burston, Norfolk, went on strike, set up their own strike school, and invited Pankhurst to come and speak.[62]

Still, none of this antiwar agitation persuaded the Labour party, the coalition government in power, or any significant number of people in the East End either to join the ELFS/WSF or to adopt many of its anti-war positions. The ELFS/WSF was a small organization working with other small organizations and battling against wartime patriotism as well as the general conservativism of the East End. Nonetheless, a small group of dedicated activists kept the issues of peace and opposition to government repression alive during this difficult political period.

FEMINIST SOCIAL WORK

During the war, Pankhurst became caught up in the contradictions of the organisation she had built. Unlike other socialists who opposed the war, she had an organisation that she could immediately mobilise to do consistent anti-war work – she was not an individual voice at the East End dock gates. But it had been built, for the most part, on the issue of women's suffrage (albeit in the context of other social issues), and it was embedded in one community. During the war, Sylvia found herself creating many social welfare agencies – substituting for government agencies that did not exist – in order to serve the pressing needs of the women of the East End. She also found herself in a dilemma similar to that which faced the shop stewards' movement or the engineers during the war: do you consistently oppose the war, or do you campaign for better wages and working conditions for workers in war production? Pankhurst came to the same conclusion as the shop stewards and engineers: she fought for the rights of the community, which in her case meant advocating equal pay for equal work for war workers.

Her concern simultaneously to continue antiwar, anticonscription, and peace agitation, as well as a limited amount of suffrage agitation, as well to build social welfare agencies, and to organise women workers pulled her in many different directions. In order to maintain its social work agencies, the ELFS/WSF had to appeal for money to middle-class supporters of the suffrage movement. At the same time, many members of the organisation became anti-war activists and took stands opposing those of their affluent supporters. Meanwhile the ELFS/WSF was losing its exclusive East End base and gradually becoming a national organisation through the *Dreadnought*, which was reaching a wider audience.

The ELFS/WSF expended a great deal of its energies in the area of public relief.[63] It was this work that shifted the Federation's focus. While it lobbied Parliament, wrote exposés in the press, and pressured individuals to do something about the conditions of women workers, the ELFS/WSF did not spend equal amounts of time and energy trying to organise these workers to change their working situation. The Federation set up day-care centres and nurseries, communal restaurants, baby clinics, and other types of services for the people of the East End; while all these were invaluable to those who benefited from them, they constituted a departure from the old suffragette tactic of organising thousands of people to force the government to provide the necessary services. As the organisation spent more time and energy providing community services, the ELFS/WSF lost a great deal of its earlier strength. Emma Boyce astutely commented that by 1917 the Federation seemed more like 'a charity organisation with suffrage tacked on'.[64]

The decision to devote so much time and effort to providing services came mainly from the real needs of East End women. Malvina

Walker, for example has described how Poplar women were faced with a shortage of many commodities during the war, especially sugar. Yet the dockers were unloading tons of sugar into the warehouses. Women of the ELFS/WSF went to see the President of the Board of Trade, but got nowhere. Walker also described the desperate potato shortage, which led women to get up at five in the morning and wait all day in line, quite often to be turned away empty-handed. They then had to face the prospect of spending the night in 'dug out' bomb shelters. Crowds of women ran past Walker's door, carrying their babies, rugs and cushions to the Blackwall Tunnel, where they stayed until daybreak. The tunnel they fled to for protection against bombs also sheltered wagonloads of munitions awaiting shipment. People were often maimed or killed when the horses went wild, frightened by the booming of the bombs.[65]

The work that was done, even though it led to greater problems, was an indication of the strong socialist and feminist convictions of the Federations. Food became an increasingly important issue as the war progressed; the food lines, the profiteering and cheating by the rich, rubbed the working class's nose in the shortages. On 8 August 1914, the *Dreadnought* called for a No Rent Strike '[u]ntil the government controls the food supply'.[66] The No Rent Strike was soon dropped. Sylvia wrote to Hannah Sheehy Skeffington, the Irish suffragette, on 24 August, that 'we are postponing the No Rent Strike until things get more acute as only a proportion of people are ready for it yet, but of course we still go on with our suffrage work'.[67]

As soon as war was declared, the Federation met and adopted a programme of nationalisation of food supplies – a programme that showed its concern for working women and worker's control. The resolution stated:

> During the war, the food shall be controlled by the government in the interests of all the people in order that we may feed or starve together without regard to wealth or social position. To make sure that the food supply is properly controlled, we demand that working women shall be called into consultation in fixing the prices to be charged for food and the way in which the food is to be distributed.[68]

One Federation member, Mary Phillips, urged direct action. She said that the ELFS should go to the shops and buy food at the old prices, or take it forcibly if the shopowners refused to sell at low prices. Sylvia claimed that this was already being done by women in the East End.[69]

Throughout the war, the Federation campaigned alone and also with other groups to control food prices. In August, Pankhurst and Mrs Drake were at the Poplar Dock Gates calling for government control of food supply with the consultation of working-class women, equal pay for equal work, and the vote.[70] In November 1914, the National Women's Council of the British Socialist Party agreed to form a joint food-supply committee with the ELFS, the Women's Industrial Council, and the Rugby Housewives Committee.[71] A few months later the ELFS and the Poplar Trades and Labour Council organised a deputation to Asquith concerning food prices. The Federation was represented by Julia Scurr and Walter Mackay; two Poplar councillors, J. Bands and S. March, spoke for the council. Nothing came of the deputation.[72]

In April 1915, the ELFS, along with the London Trades Council and the British Socialist Party, secured the London Opera House for a meeting to discuss food distribution.[73] Also in that month, a food deputation met the Mayor of Poplar, A. H. Warren, campaigning for the nationalisation of food. Charlotte Drake advocated communal kitchens for factory workers and schoolchildren; Sylvia Pankhurst told the mayor if the food supply was not nationalised, there would be general unrest. The deputation ended with the presentation of a number of resolutions: an end to private trading in food; food supply to be administered by the town or city councils; the introduction of rationing; municipal distribution of food with a ticket system for rationing; county councils to be in charge of the mills and the food preserving factories; national buying of food for the civilian population as for the military. There were other resolutions not directly concerned with food – a call for peace negotiations and a demand for votes for all.[74]

In June 1915, the ELFS further elaborated on its proposals for food distribution with another series of resolutions calling for, among other things

An advisory committee consisting of 1/3 merchants, 1/3 representatives of organised workers in the trades concerned and 1/3 representatives of working women, housekeepers and the principal consumers of the nation, [that] shall be appointed to formulate and carry out the proposals for safeguarding the supplies and limiting the prices of food and milk. This committee shall have the power to tax both prices and profits.[75]

In spite of these numerous conferences, deputations, and demonstrations, none of the plans put forward by the WSF were adopted. It was not that the population was not concerned with the food crisis. It was more that there was no working-class movement demonstrating and striking around these issues. The activities of the Federation seemed almost like forms of 'resolutionary' socialism or feminism because they did not have broad support to back them up. Given that the Federation was committed to bettering the lives of working-class women, it is not surprising that it then itself attempted to set up the necessary social welfare services.

One of the first services set up by the Federation was communal cost price restaurants. Pankhurst thought communal restaurants were an important step toward the emancipation of women in her vision of an egalitarian society.

'Cost price restaurants!' The phrase sprang into my mind. Cost price or under cost price mattered not. The name should be a slogan against profiteering and carry no stigma of charity ... Communal restaurants supplying first-rate food at cost price were in line with our hope of emancipating the mother from the too multifarious and largely conflicting labours of the home.[76]

Two restaurants were set up. Wood from Lansbury's timber yard was made into tables by his son, Edgar Lansbury, and the Rebels' Social and Political Union, another London-based socialist organization.[77] Dinner (the midday meal) cost two pence (one penny for children) and supper a penny; they were free for those who could not afford even this.[78] In one day, the cost price restaurants served 400 people, averaging 150 people at a sitting.[79] This is a sizeable amount when one considers how small the membership of the Federation was and how meagre its resources. But, popular as the restaurants were, they served only a tiny fraction of the community. Furthermore, there is no indication that the Federation made recruits or won people to its activities through the restaurants. Thus, although the Federation's stress on feeding the working-class communally – and even a degree of success was admirable – it did not inspire working-class women to organise and demand that the government set up communal restaurants everywhere.

The ELFS/WSF also set up a distress bureau in the Women's Hall in Bow, where members answered questions about food, rent, and pensions. The idea for this came about because Pankhurst and Lansbury sat on the local committees of the National Distress Bureau. They were appalled at the complacency of the local authorities and the apathy of the councillors.[80] In the *Dreadnought* Sylvia attacked the snooping investigators who judged whether or not women were 'worthy' of allowances.[81] The Distress Bureau also fought on behalf of those people who were evicted from their homes for being in arrears with their rent. It also secured the release of several people in prison, helped others through the problems of unemployment, and secured separation allowances for many wives of soldiers and sailors. The need was so great that bureaus were set up in Bromley, Canning Town, and Poplar.[82]

In response to conditions resulting from the war – including the housing cutbacks, lack of separation allowances, food scarcity (combined with the inefficiency of established bodies which distributed relief) – Pankhurst in 1915 set up the League of Rights for Soldiers' and Sailors' Wives and Relatives. She approached Lansbury with the idea, hoping to involve sympathetic trade unionists and socialists, albeit in a minimal capacity; the Federation would be responsible for the routine day-to-day work. In this area, it did involve women in the struggle for their rights. Many soldiers and sailors' wives became honorary secretaries in other branches of the League of Rights. Mrs Lansbury was persuaded by Pankhurst to be the honorary secretary of the League, but she was overwhelmed by chores and children, so she never had time to do the work.[83] Thus, Sylvia persuaded Minnie Lansbury to give up teaching and to replace her mother-in-law as honorary secretary. Minnie devoted all her time to the League, and she and Pankhurst hoped that in time it would become a national body and take over the role of the inadequate Soldiers' and Sailors' Families Association.[84] However, this organisation was not accompanied by the flashy success of the suffrage days. The meetings were attended by 'quiet, earnest little women, who joined the organisation with diffidence and in modest numbers. The dark streets were a growing deterrent'.[85] The League of Rights existed as an unofficial pressure group throughout the war and was still advertising its meetings in Walthamstow and East Ham as late as 1918 and 1919 in the *Dreadnought*. But by this time its main functions were being carried out by the other ex-servicemen's organisations.

Other community services were established by the Federation, including a baby clinic and a day nursery. For three pence a day (including food), working mothers were able to leave their children in the care of the ELFS/WSF.[86] The clinic was able to hold only about thirty children, but in 1915, the WSF took over an old pub called the 'Gunmaker's Arms', renamed it the 'Mothers' Arms', and turned it into a day-care centre and nursery run by Montessori methods.[87]

Milk centres were also organised by the Federation. The milk, or money for the milk, came from the generosity of people outside the community. At the Woman's Hall in Bow, about 1,000 nursing mothers received a quart of milk for their children, and dinner every night.[88] Unfortunately, there were many problems with the milk centres. For one, many of the babies were often so ill that they were unable to digest the milk. One of the nurses was accused of buying Nestlé milk and selling it to the mothers at a profit. She was constantly arguing about the price of milk with the women who used the centre. This nurse was also suspected of stealing money and other items from the 'Mothers' Arms.'[89]

The ELFS/WSF was particularly concerned with child welfare, an issue with which Pankhurst would involve herself for many years. One plan urged by the Federation was to send the poor children of the East End to live in the country for the duration of the war. There they would be exposed to the benefits of country life, and their health would improve.[90] (This plan was adopted by the national government during the Second World War.) The Federation also proposed to the Poplar Council that the council set up more maternity and infant centres. The motion was accepted.[91]

Every Christmas the ELFS/WSF organised a large party for the children of the East End, attended by 600 or so members and friends of the Federation – mostly working women and children, with 'a sprinkling of men'.[92] The success of the party was not completely due to the people of the East End. Maud Arncliff Sennett, a suffragist who had not been involved with the militant WSPU or the ELFS, helped arrange for gifts to be sent to the ELFS/WSF and claimed that the food and gifts had all been provided by wealthy sympathisers.[93] Later, when disagreements arose at a 1916 suffrage meeting, Sennett complained that Pankhurst and the East End women were not appreciative enough of their wealthy benefactresses.[94] Here again, we see the dilemma facing Pankhurst. She was forced to scrounge from her mother's wealthy friends for money and supplies for her projects, rather than rely on the East End community to develop programmes and services based on their own resources. What is remarkable is that the ELFS did not change its political positions in order to appease its richer and more conservative sources.

WORKING WOMEN

Contradictions were also evident in its attempt to organise working women. The first moves taken against initial unemployment were straightfoward, but as war increased the demand for labour, women were employed to release men for the army. The ELFS/WSF found itself both opposing the war and fighting for the working woman who replaced men who had been drafted.

One wartime institution particularly galled the ELFS/WSF: the Queen Mary's Workrooms. These had been set up in 1914 to give unemployed women useful work, although at abysmal rates of pay. Pankhurst wrote to the Queen on behalf of the ELFS, pointing out that in the workroom bearing her name:

> Numbers of women are working long hours each day and far into the night for wages under 10s. In factories executing government contracts for the army, women are making shirts for 2 ½d. per dozen, and finishing them, that is putting on buttons and making button holes for 2d. a dozen shirts. We are told that in your majesty's workrooms the women will be paid 3d. an hour and the maximum wage they will earn will be 10s. Many of the women employed there will have several children to keep. Even at normal times, it is impossible for a family to live in decency on such a sum, and at present the price of everything has gone up . . . [W]e would urge that a minimum wage of 11s. a week be paid to each woman and those engaged by the hour should be paid a minimum wage of 5d. an hour and 7 ½d. an hour overtime where the workers are employed for more than eight hours a day.

Pankhurst went on to urge that women with children be given 10s. extra and 5s. per child.[95]

The ELFS considered the Queen Mary's Workrooms a disgrace and called them the 'Queen Mary Sweatshops'. They were disbanded in 1915 because war work had all but liquidated unemployment, so relief work had come to an end. In the meantime, the ELFS campaigned vigorously against them but with little success or support.

Pankhurst and Julia Scurr served on the Poplar Relief Committees and used that as a way to expose the conditions in the workrooms. They called upon Susan Lawrence and Mary Macarthur, two leading trade unionists and government officials who sat on government committees, to organize a strike in protest against the setting up of sweated shops.[96] Both women refused.

In an attempt to counter the sweated shops and to provide work for unemployed women, the ELFS decided to establish its own factories to serve as models. A boot-and-shoe factory, and later a toy factory, were set up in 1914. Fifty-nine people were employed at the factory which was run on a cooperative basis; everyone was paid five pence an hour or eleven shillings a week, and no-one made a profit.[97] The boot-and-shoe factory never paid for itself; it was subsidised by wealthy supporters of the ELFS. As with many of her projects, Pankhurst found herself begging for the support from women she had known in WSPU days. She even spent one miserable weekend – trying to get support from England's wealthy – at the mansion of Lady Astor, the first woman to serve as a Member of Parliament.[98] Here, again, she came up against the contradiction: without the contributions of rich outside supporters, the cooperative factories could not have continued, but Lady Astor later wrote to her that she would never have invited her to the house or aided her toy factory, had she been aware of Pankhurst's pacifist and socialist beliefs.[99]

The toy factory prospered, although arguments arose over its method of operation. It was run by a Polish woman, Mrs Hercbergova, whose commercial expertise outweighed Pankhurst's socialist and feminist ideas of industrial organisation. She opposed the WSF's belief that the factory should have a definite constitution and run by a committee made up of its workers. Mrs Hercbergova wanted business management to be separate from this committee. The WSF decided that a special factory committee should be formed: outside people might be elected to it, but only those who held either socialist or cooperative viewpoints would be on it.[100]

The factories were set up to provide needed employment as well as to bring money into the East End, but in fact they in no way helped the community's problems of unemployment and poverty. Nor, as with the cost price restaurants, is there any indication that the people employed in the workrooms joined the Federation or were involved in any kind of agitation. Rather than setting up workrooms which totally depended upon the support and generosity of the rich, it might have been better for the ELFS to organize working and unemployed women to fight for their rights as workers, for better pay and working conditions and for more jobs.

After 1915, the WSF no longer had to deal with the question of massive unemployment for women because thousands were entering the work force, which created a new set of problems. The WSF's issues became the abolition of sweating, the protection of women workers, the upgrading and training of women, and the securing of equal pay. The *Dreadnought* played a major role in exposing their horrendous working conditions: in Limehouse, for example, one food factory was housed in a dank, steaming basement. Ironically, the factory made turtle soup for the royal family.[101] In this area, the Federation's propaganda and agitation were better received. The Labour Party, women's organisations, trade unions, and the government claimed that they wanted to do all they could to ensure safe, decent working conditions for the women who were making soldiers' uniforms or munitions. In other words, those organisations wanted to improve the conditions of women war workers in order to win the war. While the efforts of the WSF brought attention to the true position of women in industry, it was not able to bring about any real improvements.

As soon as women's war work registration was announced in March 1915, Pankhurst called for a women's conference to discuss the problems of women workers:

> It seems imperative that a National Conference of Women's Trade Union and political and social organisations should be called at once with a view to formulating demands. These include the vote so that women may have the same power as men to influence the government which controls their labour – representation on the tribunal to deal with disputes, the wages hitherto paid men for similar work and proper safeguards relating to hours and conditions.[102]

A few months later, the WSF called for demonstrations protesting against the Registration Act as well as the conditions of women workers. The WSF wrote to Lloyd George asking him to receive a deputation, and it announced that it would lobby individual MPs. However, the call was for the most part ignored by the trade union and Labour Party officials, the Women's Trade Union League, and the Women's Labour League, and Lloyd George's government refused to meet it.[103]

In March 1915, Pankhurst had written to Lloyd George demanding that the government enforce equal pay legislation. Lloyd George sent Pankhurst an ambiguous reply:

> The words you wrote would guarantee that women undertaking the work of men would get the same piece rates as men were receiving before the date of this agreement. That of course, means that if the women turn out the same quantity of work as men employed on the same job, they will receive exactly the same pay.[104]

Pankhurst thought she had wrung a concession from the government. However, the letter had been deliberately vague. A month later, attending a conference on 'Women's Organisations and the War' called by the government, Walker and Pankhurst demanded that it live up to Lloyd George's promise to pay women workers the same as men. Both Lloyd George and Walter Runciman, the president of the Board of Trade, refused to answer. Pankhurst and Walker were isolated at this conference; most of the women present looked upon the WSF as disrupters.[105]

In March 1916, Pankhurst wrote to the Prime Minister again, asking that he receive a deputation from the WSF that would address him on the question of equal pay for women workers. In her letter, Pankhurst pointed out that neither the Home Office nor the Board of Trade had included any mention of equal pay for women workers in its latest report on women's war work. Also, only four out of thirteen appointed members of the advisory committee on this question were women; of these four, none represented working women, and one had been notorious for opposing woman's suffrage.[106]

Again, the limitations of Pankhurst's work are evident. It might have been better for the WSF to concentrate on convincing women munition workers rather than Runciman and Lloyd George that they deserved equal pay. Had there been an organisation of women workers calling for equal pay, backed up with strikes, rallies, and demonstrations, perhaps more could have been accomplished. However, it must be repeated that on this issue Pankhurst and the WSF stood alone. Other Socialist, trade union, and women's organisations did little.

SUFFRAGE

During the war, the ELFS/WSF remained the only organisation that consistently pressured the government to grant votes to *all* women. Pankhurst remained dedicated to woman's suffrage; whether in the food, anti-war, or sweated industries deputations, the demand for votes for women and men was always included. Pankhurst angered many of her former suffrage allies by her determination to give all adults the vote. At a Caxton Hall suffrage meeting in 1916, she and the WSF argued for adult suffrage. The majority vote against the WSF and in response Pankhurst railed against 'comfortable middle-class women'. Maud Arncliff Sennett complained:

> Miss Pankhurst, to my amazement and disgust, seeing the sense of the meeting was going against her, began to round on us as a lot of 'comfortable middle-class women.' I am bound to say that her women did not applaud this charge and I thought it a poor return to make for those kind-hearted 'comfortable middle class women' whose money was going to support her organisation and officers in the East End, to say nothing of those splendid gifts I have seen on her platform at the Christmas proceedings.[107]

Nevertheless, the WSF continued agitation for suffrage although with new allies. The BSP (British Socialist Party), for example, which had condemned the suffragettes during the height of their militancy, praised the WSF, commenting that 'Sylvia comes on like one resurrected', and promised support.[108]

This new support was because it was clear that the new Franchise Bill drawn up by the government in 1916 was intended to give the vote to women over thirty who were either householders or married to householders. This meant, in effect, votes for women who were probably more conservative than younger propertyless women. The very fact that franchise legislation was being presented to Parliament at this time was a result of the increasing public pressure for soldiers to be enfranchised. Also, the existing occupational and residential qualifications for voting deprived many munition workers, who moved around the country doing vital war work, of the vote. This seemed grossly unfair to many people. On top of this was the feeling that all working men had contributed equally to the war effort, and therefore that the property qualification should be abolished. There was a growing demand, consequently, for votes for all men, to which was added a demand for votes for some women. To have given all women over twenty-one the vote would have made women an electoral majority, and this the government would not allow.

In a letter to the BSP newspaper, *The Call*, Pankhurst clearly pointed out why Socialists could not support the Franchise Bill:

1. A woman is not to vote until 30 years of age, though the adult age is 21 . . .
2. A woman is on a property basis when enfranchised.
3. A woman loses both her Parliamentary and her local government vote if she or her husband accept Poor Law relief; her husband retaining his Parliamentary and losing his local government vote if he accepts Poor Law Relief.
4. A woman loses her local government vote if she ceases to live with her husband, i.e. if he deserts her, she loses her vote, he retains his.
5. Conscientious Objectors to military service are to be disenfranchised.[109]

Even though the BSP had never supported, and indeed had been hostile to the demands of the woman's suffrage movement, it joined with sections of the Labour Party, and other radical and some suffrage groups to oppose this blatantly discriminatory suffrage bill, and was willing to work with Pankhurst to avoid the bill's possible effect of enlarging an older, wealthier and potentially Tory electorate. But only a minority of suffragists were interested in adult suffrage. At a WSF executive meeting in April 1917, Norah Smyth said that the WSF 'had turned the middle-class against us by our attitude toward adult suffrage'.[110]

The major reason for the change in name from East London Federation of the Suffragettes to Workers' Suffrage Federation in March 1916 was opposition to the working of the Franchise Bill. It excluded men because of poverty and their political beliefs, it discriminated against working-class women, and it excluded women because they happened to be young, poor, widowed, or deserted. Only a law that simply gave the franchise to every person over twenty-one would be acceptable, and therefore it was decided that the Federation's name would reflect this. The Federation members also hoped that with the increasing sense of grievance felt by men it was also more appropriate to an organisation of women and men, and one which was increasingly involved in struggles other than specifically women's rights issues. As Pankhurst wrote in the *Dreadnought*, 'the battle for human suffrage is part of the great struggle for upward human evolution, in the course of which dominance and compulsion, exploitation and poverty will be abolished'.[111]

Following a meeting called by Emmeline Pethick-Lawrence, a close friend and sister suffragette, under the auspices of the Women's International League, the National Council of Adult Suffrage was formed. But although it was formally committed to adult suffrage, it was inactive, and the WSF disaffiliated in November 1917.[112] With George Lansbury and other Labour leaders, the WSF then formed the Adult Suffrage Joint Committee. This consisted of four WSF members, three trade unionists, and one member of the BSP.[113] Pankhurst believed that such an organisation was necessary because the woman's suffrage movement had disintegrated. The WSF introduced a resolution in May 1917, which shows its strong socialist and feminist position on suffrage:

> We the undersigned workers, realising that if a woman can cast a shell, she can cast a vote, and that women whether in industry or as wives and mothers, have their full share of the world's work, whether or not in peace or war, call upon the government to introduce not a Registration Bill, but a Franchise Bill to give a vote to any woman and man of full age.[114]

But the days of massive frenetic suffrage agitation were over. The Franchise Bill was passed in 1918.

SOCIALISM

Pankhurst's reputation as a leading socialist antiwar agitator was further enhanced by her support of the Irish struggle which moved Pankhurst in an even more revolutionary direction. On Easter Sunday, 1916, Irish socialists and nationalists led by Padraic Pearse and the revolutionary James Connolly (with whom Sylvia had shared the speaker's platform at the Albert Hall meeting supporting the locked-out Dublin workers in November 1913) led an abortive rising against the British government. The WSF and the *Dreadnought* defended the rising and argued against Britain rule in Ireland, while other socialist groups either denounced the rebels or were silent.[115]

Pankhurst was particularly grieved over the results of the rising and the execution of Connolly. She never forgave the Labour Party's leadership for going along with Connolly's execution, for she was more aware than most socialists of the implications of Connolly's death and of the rising itself:

> To me the death of James Connolly was more grievous than any, because the rebellion struck deeper than mere nationalism. It is a truism that countries held under an alien dominance remain politically stagnant, and to a large extent are culturally repressed. Recognition of this made me a supporter of Irish nationalism. Yet after national self-government had been attained, the social problems with which we in England were wrestling would still be present in Ireland. I knew the Easter Monday rebellion was the first blow in an intensified struggle, which would end in Irish self-government, a necessary step in Irish evolution. I knew that the execution of the rebels had irrevocably ensured the ultimate success of their uprising. Yet Connolly was needed so seriously for the after building; him at the least, it seemed, fate should have spared.[116]

The influence of the *Dreadnought* also contributed to Pankhurst's growing reputation as an antiwar militant. The depth of its coverage made it arguably the most influential antiwar newspaper in England. In December 1914, Pankhurst was the first English socialist to reprint the analysis by German Marxist Karl Liebknecht that the First World War was caused by imperialists fighting over the world market.[117] In 1917, it published the famous letter from the poet Siegfried Sassoon, MC, Third Battalion, Royal Welch Fusiliers, to his commanding officer:

> I am making this statement as an act of wilful defiance of military authority, because I believe that the war is being deliberately prolonged by those who have the power to end it.
> I am a soldier, convinced that I am acting on behalf of the soldiers. I believe this war, upon which I entered as a war of defence, has now become a war of aggression.[118]

The paper also demanded the nationalisation of food as the only means to alleviate hunger. It consistently argued against all repressive measures taken by the government. It also encouraged industrial and military sabotage, as well as a peace referendum for the troops. Not surprisingly, the paper was raided by British authorities in 1916 and 1918.[119] When editions of the *Dreadnought* carried articles about British atrocities in Ireland, it was banned in Ireland.[120] Pankhurst always had difficulties raising money for the paper, and, more important, finding a printer who would risk printing possibly seditious materials.

REVOLUTION

Pankhurst and her organisation might have lost many old supporters, but as the war brought changes that transformed the WSF from a socialist relief group to a militant revolutionary organization, the group gained new adherants. As the full horror and destructiveness of the international slaughter began to hit home, Pankhurst's anti-war propaganda began to reach more receptive ears. Events in Russia were the ultimate catalyst in the transformation of both Pankhurst and the WSF. One of the first British revolutionaries to speak out in favour of the Bolsheviks, Sylvia did so consistently and enthusiastically. She demanded that Britain should negotiate a peace with Germany on Russia's terms with no annexations and no indemnities.

The Russian revolution boosted the growing militancy in Britain's factories, and the WSP found itself being swept along on a swelling tide of revolutionary unrest. Indicating the changing mood, in July 1917, the *Woman's Dreadnought* was renamed the *Workers' Dreadnought*. The Socialist Labour Party, a revolutionary organisation, welcomed the change. Its paper, *Solidarity*, wrote,

> Women and worker are synonymous terms so there is nothing very startling about the alteration of the title of the bright little rebel paper, the *Woman's Dreadnought* . . . Miss Sylvia Pankhurst has succeeded in making the *W.D.* a real force in Labour politics and we wish her every success.[121]

In 1918, rumours were circulating that Sylvia Pankhurst was interested in forming her own revolutionary organisation, in opposition to the BSP and the ILP. In a letter to a friend, she admitted that the rumours were partially correct:

> I rather think Mrs Langdon Davis' news may be that our Bow branch wants to make our new name Workers' *Socialist* Federation

instead of Workers' *Suffrage* Federation. I think the branch is right, the title describes us better, but our annual conference at Whitsuntide will decide that.[122]

The war; the futile attempts to alleviate suffering through the redistribution of food and the provision of social services; the brutal suppression of the Easter Rising; and the Russian revolution overturned Sylvia Pankhurst's world. By 1918 she was no longer a socialist suffragette but a feminist revolutionary dedicated to the struggle for socialism. She summed up this transformation in 1920, in her impassioned speech to a judge about to sentence her to six months in jail for agitating among the troops:

Because I had been a suffragette and had fought for the cause of women, the women came to me and asked me to help them. I had dying babies brought to me. I had to start clinics and find accomodation for people whose fathers were fighting for the capitalist governments of their country. I used to sit up all night writing, begging for money for these people. We had good families of people coming to my house without a penny, and with six or seven children, and I opened two penny restaurants where you could get two penny meals. These expenses used to pass through my hands. I used to spend £150 a week on that. But I know it is all palliatives. It will not do any good really. I want to change the system. I am going to fight it if it kills me.[123]

NOTES

I would like to thank the International Institute for Social History for their kind permission to quote from Sylvia Pankhurst's unpublished works. I would also like to thank Ian Bullock, Stephanie Golden, Lucia Jones and Joan Smith for all their help.

1. Sylvia Pankhurst, *The Home Front* (London: Hutchinson and Company, 1932) p. 11.
2. Ibid., pp. 14–15.
3. Ibid., pp. 38, 67.
4. This count is based on the Minute Books of the ELFS/WSF. At no time do they record the specifics of membership.

5. Minute Book of the Bow Branch, 16 October 1917, 17 November 1917, International Institute of Social History, Amsterdam, E. Sylvia Pankhurst Papers, [ESPP] 213.

6. Committee Meeting, 6 March, 1915, ESPP 206.

7. ESPP 208

8. Committee Meeting, 6 March, 1915, ESPP 206.

9. Ken Weller, *Don't Be a Soldier: The Radical Anti-war Movement in North London, 1914–1918* (London: Journeymen Press, 1985) p. 75.

10. Ibid., p. 74.

11. Ibid., p. 75.

12. Thanks to Ian Bullock.

13. 'Jessie'. Interview with Jessie Stephens by Suzie Fleming and Glodan Dallas, in *Spare Rib Reader* (London: Penguin, 1982) pp. 558–9.

14. Ibid.

15. Ibid.

16. Ibid.

17. Weller, *Don't Be a Soldier*, p. 78.

18. ELFS Executive Committee Minutes, 6 August, 1914, ESPP 206.

19. Ibid.

20. Minute Book of the WSF, 6 January, 1917, ESPP 207.

21. *Woman's Dreadnought*, 17 March, 1917.

22. *Glasgow Herald*, 29 October, 1914.

23. *Labour Leader*, 24 December, 1914.

24. Pankhurst, *The Home Front*, p. 186.

25. Ibid., p. 185.

26. *Workers' Dreadnought*, 13 April, 1918; 20 April, 1918.

27. Pankhurst, *The Home Front*, p. 186.

28. *Daily Herald*, 7 August, 1915.

29. Ibid., 21 August, 1915.

30. *East London Observer*, 14 August, 1915.

31. Ibid., 21 August, 1914.

32. *Woman's Dreadnought*, 1 January, 1916.

33. Ibid., 15 January, 1915.

34. *East London Observer*, 19 February, 1916.

35. Ibid., 3 March, 1916.

36. Committee Meeting, 6 March, 1916, ESPP 207.

37. *Woman's Dreadnought*, 15 April, 1916.

38. WSF Minutes, 27 March, 1916, ESPP 210.

39. Annual General Report, 1916, ESPP 217.

40. *East London Observer*, 8 April, 1916.

41. Ibid., 8 April, 1916.

42. *Woman's Dreadnought*, 10 June, 1916.

43. James Hinton, *The First Shop Stewards Movement* (London: Allen and Unwin, 1973) p. 44; Arthur Marwick, *The Deluge* (London: Bodley Head 1965) pp. 29–38.

44. *Woman's Dreadnought*, 23 December, 1916; WSF Minutes, 18 December, 1916, IISH P. P.; *East London Observer*, 23 December, 1916.

45. Pankhurst to George Lansbury, June 1917, Lansbury Papers, British Library of Political and Economic Science, London.

46. *Woman's Dreadnought*, 6 January, 1917.
47. *Daily Herald*, 1 September, 1917.
48. *The Call*, 8 August, 1918.
49. Anne Wiltsherm, *Most Dangerous Women: Feminist Peace Campaigners of the Great War* (London: Pandora, 1985) p. 1; Sylvia Pankhurst, *The Home Front*, p. 271, refers accusingly to the 'WSPU with its women sticking white feathers into the buttonholes of reluctant men, and brandishing little placards with the slogan, "intern them all". . .' This has become accepted as truth. Barbara Castle's popular book *Sylvia and Christabel Pankhurst*, (London: Penguin Books, 1987) repeats this: 'Emmeline Pankhurst toured the country, handing out white feathers to young men in civilian dress. Her battle cry was an attack on enemy aliens: "Intern them all".' (p. 134) David Doughey, the archivist at the Fawcett Library, told me in December 1988 that there was no corroboration for the story of the white feathers.
50. Pankhurst, *The Home Front*, p. 153.
51. Wiltsher, *Most Dangerous Women*, p. 133.
52. Minute Book, 18 October, 1915, ESPP 207.
53. 20 December, 1915, ESPP 207.
54. Wiltsher, *Most Dangerous Women*, p. 133.
55. 18 October, 1915, ESPP 207.
56. Pankhurst, *The Home Front*, p. 292.
57. Ibid., p. 153.
58. *Daily Herald*, 4 September, 1915.
59. Minute Book of General Membership, 18 October, 1915, ESPP 210.
60. Gretta Cousins to Hannah Sheehy Skeffington, n.d. 1915, National Library Dublin (NLD) 22.672.
61. *The Call*, 6 July, 1916.
62. *Woman's Dreadnought*, 19 and 26 May, 1917.
63. In *The Home Front*, Pankhurst does not mention that other groups, in particular the Women's Freedom League and the United Suffragists, did similar feminist social work in the East End. These stories need to be written.
64. Minutes of the General Meeting of the WSF, 15 January, 1917, ESPP 211.
65. *Woman's Dreadnought*, 27 January, 1917.
66. *Woman's Dreadnought*, 8 August, 1914.
67. Pankhurst to Hannah Sheehy Skeffington, 24 August, 1914, NLD MS222, 666(v).
68. *Woman's Dreadnought*, 15 August, 1914.
69. Pankhurst, *The Home Front*, 29.
70. *Daily Herald*, 24 August, 1914.
71. *Justice*, 5 November,1914.
72. *East London Observer*, 20 February, 1915.
73. *Daily Herald*, 17 April, 1915.
74. *Woman's Dreadnought*, 17 April, 1915.
75. *East London Observer*, 3 June, 1915.
76. Pankhurst, *The Home Front*, pp. 42-3.
77. Ibid.
78. *Woman's Dreadnought*, 23 August, 1915.

79. *Woman's Dreadnought*, 17 April, 1915.
80. *Daily Herald*, 4 September, 1914.
81. *Woman's Dreadnought*, 2 January, 1915.
83. Pankhurst, *The Home Front*, p. 131.
84. Ibid. Nellie Rathbone claims it was she, not Lansbury, who did all the work for Sylvia Pankhurst in this respect: 'She started this thing and I did all the work . . . [S]o the soldiers' and sailors' wives and relatives came to see me and I got such intimate information about their family life . . . [Y]ou know I spent my time writing to the War Office and goodness knows . . . [Y]ou see, they were stranded . . . [T]hey had no money coming through.' (Nellie Rathbone interview with author, 1972)
85. Ibid., p. 132.
86. *Daily Herald*, 17 October, 1914.
87. *Woman's Dreadnought*, 2 January, 1915.
88. *East London Observer*, 24 October, 1914.
89. WSF Finance Committee, 19 January, 1918, ESPP 212.
90. *East London Observer*, 12 June, 1915.
91. Minutes of the Poplar Council, November 1914.
92. *East London Observer*, 25 December, 1915.
93. Maud Arncliff Sennett, *The Child* (London: C. W. Daniel and Company, 1938) p. 110.
94. Ibid.
95. *Daily Herald*, 9 September, 1914.
96. Pankhurst, *The Home Front*, p. 58.
97. Ibid., p. 72.
98. Ibid., pp. 142–6.
99. Ibid., p. 150.
100. WSF Minute Book, 2 November, 1917, ESPP 211.
101. Sheila Rowbotham, *Hidden From History* (New York: Pantheon, 1973) p. 116.
102. *Daily Herald*, 27 March, 1915.
103. Ibid., 24 July, 1915.
104. Pankhurst, *The Home Front*, p. 159.
105. Ibid., p. 161.
106. *East London Observer*, 18 March, 1916.
107. Sennett, *The Child*, p. 110.
108. *The Call*, 6 July, 1916.
109. Ibid., 6 December, 1917.
110. Committee Meeting, 16 April, 1917, ESPP 207.
111. *Woman's Dreadnought*, 22 January, 1916.
112. Committee Meeting, 5 May, 1917, ESPP 207.
113. Committee Meeting, 19 June, 1917. ESPP 208.
114. Ibid.
115. *Woman's Dreadnought*, 22 January, 1916.
116. Pankhurst, *The Home Front*, p. 322.
117. *Woman's Dreadnought*, 26 December, 1914.
118. Ibid., 28 July, 1917.
119. WSF Minutes, 12 October, 1917, ESPP 211; *Woman's Dreadnought*, 31 January, 1917.

120. WSF Minutes, 12 December, 1916, IISH P.P.
121. *Solidarity*, July 1917.
122. Pankhurst to H. Bryan, 27 March, 1918, ILP General Correspondence, vol. 5.5, p. 157. British Library of Political and Economic Science, London.
123. Sylvia Pankhurst's *Appeal*, p. 32, ESPP 254.

5

Sylvia Pankhurst and the Russian Revolution: the making of a 'Left-Wing' Communist

IAN BULLOCK

In the spring of 1920, Lenin wrote *'Left-Wing' Communism, an Infantile Disorder*. His main target was the 'Left Communism' of the Communist Workers' Party of Germany (Kommunistische Arbeiter-Partei Deutschlands; KAPD). Apart from Germany, only Britain was given a whole section or chapter, and this was based on a critique of the writings of William Gallacher and Sylvia Pankhurst in a single issue of the latter's paper, the *Workers' Dreadnought*.

Sylvia Pankhurst, as editor of the paper, had outlined in an article in the issue of 21 February 1920 the progress of the negotiations between the various organisations, including her own Workers' Socialist Federation, aimed at forming a Communist Party. The discussions were conducted, Lenin explained,

> on the basis of affiliation to the Third International, the recognition of the Soviet system instead of parliamentarism, and the dictatorship of the proletariat. It appears that one of the greatest obstacles to the formation of a united Communist Party is the disagreement over the question of participation in parliament and over the question of whether the new Communist Party should affiliate to the old, trade unionist, opportunist and social-chauvinist Labour Party, which consists mostly of trade unions.[1]

In the article criticised by Lenin, Sylvia had listed the points on which she disagreed with what she regarded as the 'Right Wing'

121

Communism of the British Socialist Party [BSP]. While these 're-formists' stood for bolstering up capitalism, bourgeois democracy, parliaments, and partial nationalisation, revolutionaries like herself, she insisted, wanted the overthrow of capitalism, the dictatorship of the proletariat, soviets, and complete socialisation of industry under workers' control.

Her programme also meant 'revolutionary mass action' by means of the political strike, communist industrial organisation, and international solidarity. While the reformists were satisfied with 'academic preaching of State Socialism under Bureaucratic control with an attempt to remunerate employees according to their abilities and training', revolutionaries would settle for nothing less than 'Communism in which the era of equal wages and equal rationing of scarce commodities, gives place to the abolition of the wages system and the unchecked supply of needs and desires of the people as a natural right, independent of service.'[2]

All this added up to the 'Left-Wing' Communism that Lenin attacked, but at the time Sylvia wrote she saw herself as taking the orthodox Bolshevik position, since the recent Comintern meeting organised by the Amsterdam Sub-Bureau had, she argued in the same article

stated that the affiliation of no Communist Party will be accepted which has not severed its connection with the social patriotic organisations, among which, it declares, is the Labour Party, it would seem that if that meeting can be held to speak for the Third International, the Communists of Britain must either be out of the Labour Party or out of the Third International.

But it soon turned out that neither the meeting nor the soon-to-be-disbanded Amsterdam Sub-Bureau did speak for Comintern. The positions it had taken were now seen as symptoms of an 'infantile disorder'. Some sufferers from this disease were later cured by judicious administration of Comintern medicine. Not so Sylvia Pankhurst who, though at some stages she was prepared to compromise in the interests of unity, stuck doggedly to the positions she had taken.

Sylvia Pankhurst was a key figure in the British socialist response to the Russian Revolution. She was one of the very first to support the Bolsheviks – long before they took power in November 1917. Her Workers' Socialist Federation changed its name to Communist Party nearly fourteen months before the formation of the Communist

Party of Great Britain (CPGB).[3] She was expelled, in their eyes at least, by the leaders of the CPGB in September 1921, after which she aligned herself with the Left Communists of the – original – Fourth International. She was, therefore, among the first 'in' and the first 'out' of the orthodox communist movement. What had been her political evolution towards such an uncompromising position?

By the outbreak of war, Sylvia Pankhurst had already proved her great courage, determination and self-confidence and was beginning to be known internationally. Her willingness to give time and attention to the smallest detail, and her almost unbelievable energy made her an organiser of rare quality. The war brought even more work. In *The Home Front* she tells us that her routine was to dictate letters to four shorthand typists between 10 a.m. and 2 p.m. each day. The rest of her time was taken up by public and committee meetings, editing and largely writing the *Dreadnought*, and keeping up with the news and parliamentary reports. She regularly worked, she says, through at least two nights a week.[4]

THE IMPACT OF WAR

At first Sylvia and the East London Federation of the Suffragettes (ELFS) tried to assuage the effects of the war on the working-class women of the East End, rather than to oppose it outright. To begin with the *Dreadnought's* hostility to the war was oblique. The ELFS's task was to take '. . . an actively vigilant part in striving to protect women during the international crisis in which it was certain they must suffer terribly in any event'.[5] Vigilance and protection took two main forms. There were local services which the authorities failed to provide, such as milk centres, 'cost price restaurants', and nursery facilities at the renamed 'Mothers' Arms', and 'a systematised distress bureau'. Secondly, there was political campaigning, including deputations to local authorities and government departments.[6]

As early as August 1914 control of food prices was prominent in the 'Women's Charter' of the ELFS, and by the New Year it was also demanding separation allowances, the abolition of police supervision of servicemen's wives and a minimum wage for all women employed on government contract work. As the effects of the war became 'political' as well as 'economic', campaigns were initiated against the Defence of the Realm Act [DORA], the Munitions Act, conscription, and the ill-treatment of conscientious objectors. Together with other wartime developments which Barbara Winslow has described, these things constituted an almost unprecedented restriction of individual freedom.

It is difficult now to recapture the shock and anger that such draconian measures triggered off in many of those who took for granted the relative liberties of pre-1914 Britain. The result was that to the desire for peace for its own sake was added the fear of the domestic effects of a continuation of the war. 'It is urgent for the sake of humanity that the war should not go on for an unnecessary hour' said the *Dreadnought* in October 1915, urging the government to announce its peace terms. 'Every day that the War continues', it warned in April 1916, 'the bounds of tyranny are extended'.[7]

By her own account, a turning-point for Sylvia was the death of Keir Hardie. On Sunday 26 September 1915 the ELFS and other organisations were demonstrating in Trafalgar Square, calling for the abolition of sweating, equal pay and votes for women, price control and other economic and social demands. It was here that Sylvia learned of Hardie's death.

> The struggle we were waging to improve material conditions, though for the very poorest, suddenly appeared sordid, the fight against Conscription mere paltering. I wished with an intensity which seemed to burn up all other feeling, that while there was yet time, I had gone with him as a missioner through the country denouncing the War. Ruthlessly I examined myself, deciding that though I had spoken against the War the greater part of my struggle had been waged for economic conditions.[8]

While the other campaigns continued, the war itself came to seem something that had to be opposed head-on. Another Trafalgar Square demonstration in the spring of 1916 linked the – now – Workers' Suffrage Federation demand for 'Human Suffrage' (defined in the WSF's programme as 'a vote for every woman and man of full age') with 'protest against the restrictions of Popular Liberties' which reduced British workers to 'the servile state'.[9] But by the summer Sylvia was denouncing the 'capitalist war' in which international financiers were competing for the domination of 'the weaker countries which are not strong enough to protect themselves against invasion, and in which high profits can be made out of the people because they have not yet learned to protect their interests by Trade Union combination'.[10]

It was from such a position of public opposition to the war from a socialist perspective that she followed the early news of revolution in Russia. Later, she made several attempts to recapture its early impact on her.

Working in the East End of London to alleviate the hardships of the poorest people, the Russian upheaval appeared to me like the first ray of dawn after a long and painful night.

And on another occasion she described how:

Daily I rushed through the piles of newspapers searching every line of them for news of the Revolution – the Social Revolution as I at once recognised and affirmed it to be – seeing in it, not merely a Russian upheaval, but the starting point of the World Revolution, the rising of the masses against war which would usher in the Socialist order of universal fraternity – that bright hope, cherished hope of a multitude in which from childhood I had shared.[11]

EARLY SUPPORT FOR THE BOLSHEVIKS

On 19 March 1917 a WSF meeting passed unanimously two resolutions on the events in Russia, before moving on to the usual business of the suffrage and anti-conscription campaigns. The first, to be sent to Kerensky and Tchiedze (Chkeidze), congratulated the Duma on the overthrow of '. . . the autocratic dominion of the Czar' and looked forward to the early election of a constituent assembly by secret ballot and universal suffrage. The second, addressed to socialists, the press, and Russians living in Britain and France, congratulated the Russian workers on '. . . the partial measure of success which has already rewarded their efforts', rejoiced in the announcement of the Constituent Assembly and hoped the elections would '. . . result in the return of an overwhelming majority of class conscious representatives of the workers who, whilst establishing a genuine democracy in Russia will also ensure the influence of Russia will be used to bring about a speedy end to the war'.

The Russian Revolution was seen not only as opening up the prospect of peace but also as providing extra leverage in the British struggle for universal suffrage. A third resolution, clearly intended to help shame the British government into doing the decent thing, asked it to 'set aside the timid and ineffective proposals of the Speaker's Conference and introduce a measure which shall provide for complete Adult Suffrage for men and women', in the light not only of Russian intentions with regard to the Constituent Assembly but also of the German Chancellor's recent announcement on suffrage reform.[12] Within a fortnight, the *Dreadnought* was promoting a meeting to be held at the Albert Hall.

Russia Free! A Great Mass Meeting to Congratulate the Russian People on their Charter of Freedom which includes
ADULT SUFFRAGE[13]

Even before this, as she was often to remind her Communist critics in later years, Sylvia Pankhurst was one of the earliest to diagnose a 'dual power' situation in Russia and to support the soviets unequivocally. Her *Dreadnought* leader of 24 March 1917 asked 'Whose Russian Revolution?' and went on to explain that

there are virtually two Governments in Russia, the Provisional Government appointed by the Duma, and the Council of Labour Deputies which is responsible to the elected representatives of the workers and soldiers.

By the beginning of June she was predicting the downfall of Kerensky, who had '. . . failed to realise the greatness of the movement he would lead'.[14] By the end of that month she had identified herself with the Bolsheviks. Could 'a Russian Socialist Republic', she asked, 'be established and maintained in safety in the midst of a capitalist Europe with a great war raging?'

The workers' and soldiers' council might, she believed, 'become the Government of Russia if it wills'. The problem was that there were divisions on this crucial question between the more cautious Russian socialists who thought that 'until it is possible to establish a Socialist Europe it is better to have not a Russian Socialist Government, but a strong Socialist block [sic] in the Parliament to force the Liberals to do its will', and the 'Maximalists and Leninists' who wanted to 'cut adrift from the capitalist parties altogether, and to establish a socialist system of organisation and industry in Russia before Russian capitalism, which is as yet in its infancy, becomes more difficult to overthrow'. She added, 'We deeply sympathise with this view'.[15] By August she was reporting that the Petrograd

'Council' – that is to say the Soviet – was coming round to the 'position of Lenin (a position we ourselves have advocated from the first), namely that Free Russia must refuse to continue fighting in a capitalist war'.[16]

THE 'INVISIBLE' BOLSHEVIKS

Today, it is difficult to imagine how little was known in Britain about the Russian revolutionary movement in general – and about Lenin and the Bolsheviks in particular – even in sympathetic circles; something that makes Sylvia Pankhurst's early analysis of 'dual power' and grasp of the likely drift of events very impressive. However, the formulation 'the Maximalist and Leninite Socialists' used on 30 June suggests possible confusion as to whether these were one and the same or two allied groups.

Before 1917 there had only been a handful of references to Russian opposition movements in the *Dreadnought*. The first is most intriguing and significant. On Boxing Day 1914 a report on anti-war protests in Germany and Russian appeared, but while the chief protagonist in the former case is identified as 'Dr Karl Liebknecht', in the latter what today appears in Lenin's *Collective Works* as the well-known statement on 'The War and Russian Social Democracy', is described simply as 'the manifesto of the Russian Socialist Party'.[17]

Two review articles in 1915 reveal again the 'invisibility', to Western socialists, of the Bolsheviks. The autobiography of Marie Sukloff, who had assassinated General Kvostoff, traced her progression from the Bund through the Social Democratic Party to 'the new party' the 'Social Revolutionist Party'. Though the article mentions that she was 'convicted of publishing a forbidden journal, *Iskra* (the Spark), with which in fact she had nothing to do' there is no mention of the Bolsheviks as such.

The same is true of the long article on William English Walling's *The Socialists and the War*, which though it mentions that 'the 14 Socialist Members' of the Duma abstained on the war credits vote of 8 August 1914 and mentions, vaguely, disagreements amongst Russian socialists, describes the Social Democrats as the 'largest single Socialist party in Russia' without hinting at any division between Mensheviks and Bolsheviks. Indeed, except in their joint character of Social Democrats, both were less visible to the *Dreadnought* than the Tolstoyan war protesters whose trial was reported in

1916.[18] It is significant that most of the information about Russia in the paper before 1917 came from two book reviews and was presented in such a way as to suggest it was unfamiliar to both readers and reviewer.

Even after what she called 'the Lenin Revolution' had taken place – with her enthusiastic support – Sylvia Pankhurst shows little familiarity with Bolshevik attitudes or ideas. She writes, for instance of 'the Bolsheviks or Maximalists, whose best known leaders are Lenin and Trotsky, but who do not depend for their policy on any group of leaders'. She explains that 'Bolshevik' 'merely signifies that they are out for the maximum socialist programme instead of the minimum programme like the Mensheviks'. A week later – in words which would surely have astonished Lenin – she acknowledges that,

> the difficulties of those who are thus courageously attempting to put into practice the teachings of Christ are enormous. They will make mistakes in the new life of adventure, but their mistakes will never be so terrible as those of the old individualistic capitalist system.[19]

It is salutary to remind ourselves how little was known generally of Bolshevism and its leaders. Hugh Brogan has noted that 'as late as January 1920 the *Morning Post* would be asserting that Lenin was not in fact Lenin at all, but a secret organisation run by revolutionary Jews plotting the destruction of the world'.[20] Socialists might disregard such absurd – and poisonous – nonsense, but clearly those who supported the Bolshevik cause from afar had to construct their ideas of Bolshevik actions and policies partly on the basis of inference. Assumptions based on their own experience, guesswork and wishful thinking played a decisive part.

A crucial example of the unknown East being interpreted in terms of the known West was the perception of the Russian soviets. They tended to be seen in terms of the syndicalist, industrial unionist and De Leonist ideas that stressed the 'worker' rather than the 'citizen'. This is certainly the case with the *Dreadnought*. It had, early in 1916, supported the Clyde workers' revolt against the Munitions Act and their efforts – in Sylvia Pankhurst's words – 'to develop and democratise their own Trade Union organisation from within'. Commenting on the broader implications she went on:

> The new Trade Unionism, which is so active on the Clyde, wishes to emancipate the workers from the position of incoherent de-

pendent tools, whether of employers, Governments, or officials sprung from their own ranks. It wishes every worker in the trade to take his or her part in moulding the policy of the union, and each trade union to take its part in making the nation a co-operative commonwealth, managed in the interest of all.[21]

A REVOLUTIONARY ON THE 'HOME FRONT': SYLVIA PANKHURST MAY–NOVEMBER 1917

With revolution raging in Russia, Sylvia spent even more time addressing meetings all over the country. On Thursday 17 May, for example, she was the main speaker at 'a great and enthusiastic meeting'[22] in the Salvation Army Congress Hall in Brighton. Advertised as a 'Mass Meeting to Celebrate Russian Freedom' it featured what a local press report called 'some very outspoken speeches'. In a letter to the same paper the following week, 'Patriot' complained that 'Speaker after speaker insiduously advocated revolution in this country in support of the present lamentable strikes and an immediate termination of the war without requiring any indemnity from "our German comrades"'.[23]

'Patriot' would have had in mind the engineering strike against the government's unilateral withdrawal of the trade card system. Involving more than 200,000 workers this remains one of the largest 'unofficial' strikes in British history. At the Brighton meeting – attended by 1,600, claimed the organisers – Sylvia urged her audience not to be taken in by the argument that the strikes would lead to fewer guns and more British casualties at the Front. 'The truth is that the more guns you send out the more men will be killed. It does not matter to me what kind of men they are: they are all members of the human family: they are our brothers.'[24]

Two evenings before this 'Anti-Patriotic Meeting', as the local press soon called it, took place, a special and decidedly non-public meeting at the Ministry of Munitions had resolved, on the advice of F. E. Smith, the Public Prosecutor, to defer the arrest of the strike leaders until after the King and Queen, dispatched on a visit to the most affected areas, had left the north. Arrest warrants were issued on the day of the Brighton meeting.[25]

A little later, at the end of May, the WSF met for its annual conference. It declared for the abolition of capitalism and the 'establishment of the Socialist Commonwealth' and agreed its paper's title should be changed to *The Workers' Dreadnought*. Resolutions were also passed demanding adult suffrage, child 'pensions', nationalisation of food, opposition to war, repeal of the Military Service Acts, immediate peace negotiations on the basis of no annexations or indemnities, and the abolition of armies and navies.[26]

The following week the Leeds Soviet Convention, organised by the BSP, the ILP and George Lansbury's *Daily Herald*, took place. Later, Sylvia was to maintain that she regarded this initiative with great scepticism. But, with whatever reservations, she was an active participant. The WSF insisted that 'Councils of Workmen's and Soldiers' Delegates' should be amended to read 'Workers' – and claimed the offending word was in any case a mistranslation from the Russian.[27]

The Leeds conference set up a national body – the British Workers' and Soldiers' Council – which attempted to convene local conferences. The difficulties involved in wartime, with a hostile press and a government whose authority, though facing serious challenges on the industrial front, remained intact, can be imagined.[28] The *Dreadnought* suggested detailed amendments to the 'official resolution' to be moved at this series of local conferences, including inserting the words 'and Housewives' in the title of the 'Workers' and Soldiers' Councils' that it was intended to establish in the localities.

Sylvia was elected to the national council, (against her better judgement and desire, she insisted) as the delegate from the London and Home Counties. Later she would recall 'When I sat with the present PM [Ramsay MacDonald] on the Workers' and Soldiers' Council of Great Britain'. She came to believe that Lansbury and the other ILP leaders, temporarily swept away by the euphoria of the Russian Revolution, thought that 'they were forming what might be a government'. At the first meeting she 'listened in complete amazement to sentiments so revolutionary from such unexpected quarters'. But the meeting was not a great success. Provincial delegates had not even been invited – apparently because of the expensive rail fares – and Ramsay MacDonald complained of the lack of working class support and the fact that only one soldier had been elected. Sylvia

told the Council I was sorry that my presence had robbed them of a soldier or trade unionist: but I had been elected against my will. The twelve other district representatives would doubtless have said the same thing had they been present.

At the end of her account she speculates that the 'discarded leaders' who had opposed the war were out to oust their pro-war Labour colleagues and that Lansbury 'with his journalist-like sensibility to the popular news of the hour held out a prospect peculiarly attractive to politicians, who had been ostracised for so long. They rose to his bait in the hope of capturing control of the Labour movement, if not of ruling a nation in revolution'. Arriving twenty minutes late for the fourth meeting of the Council she found that

> it had disbanded and was no more. I wondered whether I had perhaps administered the death blow. I had written to the Secretary suggesting a working policy and had asked that my letter be read to the Council. The shock of a concrete policy coming before it had perhaps killed the Council. I never knew how it died.[29]

Meanwhile, the first *Dreadnought* under the new title and with the masthead slogan, 'Socialism, Internationalism, Votes for All' had appeared on 28 July. This carried the now-famous protest against the conduct of the war from Siegfied Sassoon, three days before it appeared in *The Times*. Together with the editor's 'Stop the War' leader, this precipitated an attack on the *Dreadnought*'s 'unqualified sedition' from the *Daily Express*, and a raid on its offices by five Scotland Yard detectives armed with a warrant from 'the competent military authority'. All this was reported with relish by the *Dreadnought*.[30] Alarmed *Daily Express* readers might have been relieved had they been aware of Norah Smyth's report as Treasurer of the WSF Finance Committee. All accounts were in deficit, with receipts in August of £270 to meet expenses of £371.[31]

Worse was to come. On Thursday 4 October Inspector Mclean of the City of London Police visited the *Dreadnought*'s printers, the Blackfriars Press, a subsidiary of the National Labour Press, seized the whole edition of 2,604 copies and extracted a signed undertaking from W. F. Moss, the manager, to give up printing the paper. It seems that vague but menacing threats of total closure were made. Another printer was found, who, having established that the *Dreadnought* was not being suppressed under the DORA, was prepared to take over.

This solved the immediate problem, but the following May the Finance Committee was told that the new printer 'censors the paper in an absurd manner and is most difficult to work with. He insists on being paid in advance'. In the meantime the *Morning Post* and the *Evening News* had both claimed that the *Dreadnought* was being subsidised by German gold – a very serious charge in 1917. Sylvia's response was to draw the attention of the Home Office to these accusations and invite inspection of the books of the paper and of the WSF.[32]

The outbreak of revolution in Russia in the spring had brought unexpected hope. For many, the overthrow of the inefficient and possibly secretly pro-German Tsar promised a more vigorous and successful prosecution of the war on the eastern front. The Western powers were relieved of the embarrassment of an ultra-reactionary ally, and tended to assume that with freedom and the promise of democracy in the shape of the Constituent Assembly the Russian people would redouble their war effort.

For socialists like Sylvia Pankhurst the hopes – and the perceptions – were utterly different. The revolution promised not an intensification of the war but an early peace. And she saw the soviets as the main agency for democracy and peace even before she supported the Bolsheviks. They won her support because they demanded power to the soviets and an end to the capitalist war.

At home, Sylvia's early commitment to the soviets is evident from the detailed amendments proposed by the WSF to the 'official resolutions' of the Leeds Soviet Convention. Her reservations about this initiative were indicative of a growing distrust of 'orthodox' socialist politicians. Her experience on the abortive National Council must have reinforced this. It must have seemed that, like Kerensky, MacDonald, Lansbury and the rest of the ILP leadership 'failed to realise the greatness of the movement' they would lead.

THE 'LENIN REVOLUTION'

Her initial view of the Bolshevik Revolution was that it was 'striving to complete' the February/March Revolution, of which, she asserted, the Bolsheviks had been the driving force. They had consistently demanded that the Council of Workers' and Soldiers' Delegates – 'the broadest based elected body in Russia' according to the *Daily News* correspondent in Russia, Arthur Ransome – should take over the government of the country 'until the Constituent Assembly is elected by the votes of all the men and women in Russia'.

In a long leader on 'The Lenin Revolution. What it means to democracy' in the *Dreadnought* on 17 November, Sylvia quoted Ransome again to the effect that the Bolsheviks had the support of a majority of the 'politically active population'. She went on to speculate about the fate of the new revolutionary regime.

The power of the people may maintain the Bolshevik Government, or if it should fail, the votes cast in the elections for the Constituent Assembly may reinstate it.

In the light of her subsequent attitudes, it is important to note that at this stage she saw the Assembly not as some bourgeois obstacle to Bolshevik rule but rather as a kind of insurance for it. That this was so is reinforced by her comment that, 'We can look with a confidence to the votes of the Russian people which, as yet, we cannot feel towards the votes of our own countrymen and women, because the Russian people have lately proved themselves.'

Why, she asked, was Russia so much more advanced than Britain? She thought that greater hardships had made Russia 'riper for revolution'. But there was another reason. In Russia, 'the politics of advanced politicians' were 'more definite and scientific *and above all more democratic*' [emphasis added]. Notoriously, democracy is open to many interpretations, but we know what it meant to Sylvia at this time, for she goes on;

In the political field we believe we are right in saying that neither a Labour Party, Trade Union, or ILP Conference has discussed at any rate within recent years, such essential democratic institutions as the Initiative, Referendum and Recall, institutions which are all actually in being in the Western States of the USA, and which are partially established elsewhere. A Russian Socialist woman said to us: 'People here are actually discussing whether the Referendum is democratic; why, I realised the democratic importance of the Referendum when I was fifteen years of age'.[33]

DIRECT DEMOCRACY

With hindsight it seems strange, even ironic, that in welcoming the Bolshevik seizure of power she should link this with devices like the referendum and initiative more associated with Switzerland than Leninst Russia; and that her immediate source of inspiration should be the United States. While she may have been correct as regards 'recent years', she was certainly not introducing direct democracy as a new idea in British socialism.

In the 1880s, and especially the 1890s, support for the referendum and initiative had divided the Social-Democratic Federation and Robert Blatchford's *Clarion* from the Fabians and the ILP leadership, including, ironically, her mentor and friend Keir Hardie. The Fabians had been the most consistent opponents of such 'primitive expedients', and indeed the *Dreadnought* itself was to carry an attack on the referendum by George Bernard Shaw in its issue of 15 December 1917. After 1900 rather less was heard of the debate, although discussion did surface from time to time in the socialist press, notably during the period of 'constitutional crisis' in 1910–11.[34]

It seems likely that, preoccupied with the suffrage issue in earlier years – and perhaps shielded from contact with the socialist proponents of direct democracy by her association with Hardie – she was only vaguely aware, or even totally unaware, of the part played by such issues in pre-war British socialist debate. Nevertheless, her championing of the referendum preceded the Russian Revolution.

The first mention of anything of the sort in the *Dreadnought* was in June 1916, a short while after the Easter Rising, when she supported the idea of a referendum to decide the future of the 'six counties'.[35] At the end of that year, in discussing the possible German peace offer, she wrote:

> We must determine that if the offer to negotiate be not accepted by the British Government, a referendum vote of the men and women of the country shall be taken to decide the matter. The jingoes pretend to speak for the people, we assert that they do not.[36]

The 'initiative' and 'recall' made their first *Dreadnought* appearance in her criticism of the Speaker's Conference report on electoral reform early in 1917. She urged that Britain should follow the example of 'forward moving democracies' like Australia, New Zealand, Canada and many of the American states which had adopted complete adult suffrage and were moving towards 'a still more direct means of popular control'. She went on:

> To this end, as State after State from time to time revises its constitution, such innovations as the Initiative, Referendum and Recall are introduced. If Britain would break away from amongst the autocracies of the past and take rank with the new democracies, with which the hope of the future lies, she must be prepared to give equal political rights to all her people.[37]

The revival of the franchise issue in Britain as a matter of urgent political debate led the London Labour Council for Adult Suffrage to call a conference at Holborn Hall on Saturday 17 February. It reiterated the demand for 'the speedy enactment of adult suffrage'. But Sylvia wished to go much further. She seconded a motion moved by G. A. Hobson which was short and to the point.

This Conference urges that provisions for
a) Establishing the Referendum
b) the Initiative
c) the Recall
be inserted in the forthcoming Reform Bill.[38]

She recalled later that:

So unfamiliar were these institutions here that in drawing up the agenda I found it necessary to add a note explaining that under the Initiative a small percentage of the electorate is entitled to claim by petition that a Referendum vote of the whole electorate shall be taken to decide whether any measure shall be enacted or repealed or whether any Minister of state [sic] shall be Recalled from office.[39]

The note on the Conference programme claimed that 'The Initiative and Recall have been established in a growing number of American States. A Referendum vote is necessary to confirm the passage of all important legislative measures in the United States'. It is certainly true that between 1898 and 1918 the referendum and initiative was adopted by nineteen states while another three introduced the referendum only.[40]

One copy of the programme in the Sylvia Pankhurst Papers has a handwritten addition to the motion: 'That the Prime Minister and Cabinet Ministers be elected by ballot of the whole electorate'. It is not clear from the *Dreadnought* report whether the resolution was passed with or without this addendum. Whatever the theoretical and practical difficulties of such instruments of direct democracy, the appeal for those wishing to achieve 'real' democracy is clear.

The 1917 WSF conference not only urged the enactment of the three measures – with 'the recall and the election of Ministers and Judges by referendum vote', but also resolved 'That the referendum be used within the Federation for the ratification of resolutions adopted by the Annual Con [sic] – new departures in policy where urgency and rapidity of action are not essential'.[41]

It is not clear whether this provision was ever used, but among the amendments suggested soon afterwards to the 'official resolution' for the local 'soviets' that the Leeds Convention intended to set up was one which expressly demanded an 'adult suffrage referendum vote' by the people of the nations to decide their own affairs as a basis for peace, the application of this principle throughout the British Empire, and the inclusion of the referendum, initiative and recall in the proposed 'charter of liberties'.[42]

Moreover, this brand of direct democracy continued to be presented as desirable for some time after the 'Lenin Revolution'. In January 1918 the *Dreadnought* reported that the Bolsheviks at the Brest Litovsk peace talks were demanding a referendum in Lithuania. In March the Labour Party was criticised for failing to include the referendum, initiative and recall in its manifesto *Labour and the New Social Order*. G. D. H. Cole was also criticised for failing to include them in his Guild Socialist plans, and the *Dreadnought* went on to claim that 'no system of representative Government can be genuinely democratic. We urge on all Socialists the need for incorporating this useful machinery in any scheme for a socialist community'.[43] The referendum, 'the most direct and democratic means of popular expression', was, said an editorial advocating abolition of the House of Lords, the only acceptable check on the elected chamber, whether that was the House of Commons or a future 'Industrial Parliament'.[44]

Such views were never repudiated, but after the summer of 1918 the referendum disappears from the pages of the *Dreadnought*. An explanation is suggested by the question and answer exchange on the 'New Russia' that August. Readers' queries had been invited three weeks earlier. To the – inevitable – question 'Is the Referendum in force?' the reply was 'Yes, but it has not yet been applied, though it is being demanded to express national self-determination in provinces now occupied by Germany, Esthonia etc'.[45]

THE CONSTITUENT ASSEMBLY AND ITS DISSOLUTION

As we have already seen, Sylvia Pankhurst's initial reaction to the Bolshevik Revolution, though totally supportive, had seen it as provisional pending the election of the long-awaited Constituent Assembly – a body which might even 'reinstate' the Bolsheviks if they were overthrown in the meantime. She still seems to have seen the Assembly as the ultimate expression – barring, presumably, the result of a referendum – of the democratic will of the Russian people. The action of the Bolsheviks was justified on democratic grounds; since they derived power from the elected soviets which was a more democratic basis than that of the provisional governments of the Duma parties. But had not the Bolsheviks themselves criticised the delay in holding general elections for the Assembly?

The *Dreadnought* had been eagerly drawing attention to signs that the Socialist parties were going to do well in these elections. The Petrograd municipal result augured well, readers were told in June, and 'the Socialists confidently expect a big majority' in the Assembly elections'.[46] In October the paper was complaining of further delays, 'but it seems to us that the mass of the people in Russia should demand the holding of these elections, in which all will have a voice'. It concluded that '"Trust the people" is in the ultimate resort, the only satisfactory motto'.[47] Soon after the Bolshevik takeover, details of early election returns from Petrograd and elsewhere appeared which, the paper suggested, made it likely the Bolsheviks were on their way to a majority in the Assembly. The *Dreadnought* added that:

Petrograd public opinion in support of peace and Socialism has grown tremendously since the Municipal Council was elected. The Government is therefore wisely acting in the interests of democratic representation in calling new elections. The Initiative, Referendum and Recall would provide the people with the means of meeting the situation without the intervention of the Government.[48]

By the following week the results looked less promising for the Bolsheviks but 'it is certain that whether the Bolsheviks have a clear majority or not, the various Socialist parties command a vast majority in the Russian Parliament'.[49]

In all this there is absolutely no suggestion that the Assembly represented a now superseded bourgeois form of democracy. If such a form was to be transcended it would be by the most direct forms of democracy – the referendum, initiative and recall. For Sylvia Pankhurst the dissolution of the Assembly, rather than the October

Revolution itself, was the 'Rubicon'. Her response to it set her definitely on the path that was to lead to 'Left Communism'. 'What About Russia Now?' asked the *Dreadnought* leader on 26 January 1918 following the forcible dissolution of the Constituent Assembly.

'There's the democracy of your Socialists.' 'Substituting one tyranny for another.' 'Bolshevik autocracy.' 'What about Russia now?' such are the cries that assail us. And what have we to answer?

In reply, Sylvia quoted the Bolshevik decree stating that 'the old bourgeois parliamentarianism has seen its day', and was unable to cope with the tasks of Socialism, while the soviets, 'as the only organisation of the exploited working classes', were 'in a position to direct the struggle of these classes for their complete political and economic emancipation'. It had been, she said, from the beginning the soviets' revolution: 'They sprang into being at its outbreak, they carried through the disposition of the Czar in March, and every subsequent advance has been initiated by the Soviets.'

Returning to the Bolshevik decree, she quoted it on the gradual dissillusionment of the soviets with bourgeois parties and institutions. Eventually,

Perceiving the illusion of an understanding with the bourgeoisie and the deceptive Parliamentary organisations of the democratic bourgeoisie, they arrived at the solution that the liberation of the oppressed classes was an impossibility without a complete rupture of every kind of understanding. Therefore the Revolution of October arose.

Following this is a highly significant comment which helps us understand how she was able to cope with such a 'U turn'. In interpreting it we must bear in mind her remarks on the 'new Trade Unionism' of the Clyde workers quoted earlier.

All this we have watched with interest, observing the strong support which the trend of events in Russia has been lending to those calling themselves Syndicalists, Industrial Unionists, or simply Marxian Socialists, who interpret the great teacher's doctrine from the industrial standpoint, who believe Parliaments as we know them are destined to pass away into the limbo of forgotten things, their places being taken by organisations of the people built on an occupational basis.

The failure of the elections for the Constituent Assembly even though decided on an adult suffrage ballot, to return members prepared to support the policy of the Soviets, is strong evidence that the industrialists have found the true path.

There remained the problem of explaining why, if all this were true, the Bolsheviks allowed the Assembly elections to go ahead. Sylvia was clearly unsure of the answer, but suggested three possibilities. Perhaps it was to demonstrate 'that the capitalist parties have no following in Russia', or to make clear to the people the division between 'the politicians who are in favour of Socialism but do not want to have it in their time' and those who are 'striving for its immediate establishment'? Or, perhaps, the Bolsheviks expected it to turn out differently and had been disappointed with the result?

This last explanation, she said, was supported by the decree's statement that 'the people who voted for the Revolutionary Socialists [that is the Social Revolutionaries or SRs – IB] were unable to distinguish between the Revolutionary Socialists of the Right, partisans of the bourgeoisie, and the Revolutionary Socialist of the Left, partisans of socialism'.

She is quite clear and explicit about the reasons why soviets constitute a superior form of democracy.

> As a representative body, an organisation such as the All-Russian Workers', Soldiers' and Peasants' Council is more closely in touch with and more directly represents its constituents than the Constituent Assembly or any existing Parliament. The delegates...are constantly reporting back and getting instructions from their constituents; whilst Members of Parliament are elected for a term of years and only receive anything approaching instructions at election times. Even then it is the candidate who, in the main sets forth the programme, the electors merely assenting to or dissenting from the programme as a whole.

The soviets were to be preferred, then, for exactly the same reason as the referendum and initiative; directness. Both, in principle, avoided the distortion of representation – the referendum by allowing the elector to speak without mediation; the soviet by working through mandated delegates. But the soviets had the further advantage that, elected by occupational groupings, they were a working-class institution.

Some people complained, Sylvia went on in the same editorial, that they represented only the working classes. But this was precisely the Bolsheviks' intention and should be supported by all socialists since 'you must recognise that under Socialism everyone will be a worker and there will be no class save the working class to consider or represent'.[50]

Yet despite her unequivocal and immediate support for the dissolution of the Assembly, Sylvia seems to have felt the need to reinforce this with the explanations of Bolshevik leaders and eye-witnesses, such as Louise Bryant and Philips Price, whose views would carry weight with *Dreadnought* readers. This process of justification continued for a considerable period and suggests an underlying unease.[51]

SOVIETS – EVERYWHERE: 1918–1922

Following the dissolution of the Constituent Assembly, soviets became absolutely central to Sylvia Pankhurst's politics. They were the 'most democratic form of government yet established'.[52] Accounts of the soviets and how they worked – or were supposed to work – appeared frequently in the *Dreadnought*, particularly between the summers of 1918 and 1920. There were accounts both by the Bolshevik leaders – Litvinov, Bukharin, Zinoviev and Lenin himself – and by foreign sympathisers like Arthur Ransome and John Reed. As well as general theories and justifications of the soviet system, there were detailed descriptions of how it worked, sometimes illustrated with complex charts.

Not that soviets were confined to Russia. On the contrary, they were becoming ubiquitous. Promising developments were reported in Italy in August 1919, in Germany the following December, in Ireland, and in Bulgaria in 1922. At various times distinctions were suggested or inferred between 'political', 'economic' and 'social' soviets, as well as 'soviets of the street', 'household soviets' and 'workshop soviets'. Even the National Union of Teachers was seen as prefiguring 'occupational soviets' in April 1924. As Lucia Jones has commented, 'The lack of clarity as to the meaning and function of a soviet, as distinct from a workers' committee or a political party seems extraordinary ... it would seem that soviets could be set up regardless of the political and revolutionary climate'.[53]

For Sylvia, it seems, a soviet was any sort of workers' committee, with of course the important qualification that housewives were to be explicitly recognised as workers and included accordingly. This led to a drift from the initial occupational basis, so that by 1920 'soviets of the street' and 'the formation of household soviets' are being discussed and advocated.[54] Every grass-roots movement was a candidate for soviethood. Socialism meant the whole society, ultimately the whole world, organised on such a basis, not as any temporary expedient but as its permanent and authentic expression.

So alarm bells rang when, replying to a question on the dissolution of the Constituent Assembly from a correspondent of *Avanti*, Kamenev and Zahkind justified the soviet system as an essentially temporary expedient in the fight against the capitalists. While this struggle continued, the soviets must be 'the fighting organisation of the workers. When all have submitted, the diverse social strata will again be able to send their legitimate representatives to the legislative and administrative assembly'. This was not at all what the editor of the *Dreadnought* expected – or wanted – to hear: 'We are surprised by this answer for it seems to us that the Soviet form of Government is a more modern and democratic form than the old Parliament elected on a territorial basis'.[55]

This commitment to her vision of the soviets as a truly democratic system remained constant through the rapid changes in Sylvia's political life during the next few years. In June 1918 the WSF became the Workers' Socialist Federation. In the meantime she had begun to work closely with Litvinov, and, after his deportation in September 1918, Rothstein, who took over as the 'Eye of Moscow' in Britain. In October 1918 she was fined £50 under the DORA regulations. She was the mainspring of the People's Russian Information Bureau, which was used to propagate the Bolsheviks' version of events in Russia, and she was active in the 'Hands off Russia' campaign against the continued Allied intervention.

In July 1919, impatient with the slow progress of attempts to unite various left-wing groups to form a Communist Party, the WSF adopted the name itself. But, on the advice of the newly-formed Comintern, it agreed to delay implementing its decision in the interests of facilitating unity. Later that year, denied a passport valid for Germany, Sylvia attended the Bologna conference of the Italian Socialist Party and then, with enormous physical courage and endurance, made illegal crossings of the Alps – a feat which took three days and two nights – and the Swiss/German border to attend a clandestine Comintern conference in Frankfurt. A little later she also attended a meeting called by the short-lived Sub-Bureau of Comintern in Amsterdam.

She was firmly opposed to uniting with the 'Right Wing' communists unless they totally rejected parliamentary participation and affiliation to the Labour Party: the views for which she was to be criticised by Lenin in *'Left-Wing' Communism*. The WSF maintained this position for some time. Having decided against attending the 'unity conference' which was to form the CPGB, the WSF tried to preempt this by calling an 'Emergency Conference of Anti-Parliamentary Groups' which merged the WSF and other small groups to form the Communist Party (British Section of the Third International) on 19 June 1920. On behalf of this body Sylvia attended the later parts of the second Comintern Congress in August. This involved further dangerous clandestine travel, this time to Russia.

In Russia she was persuaded by Lenin and other Bolshevik leaders that, in spite of her continuing doubts, an accommodation with the CPGB was vital in the interests of international communism. Returning home she accomplished the necessary 'U-turn', but was almost immediately involved in another DORA prosecution. This time she was given a six-month prison sentence. She appealed unsuccessfully and began her sentence on 5 January 1921. As soon as she was out of circulation the scene changed dramatically. Internal conflicts and suspicions rent her organisation and the CP [BSTI] Executive Committee disowned the *Dreadnought* within a fortnight and merged with the CPGB at the end of the month.

Released from Holloway at the end of May, she found that she was regarded as a member of the new merged party and under pressure to hand the *Dreadnought* over to it unconditionally. She refused to do this and insisted on her right to criticise the Communist Party if she thought it necessary. She was expelled by the CPGB Executive Committee on 10 September 1921. Later, she would argue that since the merger of the parties had taken place when she was 'inside', and she had never signed an application form or membership card, she had never been a member and therefore could not be expelled.

From this point on, she identified increasingly with the 'Fourth International' of dissident communist groups of which the KAPD – the German Communist Workers' Party – was the most prominent. The hallmark of these groups was the commitment to the soviet system understood as one in which power was held at all levels by genuine workers' councils. For this reason their members are frequently described as 'council communists'.

Ever more critical about the turn of events in Russia, the *Dreadnought*, now more than ever the work of Sylvia herself, serialised Rosa Luxemburg's *The Russian Revolution*, and writings of Alexandra Kollantai on the Workers' Opposition between April and June 1922. Another important influence and contributor was Herman Gorter, the Dutch poet and 'Left Communist', whose writings appeared frequently in the paper during its last months of publication in 1924. By that time Gorter saw the Bolsheviks and Comintern as 'the greatest enemies of the world revolution'.[56]

For her own part, Sylvia had detected the restoration of capitalism in Russia by July 1922 and by the end of that year she accused Lenin of 'hauling down the flag of Communism'.[57] Her own position, which had remained firmly anti-parliamentary, is well summed up in a 'What We Stand For' piece in March 1924 advocating workshop councils on the grounds that 'the only genuine self-government is literally self-government, in which free individuals willingly associate themselves in a common effort for the common good.'[58]

A similar statement appeared a few weeks later which emphasised that 'A centralised Government cannot give freedom to the individual: it stultifies initiative and progress. In the struggle to abolish capitalism the workshop councils are essential'. Her Communist Workers' Movement aimed, therefore, at the creation of an 'All-Workers' Industrial Revolutionary Union' covering both employed and unemployed and 'Built up from a workshop basis, covering all workers . . . who pledge themselves to work for the overthrow of Capitalism and the establishment of Communism administered by workers' councils'. Not only were Parliament and the Labour Party – and of course the CPGB – rejected but also the trade unions 'which are mere palliative institutions'.[59]

CONCLUSION: THE MAKING OF A 'LEFT-WING' COMMUNIST

For Sylvia Pankhurst the initial attraction of the Russian Revolution in the spring of 1917 lay in its promise of peace and social revolution. More immediately, it gave a boost to the struggle for adult suffrage and for democracy generally. For Sylvia there was from the start a strong emphasis on the goal of democracy. Their firmness on the issue of peace and their support for the soviets – the most broadly-based representative institution yet in being in the country – led to a sympathetic, if hazily perceived, view of the Bolsheviks, who seemed to promise a determined drive to social and economic equality.

But for Sylvia the emerging soviet model was not the only possible road to democracy and socialism. Until the drawing-power of the Russian magnet became irresistible, a potential alternative could be seen in the 'new democracies' such as the USA and Australia. For Sylvia the major attraction of such countries was their development, actual or potential, of forms of direct democracy – the referendum, initiative and recall. Her preference, by no means unusual in socialists of that era, for such forms, predisposed her to be able to get over the crucial hurdle of the dissolution of the Constituent Assembly as long as the soviets could be seen as a more directly democratic institution.

We must also remember that her long, close – and frustrating – dealings with the British Parliament and parliamentarians both before and during the war, and her more recent experiences with some of the leading exponents of parliamentary Socialism in the 'British Soviet' set up by the Leeds convention was not calculated to enhance the standing of parliamentary government in her eyes. And as a woman she was still denied full citizenship by the parliament she knew best.

With their system of delegation as distinct from representation, the soviets seemed, like the initiative and referendum, to be a form of *direct* democracy. And they had the additional appeal as *class* institutions representing workers rather than citizens. In the WSF Minute Book for 1918-20 are some notes – presumably for an article or a speech – on 'Why I Want the Soviets' which illustrate these points.

> The Soviet system of government which has been adopted in Russia is the most democratic yet devised. Its structure is similar to that of the organisations which the working class has built up for itself in every country in the world, but the Russian plan gives fuller control over the delegates. Those who study scientifically the progress of evolution must see that the capitalist system is nearing its end and that the Socialist or Communist era is dawning upon the world.[60]

The soviets embodied not only the most genuine democracy; they were also the form taken by the 'dictatorship of the proletariat'. Left-

wing socialists demanded both complete democracy and the abolition of capitalism. The soviets seemed to solve the problem of the
possible conflict between these two aims. As working-class institutions, it was assumed, they could be trusted to combat capitalist
exploitation, while their delegation and recall provisions seemed to
exemplify real, participatory, democracy.

What of the democratic rights of those excluded? The solution
was to regard the disfranchisement of the bourgeoisie as entirely
voluntary. That enabled the question to be moralised. Since 'Under
Socialism no one will live on profits and dividends drawn from the
labour of others; there will be no leisured classes',[61] it followed that
those bourgeois individuals willing to accept honest work could do
so freely and would thus automatically find themselves within the
scope of the soviets. The dictatorship of the proletariat simply meant
'the refusal of any share of political power to those who, instead of
joining the general companionship of workers, employ others to
work for them for private gain'.[62] This was not simply Sylvia's own
interpretation. She was able to quote the Hungarian Communist,
Albert Santos, who stressed that those excluded from the soviets
could easily acquire political rights 'by engaging in fruitful labour'.[63]
Only recalcitrant drones, then, would really remain outside the soviet system. And their exclusion would be a result of their own free
choice and no more undemocratic than allowing electors to abstain
from voting.

At first sight it may seem strange that one who worked so hard
and suffered so much in what was – whatever else it may have also
been – a struggle for the parliamentary vote, should adopt such a
vehemently anti-parliamentary stance. Yet having come, by the route
we have retraced, to the conviction that soviets were so highly
superior as democratic institutions, how could their supporters possibly contest *parliamentary* elections? How could they even consider
affiliation to a Labour Party embedded in the parliamentary system?
Would not any short-term advantage be more than cancelled by the
confusion and cynicism planted in the minds of the workers? There
was something close to inevitability in Sylvia Pankhurst's evolution
towards the 'disorder' of 'Left Communism'.

The crucial turning-point had been the dissolution of the Constituent Assembly. Had she read this as an authoritarian and anti-
democratic act by the Bolsheviks and opposed it, she might well
have gravitated back to the world of the ILP and the left-wing of the
Labour Party. But she supported the dissolution. She was only able

to do so in the belief that 'bourgeois democracy' with all its well-known defects was being supplanted by a higher form – that of the soviets. As it became clear gradually that her perception of how soviet democracy was supposed to operate was very different from Russian reality, her breach with 'orthodox' communism became a matter of time.

There were few alternatives left. At first the dissident 'Left' or 'council' communists could see themselves as an opposition *within* the Communist movement, but the latter increasingly left no room for dissident. The hammer and sickle that appeared in the *Dreadnought* masthead at the end of January 1920 vanished in February 1924. Within a few months the paper itself was no more.

Yet if it seemed like a dead end, that was only partly the case. Sylvia's early warnings about Mussolini's fascism prefigured the anti-fascist and anti-imperialist campaigns that were to occupy so much of her life from the 1930s. The first mentions of Italian fascism in the *Dreadnought* were on 25 November and 13 December 1919. How 'acceptable' Mussolini was even after 1922 – and Sylvia Pankhurst's unusually adamant early opposition to fascism – can be judged by her criticism of George Lansbury's speech to a group of ex-service trainees. She commented scornfully on his reported speech: '"If I were Mussolini" (observe, by the way, pacifist Mr Lansbury does not shrink from comparing himself with the renegade murderer) "I would put a tax on every able-bodied man in the country . . . ."'[64]

By 1924 Sylvia Pankhurst may have been, politically, 'down'. Time would show she was certainly not 'out'.

NOTES

1. V. I. Lenin, *'Left-Wing' Communism, An Infantile Disorder* [1920] (Peking: Foreign Languages Press, 1970 edition) pp. 77–8.
2. *Workers' Dreadnought*, 21 February 1920.
3. After representations from Rothstein, the Comintern representative or 'Eye of Moscow' in Britain, the WSF agreed to *delay implementation* of the conference decision to change its name in the interests of 'communist unity'.
4. E. Sylvia Pankhurst, *The Home Front: A Mirror to Life in England during the World War* (London: Hutchinson, 1932), p. 83.

5. *Woman's Dreadnought*, 2 January 1915.
6. *The Home Front*, p. 43.
7. *Woman's Dreadnought*, 9 October 1915; 8 April 1916.
8. *The Home Front*, p. 230.
9. *Woman's Dreadnought*, 18 March; 1 April; 6 May 1916;. Confusingly, the ELFS gave way to the *Workers'* Suffrage Federation in February 1916, while the paper remained the *Woman's* Dreadnought until 28 July 1917. The phrase 'servile state' had been popularised by Hilaire Belloc's pre-war book of that title, which in spite of being an argument against *inter alia* state socialism, was influential among socialists in Britain. (Hilaire Belloc, *The Servile State* (London: T. N. Foulis, 1912)).
10. *Woman's Dreadnought*, 3 June 1916.
11. E. Sylvia Pankhurst Papers (ESPP], International Institute of Social History, Amsterdam. The first quotation is from one of several synopses of the projected *In the Red Twilight*; ESPP 146-50. The second is from a handwritten notebook of the same title dated February 1922. ESPP 83, p. 65.
12. WSF General Meeting Minute Book, 19 March 1917. ESPP 211.
13. *Woman's Dreadnought*, 31 March 1917.
14. *Woman's Dreadnought*, 2 June 1917.
15. *Woman's Dreadnought*, 30 June 1917.
16. *Woman's Dreadnought*, 11 August 1917.
17. *Woman's Dreadnought*, 26 December 1914. V. I. Lenin, *Collected Works*, vol. 21- August 1914-December 1915, pp. 27–34.
18. *Woman's Dreadnought*, 24 April; 18 December 1915; 20 May 1916.
19. *Workers' Dreadnought*, 17; 24 November 1917.
20. Hugh Brogan, *The Life of Arthur Ransome* (London: Cape, 1984), p. 238.
21. *Woman's Dreadnought*, 8 January 1916.
22. *Woman's Dreadnought*, 26 May 1917.
23. *Brighton Gazette*, 19; 26 May 1917.
24. *Brighton Herald*, 19 May 1917.
25. Walter Kendall, *The Revolutionary Movement in Britain, 1900-1921. The Origins of British Communism* (London: Weidenfeld and Nicholson, 1967), pp. 157-8. See also for details of Sylvia Pankhurst's part in the events leading up to the foundation of the CPGB.
26. *Woman's Dreadnought*, 2 June 1917.
27. *Woman's Dreadnought*, 9 June 1917.
28. Kendall, *The Revolutionary Movement*, pp. 174–6.
29. Undated draft article, 'When I sat with the present PM on the Workers' and Soldiers' Council of Great Britain', ESPP 160.
30. *Workers' Dreadnought*, 28 July; 4 August 1917. *The Times* reported Sassoon's statement on 31 July after it had been read to the House of Commons.
31. WSF Finance Committee Minutes, 16 August 1917. ESPP 212.
32. WSF Committee Minutes, 12 October 1917; ESPP 208. Documents relating to the seizure of the *Workers' Dreadnought*, October 1917; ESPP 253. WSF Finance Committee Minutes, 9 May 1918; ESPP 212.
33. *Workers' Dreadnought*, 31 March 1917. For an up-to-date appraisal of the American experience see Thomas E. Cronin, *Direct Democracy, The Poli-*

tics of Initiative , Referendum, and Recall (Cambridge, Mass.: Harvard University Press, 1989).

34. Ian Bullock, 'Socialists and Democratic Form in Britain, 1880–1914: Positions, Debates and Conflicts', unpublished D. Phil. thesis, University of Sussex, 1982.
35. *Woman's Dreadnought*, 17 June 1916.
36. *Woman's Dreadnought*, 16 December 1916.
37. *Woman's Dreadnought*, 3 February 1917.
38. Conference programme, ESPP 234.
39. ESPP 67 [undated] handwritten notes.
40. Cronin, *Direct Democracy*, p. 51.
41. *Woman's Dreadnought*, 2 June 1917.
42. *Woman's Dreadnought*, 21 July 1917.
43. *Workers' Dreadnought*, 19 January; 26 January; 9 March; 27 April 1918.
44. *Workers' Dreadnought*, 4 May 1918.
45. *Workers' Dreadnought*, 24 August 1918.
46. *Woman's Dreadnought*, 23 June; 30 June 1917.
47. *Workers' Dreadnought*, 13 October 1917.
48. *Workers' Dreadnought*, 8 December 1917.
49. *Workers' Dreadnought*, 15 December 1917.
50. *Workers' Dreadnought*, 26 January 1918.
51. Explanations and accounts of the dissolution of the Constituent Assembly in the *Workers' Dreadnought* included those of Kamenev (8 June 1918), Litvinov (6 June 1918), Price Jones (2 August 1919), Louise Bryant and Bessie Beatty (20 December 1918), and Lenin (7 August 1920).
52. *Workers' Dreadnought*, 3 August 1918.
53. Lucia Jones, '"In the Red Twilight': Sylvia Pankhurst and the Russian Revolution', unpublished University of Manchester MA thesis, 1972.
54. *Workers' Dreadnought*, 27 March; 28 August 1920. SPP – CP [BSTI] Branch Circular No. 5. Signed by Edgar Whitehead as Provisional Secretary, ESPP 239.
55. *Workers' Dreadnought*, 8 June 1918.
56. *Workers' Dreadnought*, 10 May 1924.
57. *Workers' Dreadnought*, 1 July; 4 November 1922.
58. *Workers' Dreadnought*, 24 March 1924.
59. *Workers' Dreadnought*, 10 May 1924.
60. ESPP 209. Notes for 'Why I want the Soviets'.
61. *Workers' Dreadnought*, 26 January 1918.
62. *Workers' Dreadnought*, 10 May 1919.
63. *Workers' Dreadnought*, 17 May 1919.
64. *Workers' Dreadnought*, 9 June 1923.

6

Sylvia and *New Times and Ethiopia News*

RICHARD PANKHURST

Travel to Italy, as an art student and later as an internationally-minded socialist, caused Sylvia to develop an abiding love of that country. Watching the post-World War I Italian scene with keen interest, she was disturbed by the civil strife, violence and intimidation of opponents which preceded Mussolini's 'March on Rome' in 1922; and shocked by the subsequent establishment of the fascist dictatorship. Mussolini's regime, with its penal islands and controlled press, was the antithesis of everything she held dear.

Imbued with feminist, humanitarian, democratic, socialist, pacifist and internationalist ideals she was repelled by the chauvinism, authoritarianism and militarism of the fascists. She regarded fascism as a reactionary movement which sought to preserve Italy's unjust and inegalitarian social order by crushing the socialist and workers' movements – and arresting all hopes of progress and human betterment. She saw that the fascists, who were murdering and imprisoning their opponents (several of whom she had known personally), as gangsters, who rejected the principles of free speech to which she subscribed; and she believed that their glorification of war – and desire for cannon-fodder – made them wholly inimical to the emancipation of women to which she was committed. She therefore regarded fascism as a supreme evil, with which rational discussion was impossible, and which, if not resisted, would spread throughout the world. She believed that the movement was so aggressive that it could be resisted only by force of arms. Faced with the violence of fascism she gradually found herself obliged, willy-nilly, to abandon her pacifism.

Revulsion against fascism in the early 1920s led her to found a Women's International Matteotti Committee, named after the Italian

149

Socialist deputy murdered on Mussolini's orders. She served as its honorary secretary, and corresponded with anti-fascists in many countries.[1]

As a passionate opponent of fascism, aware of its expansionist character – which had become increasingly evident after Hitler's rise to power in 1933 – she took a keen interest in the dispute between Mussolini's Italy and Ethiopia (then internationally better known as Abyssinia) which hit the headlines of the press in the winter of 1934–5. The quarrel came to a head when it transpired that Italian troops from the colony of Somalia had penetrated deep into Ethiopian territory. Though the Ethiopians exercised exemplary patience a skirmish almost inevitably occurred. The Duce, who had for years dreamt of carving an Italian empire in Africa, used this incident as a pretext for pouring soldiers into Eritrea and Somalia, the two neighbouring Italian colonies.

Sylvia, aware of the aggressive character of fascism, was convinced that Mussolini would embark on an invasion of Ethiopia. Still in spirit largely a pacifist – as well as a bitter opponent of fascism – she began writing and speaking in support of Ethiopia (whose long history of independence appealed to her anti-colonialist sentiments), and emerged as a strong supporter of the League of Nations.

LETTERS TO THE PRESS[2]

One of her first published letters on the subject appeared in the *Manchester Guardian* of 22 February 1935. In it she argued that secret commitments to Italy had prevented Britain from giving support to Ethiopia, and that this was the main reason why the Foreign Office had prevented Ethiopia from purchasing aircraft to bomb Italian concentrations of military supplies.

Four months later, on 20 June, she wrote a further letter to the *Guardian*, observing that as a result of the British government's failure to support the League: 'The first victim . . . is to be Abyssinia, who . . . is to be cast into the rapacious jaws of Italian Fascism'. Describing the 'dictatorships of Germany and Italy' as 'poisonous snakes', which, 'warmed in the bosom of the democratic states', would 'wound them to the death', she declared: 'The Italo-Abyssinian war is upon us. Unless the peoples of Europe will rise to the menace overhanging them, another greater catastrophe will shortly follow'. Emphasising the need for resolute action she wrote to the paper, on 2 July, declaring, 'I urge very emphatically that British public opinion . . . should make itself heard'.

In the following months she wrote a flood of letters on the crisis. They appeared in many British newspapers, including *The Times*, the *Manchester Guardian*, the *Daily Telegraph*, the *News Chronicle*, the *Daily Herald*, and the *Daily Express*, as well as a number of evening, provincial and foreign papers.

Sylvia's position in mid-1935 can be seen from a letter in the *News Chronicle* of 12 July. Writing as an anti-imperialist she recalled that 'it was Kipling who coined the phrase: "Bearing the white man's burden" to indicate that it was the mission of the peoples of modern civilisation to civilise the less advanced peoples', and commented that the white man, in the shape of fascist Italy, was 'to be engaged in civilising the Abyssinians by the atrocities of the gas bomb and the shell'. Turning to the threatened outbreak of war she continued:

the Fascist Government, which does not believe that the Italian people are fit for freedom, does its devilish work and consigns, not merely Abyssinians to slaughter, but the youth of the gifted Italian race . . . all we who in 1918, cried 'Never Again', know that to-day the mothers of Italy weep for their departing sons. For my part, whatever the colour of the skin, I make no distinction between mother love, whether it be in Africa or Europe.

She went on to note that though Ethiopia was prevented from importing defensive weapons Italy was obtaining from abroad all the military requirements it needed for an 'attack upon a defenceless people', and that the 'greater part' came directly from Britain, Italy was thus being supplied with coal from South Wales coalfields, while for every Italian soldier passing through the Suez Canal the British-based Suez Canal company netted £1 sterling, 'a little by-profit out of the intended massacre'.

Emphasising the importance of Ethiopia to the cause of peace, appealing for justice-loving people to come to Ethopia's aid – and rebutting the widely-propagated fascist claim that the country was the 'last stronghold' of slavery, she declared that 'the question of Abyssinia was the acid test of the League of Nations', and:

Let us put away the hypocrisy of compelling the Abyssinians also to keep the peace, for here we have the spectacle of this small country, which is a member of the League of Nations, pleading piteously to the League to intervene, and the great League of civilised powers, which was set up to prevent questions in dispute ever again being decided by the arbitrament of war, turning a deaf ear to the plea of one of her own members.

She added:

> Is the conscience of Europe dead? Is there no honest thinking left in Britain? Cannot an appealing voice which the Government dare not disregard, insist on the Italo-Abyssinian question being taken up by the League of Nations with real determination? . . . Let us tear away hypocrisy. Italian Fascism has said, ever since it took power, that it intended to obtain an extension of Italy's colonial dominions . . . The talk of slavery in Abyssinia should make all honest people blush, for no one cared about it until Italy desired to put the slavery of a nation equipped with modern arms upon the Abyssinian neck.

Other letters sought to answer other Fascist claims, such as that Italy needed an empire for its surplus population. To this she replied, in the *Daily Telegraph* of 31 July, that most Italians had no desire to settle in Africa, and that Italian emigrants had always 'flocked to the United States, not, despite all Government persuasions, to Eritrea'. Later she wrote in the *News Chronicle*, of 19 September, that 'Our duty is to stand by Abyssinia'.

Sylvia's credo was forcibly stated again in *The Times*, of 30 September, in which she forcefully declared:

> Those like myself, who from its first inception, uttered warning against the theories and practice of Fascism, which has since spread with so disastrous results to Germany, and who pointed out from the start that the policy of Fascism was first civil war and then foreign war, must now sadly say: 'We told you so'. In doing so another warning must be issued. If the Fascist Government is allowed by the rest of the world to succeed in its aggression against Abyssinia, this will be but the prelude to yet more terrible aggression.

Gravely disturbed by the League's failure to prevent the threatened invasion, she wrote again to the *Guardian*, on 3 October, after the opening of hostilities, to observe:

Every honest citizen must to-day feel ashamed that the declaration of the British representatives, and the majority of the nations assembled at the League Conference, that aggression would be prevented and the League Covenant adhered to, has thus far come to naught. Criminal indeed is the sloth which has permitted the situation to drift on until Italy has invaded Ethiopia and begun the war.

She urged that 'all necessary sanctions be immediately imposed against the Italian aggression', and added: 'Failure or hesitancy now would be the deepest possible dishonour'. Writing at this early stage as a friend of Italian freedom, rather than of Ethiopia as such, she concluded that 'immediate action is not only a duty towards Ethiopia, but the greatest good that can be done to the people of Italy' whose 'best interest' would 'undoubtedly be served by stopping this wanton war'.

The invasion of Ethiopia was duly condemned by the League of Nations, on 10 October, by fifty votes against one (Italy). The international organisation nevertheless imposed only mild economic sanctions against the aggressor – and excluded from the ban the all-important item of petrol, without which the invader's airforce could not have flown, and its tanks and armoured vehicles would have ground to a halt. Nor was any action taken to close the Suez Canal through which Italian soldiers continued to pass.

The invaders, though enjoying overwhelming superiority in arms, encountered fierce Ethiopian resistance, and therefore at first advanced only slowly. Mussolini thereupon ordered his commander-in-chief, General Badaglio, to use poison-gas, which was dropped in bombs and sprayed from the air, killing and maiming innumerable Ethiopian soldiers, civilians and livestock. This unexpected aerial onslaught broke the defenders' morale. The Italian air-force also bombed British and other Red Cross ambulance units, which were obliged to withdraw.

As the Fascist army advanced towards the Ethiopian capital, Sylvia joined in demands for more effective League action. Appealing for British support for Ethiopia, the victim of fascist aggression, she wrote in the *Cornish Guardian*, of 9 April 1936:

The honour of the League of Nations and of this country is at stake . . . Abyssinia, a loyal member of the League of Nations, has trusted the League to uphold the Covenant and defend her independence . . . . Thus far the League has failed. Failure . . . means that this bulwark, towards which a peace-loving people looks for safety, will crash down, leaving humanity defenceless against the menace of an international conflict, yet more hideous and devastating than that which afflicted us in 1914–18.

Sylvia's press campaign helped to rally not a few women to the cause of collective security. Writing as a former suffragette in the *Daily Herald*, of 17 April, she recalled:

Daily I receive letters from women thanking me for my repeated protests against the inaction of the League . . . and of the British Government in face of Italy's breach of the Covenant and diabolical attack on a Member State of the League . . . All these women appeal to me to know what they can do and urge me to give a lead which will enable them to come together to struggle for international justice as women struggled for national justice in their fight for the vote.

Urging them to struggle in this cause, she added: 'There never was a time when it was more urgent than this for women to make use of the great influence they gained when they became enfranchised citizens'.

THE ESTABLISHMENT OF THE NEWSPAPER

In April 1936, Sylvia became convinced that the Fascist armies would soon enter the Ethiopian capital. Fearing that Ethiopia, though then a matter of world attention, might soon be forgotten as other events captured the headlines, she decided, as earlier in her life, to establish a weekly newspaper. Modelled, perhaps unconsciously, on her earlier publication the *Woman's* (later *Workers'*) *Dreadnought*, she determined that through it she would keep the question of Ethiopia alive within the context of anti-fascism and support for the principle of international justice enshrined in the League Covenant.

Sylvia's choice of title was influenced partly by Charlie Chaplin's film *Modern Times*, which then enjoyed great popularity, and partly by an awareness that the people whose cause she espoused spoke of their country not as Abyssinia, but as Ethiopia. The newspaper was thus christened *New Times and Ethiopia News*.[3] Though its editor could not have guessed so at the time, it was to occupy her for a third of her working life – and was to take her along many unimagined paths.

The first issue was printed in Walthamstow, an hour's journey from its editor's house at Woodford, Essex. This issue went to press on 5 May 1936, the day the Fascist armies entered Addis Ababa, but was dated 9 May, the day that Mussolini (falsely) proclaimed the victorious end of the war, and the establishment of a Fascist Empire in Africa.

The paper's anti-fascist position was laid down in the first issue which bore two banner headlines: 'REMEMBER: Everywhere, Always, Fascism means War'; and 'WE STAND FOR INTERNATIONAL LAW AND JUSTICE'. This stance was annunciated in an editorial which declared:

'New Times and Ethiopia News' appears at a moment when the fortunes of Ethiopia seem at their lowest ebb; the greater then the need for an advocate and a friend.

We know that the difficulties facing her are grave, but we will not falter, either in faith or determination that they shall be overcome.

The cause of Ethiopia cannot be separated from the cause of International justice . . .

As friends of Ethiopia we most solemnly protest against the attack on her millennial independence; we condemn the atrocious barbarities employed against her, the bombing of her undefended villages, the use of poison gas, by which thousands of innocent women and children have suffered agonising death.

Emphasising that Italian victories were to be expected because Ethiopia was 'virtually unarmed', the article declared that the fascist government had 'already launched an intensified propaganda to secure the lifting of Sanctions, and to justify the conquest of Abyssinia'. As for *N.T. & E.N.*, the editorial continued:

We shall set ourselves resolutely to combat fascist propaganda, to secure the continuance and strengthening of sanctions . . . We shall strive to induce measures by the League to resist the Fascist usurpation, and to aid and defend Ethiopia, and will persistently urge that Britain take the responsibility of initiating an active League policy . . .

We shall urge that Britain shall herself individually give aid to Ethiopia . . .

As for Italy, it announced:

> We shall urge, in season and out, that the facts of the Italo-Ethiopian war and the reason for League intervention . . . be broadcast in all languages to inform all peoples thereon, and especially those of Italy where free information is denied.
> 'New Times' is opposed to the conception of dictatorship. It understands that fascism destroys all personal liberty and is in fundamental opposition to all forms of intellectual and moral progress.
> We draw a profound distinction between the Italian Fascist Government and the Italian people, who are enslaved today, but whose freedom is slowly but surely being prepared by the martyrdom of thousands of heroic men and women, guardians of an inextinguishable faith: murdered, tortured, imprisoned, exiled in poverty and sorrow, they keep high and untarnished the ideal of justice.

In accordance with this policy *N.T. & E.N.* published a series of moving articles by the Ethiopian Minister in London, Azaj Warqneh C. Martin, with such titles as 'We Trusted the League', and 'Wait and See while Murder is Done'. Other contributors included writers with widely differing backgrounds, ideologies and interests. Among them was a British academic, professor F. L. Lucas, and three students of international affairs, Colonel Maurice Spencer, W. Arnold Foster and Leslie Carruthers, as well as a number of British supporters of Ethiopia: Helen Napier of the Friends of Abyssinia (Ethiopia) League of Service, Cecil Turner, who had served during the invasion in the British Red Cross Unit, Mary Downes, a teacher from Wales, and Francis Beaufort-Palmer, a friend of all oppressed peoples.

Several Italian anti-fascist refugees in London were also involved with the paper, most notably Sylvia's companion, Silvio Corio, who, though often preferring to remain anonymous, acted as *de facto* co-editor, spending one day a week directing the lay-out at the printing press, as well as writing articles, largely on Italy, under the *nom de plume* 'Crastinus'. Another Italian anti-fascist refugee, Professor Angelo Crespi, was also a keen contributor. Support was likewise received from two Italian anti-fascists in Paris, Carlo Rosselli, founder of the journal *Guistizia e Libertà*, and Dr. G. E. Modigliani, as well from Professor Gaetano Salvemini in the United States. Active contributors also included a number of anti-Nazi refugees from Central Europe, notably an Austrian, Dr Ruth Schulze-Gaevernitz, and a Hungarian, Bela Menczer. Articles were also published from two Swedes with Ethiopian experience, Count Carol von Rosen and General Eric Virgin, and an American aviator, Count Hillaire du Berrier.

Sylvia was, however, the most prolific, as well as the most frequent, contributor. She produced a weekly editorial of two or three thousand words, and a succession of articles, several serialised through many issues. The first, 'Fascism As It Is', contained over 120,000 words, and ran through almost fifty instalments. (As long as I can remember she would stay up at least one night a week, and would still be writing at her desk when I came down for breakfast. Contrary to the impression given in a recent film she did not type, but sent her hand-written script directly to the printer.)

The paper sought, in articles, photographs and cartoons, to expose the iniquity of the fascist invasion, and occupation, of Ethiopia. The issue of 16 May, for example, listed seventeen occasions on which the Italian air force had used poison gas, while later issues reproduced photographs of the fascist bombing of the British Red Cross, as well as of a fascist portable gallows on which six Ethiopian patriots had been hanged.

Extensive publicity was also given to the statements by the Ethiopian government in exile, which received but scant attention in the rest of the press. In June the paper published questions submitted to Emperor Haile Sellassie, who had by then arrived in London, and his replies, *N.T. & E.N.*, alone of its contemporaries, later also published the full text of his famous address to the League of Nations in which he outlined the atrocities committed against Ethiopia, and concluded: 'Representatives of the world, I have come to Geneva to discharge in your midst the most painful of the duties of the head of State. What reply shall I have to take back to my people?'

N.T. & E.N. rapidly achieved a circulation of 10,000, which, together with donations from subscribers, enabled complimentary copies to be despatched to members of both Houses of Parliament and other persons of influence. During the Peckham and Balham by-election of July, 1936, the paper opened a shop for the sale of pro-Ethiopian and anti-fascist publications, and throughout this time helped the Ethiopian minister in London to raise money for a fund of mercy for Ethiopia.

The paper evoked immense interest in Africa and among peoples of African descent. It developed an extensive circulation in West Africa and the West Indies, and was widely quoted in the emerging African nationalist press – which reproduced many articles from it, often without attribution of the source. Typical of the African response was a letter from a West African student in Britain, who wrote: 'the young people of African descent feel that Italy has invaded our fatherland', and added: 'if it were not for your paper the young Africans would not know what is happening in Africa today, as the whole of the press in Europe has no room to publish the Ethiopian case'.[4] No less characteristic was a message from a teacher at Accra City School in the Gold Coast (later Ghana) who observed that copies of the paper were 'highly valued', for they contained the 'real truth' of the Ethiopian war, and were the 'truest papers we have ever read'. A series of articles entitled 'Africans to Africans' later also attracted considerable attention in Africa.

THE SPANISH CIVIL WAR – AND CONTINUED ETHIOPIAN RESISTANCE

Sylvia, like anti-fascists the world over, was deeply moved by the outbreak in the summer of 1936 of the Spanish Civil War. *N.T. & E.N.* in August carried the heading, 'Two Victims of Fascism – Spain and Abyssinia', together with sarcastic cartoons exposing the pretence that the support of Franco by fascist Italy and Nazi Germany was limited to the despatch of volunteers, while a later issue, under the heading 'FASCISM AT WORK', reproduced photographs of Spanish children killed by German and Italian bombing.

Meanwhile in the autumn the paper reported continued Ethiopian resistance. A front-page story, based on news received by the Ethiopian legation in London, was published under the headlines: 'Ethiopian Armies Still in the Field. Vast Territories Still Unoccupied . . .'. Another article bore the heading: 'Terrible Warfare Now Raging in Abyssinia'.

Besides publicising Ethiopian patriot resistance, the paper issued a number of Amharic editions for clandestine despatch to Italian-occupied Ethiopia; and the present writer, many years later when Director of the Institute of Ethiopian Studies, was presented with one by an Ethiopian patriot who had received it in the far-off province of Gojjam a quarter of a century earlier. Sylvia also assisted

Carlo Rosselli in smuggling anti-fascist pamphlets printed in Italian for perusal by Italians in Mussolini's empire. These writings were assumed to emanate from Italy, with the result that one consignment was seized during sanctions by over-zealous British customs officials.

By 1937 the paper had gained the attention of readers in many parts of the world – including Italy, where Mussolini, perhaps confusing Sylvia with her deceased mother Emmeline, sneeringly attacked her in the *Popolo d'Italia* of 4 February. He claimed that the suffragette of forty years earlier had sought the embraces of the British police, and, by now an octogenarian, had 'sworn "Ethiopia or Death" in the name of all Negroes and Negresses' (Sylvia was then fifth-five).

THE GRAZIANI MASSACRE AND THE MURDER OF CARLO ROSSELLI

The year 1937 was a sad one for Ethiopia. An attempt on the life of the fascist Viceroy, Graziani, by two young Eritreans, was followed by the three-day Addis Ababa massacre of 19 to 21 February, in which thousands of defenceless Ethiopians were wantonly killed. News of this event, which was followed by numerous summary executions, only slowly filtered through fascist censorship, but early in March the paper published its first detailed report. It came from its Jibuti correspondent, an Indian journalist called Wazir Ali Baig (who had earlier been a news-gatherer for Evelyn Waugh). It appeared under the heading:

THOUSANDS MURDERED IN ADDIS ABABA
Corpses Burnt, Soaked in Petrol . . . Fascism Stamped with Eternal Infamy

The account, based on news carried verbally across Italian-occupied territory, inevitably contained some errors, mainly resulting from the absence of official reporting. Several prominent Ethiopians who had not been seen since the massacre were incorrectly assumed to have been among the dead. The main features of the article were, however, later verified. Sylvia's own reaction was stated in a leading article which began:

The awful holocaust of Addis Ababa has stirred the world. Even the diplomats in their chanceries betrayed their horror. They protested to the Italian aggressors, ignoring all fear of diplomatic incidents, and sent through to Europe the news of the slaughter, which the Fascist Press censorship would have hidden from the world, as it has hidden so much else of cruelty and wrong.

The horror of this foul massacre of six thousand souls – the United States correspondent put it at fourteen thousand . . . confounds description . . .

Yet the tragedy of Ethiopia is deeper and more extensive than even the horror in Addis Ababa on the cruel 19th of February, which will pass darkly into history among the crimes of all time. It is the tragedy of a people who longed for peace, who joined the League of Nations created by the Western Powers, believing it the League to end war.

N.T. & E.N. subsequently despatched a petition to Mr Avenol, Secretary-General of the League of Nations, appealing for his help in obtaining the release from detention in Italy of Ras Imru, one of the very few pre-war Ethiopian leaders who had not been shot by the fascists. This appeal was signed by a galaxy of forty prominent British men and women, but was ignored by the pro-fascist functionaries in Geneva.

Three months later, on 10 June, Carlo Rosselli, the editor of *Giustizia e Libertà*, was assassinated in Paris. *N.T. & E.N.* published the news under the banner heading:

Carlo Rosselli and his Brother Nello Assassinated . . . by Order of Fascist Rome . . . on the Anniversary of the Murder of Deputy Giacomo Matteotti

An article recalled Rosselli's famous message, 'Today in Spain, tomorrow in Italy', uttered when going to fight in the Spanish Civil War, and added:

The Rossellis live; they enter history in the immaculate garment of martyrs: They live, and will live, as long as memory lasts, in the heart of all lovers of Liberty.

N.T. & E.N. never forget Carlo Rosselli. It frequently reproduced his portrait, and later adopted his paper's symbolic representation of a fiery sword of justice as part of its own logo.

Later that year the paper held a number of publicity events, including the first of a series of garden fetes in aid of Dr Martin's Fund of Mercy, and a political meeting in support of Ethiopia at Central Hall, Westminster. This latter event, like many which followed, was attended by representatives of the League of Nations Union, the Friends' Peace Council, the Federation of Peace Councils, Cooperative Women's Guilds, Trades Councils, and Church of England and Free Church organisations, as well as by the India League, the League of Coloured Peoples, the African Service Bureau, the Negro Welfare Association, and the Kenya Association. Among those moving resolutions were the Dean of Winchester, the Quaker humanitarian Isabel Fry, Krishna Menon (who brought a message from the President of the Indian National Congress, Jawarhlal Nehru), Wallace Johnson of Sierra Leone and Jomo Kenyatta of Kenya, the Rev. Dr Hugenholtz, a clergyman from Holland, and the elderly suffragette Mrs Gillett-Gatty of Action Feministe Internationale.

The paper subsequently also held a bazaar and fete at Victoria Palace Rooms. Opened by Haile Sellassie, it was addressed by the Dean of Winchester, Eleanor Rathbone and Francis Noel-Baker MP. Films on the Ethiopian war were also shown at the Regal Cinema, Marble Arch, and elsewhere. On one occasion the paper also attempted to project a Fascist documentary film 'The Birth of an Empire', but the Italian Embassy, realising the use to which it was to be put, had it withdrawn.

THE LEAGUE OF NATIONS, CONTINUED ETHIOPIAN RESISTANCE, AND THE PROPOSED RECOGNITION OF THE FASCIST 'CONQUEST'

When the League Assembly convened again in September 1937 Sylvia travelled to Geneva to report events – and lobby delegates. *N.T. & E.N.* gave the session extensive coverage, and published an editorial interview with the Chinese representative Wellington Koo, whose country was then suffering from Japanese invasion. To publicise the country's case the paper issued several supplements entitled *China News*.

News meanwhile continued to be received from Jibuti, and elsewhere, of continued Ethiopian resistance. Almost a year and a half after Mussolini's declaration of the end of the war, the paper thus ran such headlines as 'Ethiopians Fighting Everywhere' and 'Unconquered Ethiopia Fighting Tooth and Nail for Independence'. Though most articles concentrated on political issues, others focused on Ethiopian history and culture. One such was an editorial supplement, 'What Modern Ethiopia Achieved for Herself' which chronicled the country's progress prior to Mussolini's so-called 'Civilising Mission'.

The cause of Ethiopia fell on hard times in 1938 when the countries which had condemned the Fascist invasion, but had failed to stop it, began to recognise Mussolini's 'conquest'. Confronted with this development, *N.T. & E.N.* joined with several other anti-fascist organisations in holding a Trafalgar Square demonstration on the theme 'Save Abyssinia and the League'. Speakers included Sylvia and Mary Downes as well as the radical lawyer D.N. Pritt MP, the publisher Victor Gollancz, and representatives of several peace councils and trade unions.

Throughout this diplomatically critical period the paper reported continued Ethiopian patriot resistance. One issue announced that the provinces of Wollo, Tigre and Gojjam were almost entirely 'free of the Italians', while another revealed that the invaders were again using poison gas.[5] Prominence was also given to a leaked report by the Duke of Aosta, the fascist Viceroy, which stated that Italian influence extended only as far as machine-gun bullets could reach, and that 'in the event of a European war, the invasion could not last a month.'[6]

Notwithstanding Ethiopian resistance, the British government, determined on appeasing Italy, began talks in Rome to conclude an Anglo-Italian agreement involving recognition of Mussolini's 'conquest'. To oppose this policy the paper held a Central Hall meeting, with the slogan 'No Recognition of Italy's Invasion of Ethiopia'. Speakers included Sylvia as well as the Emperor's daughter, Princess Tsehai, Arnold Foster, and Mrs Corbett Ashby. Support was also expressed by other worthies, including the singer Paul Robeson, and a representative of the India League. Messages of support were read out from Lord Cecil and the Bishop of Durham. On the following day the paper published an editorial, which, discussing the proposed treaty, commented:

> The outstanding feature of Mr Chamberlain's shameful pact with Mussolini was his cynical and callous thrusting aside of the principle of justice and the rights of the Ethiopian people who are now fighting bravely with extraordinary success . . .

His eulogy of 'the New Italy', as he termed it, is surely the crowning insult to Ethiopia and to the British Parliament and people.
The mask is off! Mr Chamberlain has revealed himself as a supporter of Fascist theory and practice.

Sylvia also despatched numerous letters to various newspapers, M.P.s, and statesmen in Britain and elsewhere.

THE MUNICH CRISIS, AND BRITISH RECOGNITION OF THE 'CONQUEST'

The crisis over Czechoslovakia in the autumn of 1938 was another turning-point in the anti-fascist struggle. The position of *N.T. & E.N.* was stated in its issue of 1 October which carried the banner headlines:

STAND BY CZECHOSLOVAKIA
Peace Can Only Rest on Justice and Respect to Treaties
Further Concessions to Dictators will Destroy Us All.

Reiterating the paper's stand, the front page declared: 'In the Event of War it is the Bounden Duty of All Freedom-loving Persons to work with determination for the Defeat of the Fascist States'.
The subsequent Munich agreement between Hitler and Chamberlain was viewed by the paper as a betrayal. On the front page Professor F.L. Lucas wrote on what he termed 'The BASEST DAY in BRITISH HISTORY', while the editorial was headed: 'DICTATORS AGAIN TRIUMPH'.
The question of British recognition of the Italian 'conquest' came finally to the fore towards the end of 1938. The paper organised a petition to the Prime Minister, and a protest meeting in Trafalgar Square. The speakers included Sylvia, as well as the Rev. Reginald Sorensen M.P., the Rev E.O. Iredell, Lady Layton, and Jomo Kenyatta.
The British government duly recognised the 'conquest', whereupon an *N.T. & E.N.* editorial commented that Ethiopia's struggle would not be affected, and continued:

We appeal to our readers to continue their support of that heroic fight . . .

By their courage and endurance these people of the 'Dark Continent', as it is sometimes termed, are proving to the world that even the might of modern arms against a disarmed people cannot persuade valiant human souls to bow to slavery.

As for the Chamberlain-Mussolini agreement, the article declared:

The violation of Treaties and Covenants has gone so far in these recent years of shame and treachery that even Mr Chamberlain can have but little faith in the permanence of any pact he may frame . . . The pact will not stand. We pledge ourselves to work for its destruction, and many a thousand with us.

The paper shortly afterwards held another fete and bazaar, at Westminster Palace Rooms. It was addressed by Dr Martin, the Deans of Winchester and Canterbury, and two Members of Parliament, Eleanor Rathbone and Francis Noel-Baker. Sylvia, though having long abandoned her artistic career, designed a programme cover based on Ethiopian motifs. She also began a new serial entitled 'How Hitler Rose to Power' which ran to 80,000 words. The fete, a continued manifestation of Ethiopia's presence in the world, evoked an outburst of anger in Rome where the fascist journal *Azione Coloniale* complained that *N.T. & E.N.* was full of 'nonsense' and 'poisonous recriminations'.

In Ethiopia, meanwhile, the resistance of the patriots continued, and in January 1939, the paper published petitions which Haile Sellassie had received from Ethiopian freedom fighters. One explained that in three provinces the Italians were in possession of only six towns, while others reported the continued fascist use of poison-gas. Reports were also published on the seemingly incredible (but later authenticated) Italian attempt to negotiate with the patriot leader Ras Abbebe Aregay, while a subsequent article from the Jibuti correspondence reported that the Italians were largely confined to fortified garrisons.[7]

FRANCO'S VICTORY, ANGER IN ROME, AND NEW TIMES BOOKSHOP

Though the Ethiopian patriots continued their struggle, in Spain armed resistance to Franco collapsed at the beginning of 1939. Anti-fascist volunteers were obliged to flee. Those from free countries returned home, but those from Fascist Italy, Nazi Germany, and Falangist Spain were placed in French detention camps and suffered great hardship. This was a matter of much concern to *N.T. & E.N.* whose editor joined a women's deputation to press the Foreign Office to allow refugees entry into Britain. The paper gave much publicity to the plight of the detainees, which was investigated by Nancy Cunard in several reports, one headed:

TERRIBLE CONDITIONS AT PERPIGNAN
Refugees Die of Hunger and Cold . . .

In August, the twenty-fifth anniversary of the outbreak of World War I, the paper published a leader, which, recalling that the world was once more 'under the shadow of the guns', declared: 'The enemy is Fascism. There can be no respite from it till it is overthrown'.

Other articles continued to draw attention to Ethiopian resistance – and to the repressive character of Fascist colonialism. This led to a vitriolic attack from Rome radio.

N.T. & E.N. embarked on a new initiative in April 1939 when it opened New Times Bookshop, in London's Farringdon Street. It stocked many pro-Ethiopian and anti-fascist publications, and served as the site of the paper's annual bazaar. The bookshop also held a series of weekly meetings, known as 'Meet the Author Thursdays' at which writers spoke about, and autographed their works. Those doing so included the veteran British journalist Henry Nevinson and the anti-imperialist theoretician H.N. Brailsford; two writers on Ethiopia, Enid Starkie and George L. Steer; John Langdon-Davis, sometime editor of the magazine *Picture Post*; Prince Kessie of Ashanti; and Peter and Irma Petroff (whom Sylvia had met in Soviet Russia many years earlier). Women writers were represented by Vera Brittain, the interviewer Betty Ross, the New Zealand novelist Robin Hyde, and Sylvia herself – who discussed her translation of the Romanian poet Mihai Eminescu. Such activities, however, came to an end when the bookshop was destroyed by German bombing.

THE OUTBREAK OF THE EUROPEAN WAR

Hitler's demands on Poland in the summer of 1939, and the probability of a European conflagration, led meanwhile to the recall of the British parliament, on which occasion the paper declared: 'The Prime Minister preferred his personally conducted policy of appeasing the dictators to collective international action through the League . . . His personal policy has led us to the pass at which we stand'. The article then turned to the recent Hitler-Stalin pact, on which, it pointed out, neither the Russian nor the German people had been consulted. Recognising that it had led to 'a great shattering of hopes', it continued:

> One cannot but commiserate the many who have staked well nigh their whole store of hope upon the entry of Soviet Russia into a Peace Front . . . The Communist Parties of Britain and France will doubtless find some method of justifying this Pact to their own satisfaction, but their non-communist allies, who had great faith, are dismayed.
>
> It is a stunning blow. Yet for ourselves we are not stunned by it, nor wholly surprised. We knew that there was always a risk that the Soviet Union would even now hold aloof from the struggle – the desperate struggle – between all that is best in European democracy and the brutal forces of fascism.

After outlining other examples of Stalin's complicity with fascism, the article declared: 'That Russia has not been permitted by her Dictator to take up the mission, which might have been hers, of leading the defence of freedom against the onslaughts of fascism, will be regretted by many. It must not occasion despair'.

The paper's policy was stated more explicitly in the issue of 2 September, which stated that 'IN THE EVENT OF WAR' it was 'THE DUTY OF ALL ANTI-FASCISTS':

> To promote resolutely by every possible means the downfall of the fascist dictatorships;
>
> To ensure that the liberties of Britain and of all democratic nations shall not be encroached upon;
>
> To strive, in season and out of season, flinching at no obstacle, that the Member States of the League, Ethiopia, Spain, Czechoslovakia, China and Albania, shall be freed from invaders and restored to their former liberty and independence;
>
> To prepare public opinion so that no Peace shall be concluded with any State denying free and untramelled expression of opinion;

To restore the authority of the League of Nations and its Covenants against aggression.

In accordance with these principles the paper carried such slogans as 'UNITY AND COURAGE', 'FASCISM TO BE FOUGHT TO A FINISH' and 'RESTORE TO INDEPENDENCE ALL NATIONS SEIZED BY THE AGGRESSORS'. The first issue after Britain's declaration of war declared: 'Ourselves, each and all, let us resolve to be worthy of the cause of freedom and justice. Let us sacredly resolve that this cause, and not some selfish end, shall triumph'. This injunction, which struck a cry already voiced in her student days, was perhaps more significant than Sylvia then realised, for within a year she would be castigating the British government for transgressing it!

The outbreak of war also led the paper to launch a Women's War Emergency Council, which was founded by Sylvia, Councillor Mrs J. Davey and Mrs E. F. Harburn on 3 October. Its objectives recalled those of Sylvia's movement in the East End in World War I, and included better soldiers' pensions and separation allowances, and the control of food prices. These policies were soon adopted by the coalition government, so the council operated at a low key, with the distribution of children's clothing.

Mussolini meanwhile had avoided entry into the European war, and described himself as 'pre-belligerent'. The British government, hoping that he could be persuaded from entering the conflict, found *N.T. & E.N.*'s anti-fascist position embarrassing, and, to placate the Duce, sought to prevent the paper from reaching Italy, by forbidding its postal despatch to neutral countries. Copies nevertheless reached Rome, and led to an outburst from the Italian *Rassegna Sociale dell' Africa Italiana*, which declared the paper a violation of the 1938 Anglo-Italian treaty which was supposed to restrict hostile propaganda between the two countries.

N.T. & E.N.'s critique of Italian fascism and colonialism, however, continued unabated, and in April 1940, it published an article by the Australian ex-Senator Arnold Weinholt, who had secretly visited Ethiopia and contacted the Ethiopian patriots. His article, 'Unconquerable Ethiopia', also issued as a pamphlet, reproduced photographs of Ethiopian leaders in the field. The first such pictures ever published, they provided proof that Ethiopia was still unconquered.

During this period *N.T. & E.N.* also published much criticism of Stalin's Russia. It attacked Russia's invasion of Finland, and serialised a history of the Spanish civil war by a defector from the Soviet army, General Krivitsky, who showed that Russian support for the Spanish Republic had been far from altruistic. This was confirmed in subsequent articles by Louis Araquistain, a former Spanish Republican ambassador. An article by Krivitsky on 'The Execution of the Old Bolsheviks', several of whom Sylvia had met many years earlier (and greatly admired), was also published.

MUSSOLINI'S ENTRY INTO THE EUROPEAN WAR

Mussolini's entry into the European War, on 10 June 1940, was a major event for *N.T. & E.N.* which had long been campaigning against the dictator who it regarded as the founder of fascism, as well as the first to flout the League. There was thus satisfaction in Woodford that fascist Italy, the weaker of the Axis powers, had at last entered the armed conflict in which, Sylvia felt sure, he would inevitably be overthrown. The next issue carried the banner heading:

ABYSSINIA OUR ALLY
Help to Speed the Victory!
Mussolini's Declaration of War Assures:
ABYSSINIA'S FREEDOM:
THE FALL OF FASCISM;
AXIS POWERS WILL PERISH TOGETHER

A further paragraph drew attention to the fact that Mussolini had declared war on the anniversaries of the murder of both Matteotti and Carlo Rosselli.

The importance for the Ethiopian cause of Mussolini's action was emphasised in an editorial which affirmed:

Ethiopia is our ally in the struggle against the Axis Powers.
    She must be officially recognised as such by the Governments of Britain and France, and their Allies.
    The infamous Anglo-Italian Agreement, recognising Italy's occupation of Ethiopia . . . and all such recognition by other Allies must be declared null and void . . .
    The Government of the Emperor Haile Sellassie I, here in Lon-

don, must be recognised by the Allied Governments without delay or circumlocution, and welcomed to the Allied Council.

The full support of the Allied Governments in arms and munitions, and particularly in planes, as well as in the field, must be furnished to Ethiopia . . .

She must be given the full status of an ally, entitled to the full and honourable treatment she has so often missed in her past dealings with Europe.

The editorial also urged the need for the liberation of Albania, and the Dodecanese islands which had 'suffered grievously under Fascist rule', and whose inhabitants' desire for reunion with Greece demanded recognition.

Another section of the article spelt out the paper's attitude to Italy, declaring: 'It cannot too often be emphasised that the Government of Italy is an autocracy maintained by military force, and that it does not represent the Italian people over whose "corpse" of democratic liberties Mussolini boasts he "marched"'. Recalling that some members of the British House of Lords had commiserated with the King of Italy, who, they had claimed, was not responsible for Mussolini's war, the editorial continued:

Victor Emmanuel of Italy cuts certainly a pitiable figure lacking the moral courage to withstand the crimes of the dictator. Yet he called Mussolini to office and made no open protest against the dictator's many crimes. He accepted from Mussolini the title, Emperor of Ethiopia, to which he had no right. Even while British Lords were endeavouring to whitewash him Victor Emmanuel was making a speech commending the war.

The editorial also expressed regret for the outbreak of violence in Britain against Italian shopkeepers, who, it insisted, were 'in no way responsible for the doings of Mussolini and his gangsters'. Paying homage by contrast to the Italian 'heroes and heroines' of the long reign of Fascism, and recalling the many Italians who had been placed in Mussolini's penal islands, the article declared: 'Ardent anti-fascist exiles are ready to fight to liberate Italy from the shameful yoke of Fascism, as they fought, ill-equipped, against its extension in Spain'.

This latter theme was echoed by Silvio Corio, who, in an article also published in Italian, declared:

At Last! The long agonising vigil is over.
The Fascist regime is to-day an open and declared enemy . . .
The crowning deed of infamy committed by Fascism in declaring war against Britain and France restores to us our complete freedom of action.
We shall use it!

Emphasing the need to reject 'false patriotism' and to be responsible to justice, he went on:

There is not a single thread of solidarity between us Anti-Fascists and those who have fettered into abject slavery the Italian people. Mussolini is the traitor, not we!
To his call to arms we answer: 'Yes, we shall fight, proud to do so, at last – against you!
We shall avenge Matteotti and Rosselli and other victims of your tyranny.
You have stolen the freedom of our native land; we shall reconquer it, arms in hand.
Ere long, by the side of the Allied forces, we shall enter victorious in Rome, free once more, and exact the punishment fitting for your crimes.
We shall free the Italian name from the shame you have cast upon it.
Hitler and Mussolini are now one: united in crime and dishonour they shall fall together.

The paper now carried the page-heading 'FOR VICTORY' – and after the arrival of French exiles in Britain published some articles in French. Warm support was voiced for General De Gaulle.

POLICIES RESULTING FROM ITALY'S ENTRY INTO THE EUROPEAN WAR

Fascist Italy's declaration of war raised many new questions, which the paper regarded as major matters of principle, and to which it was to devote many columns in the months – and years – to come. The first was the need to ensure recognition of the full independence of Ethiopia and other countries occupied by fascist Italy. This was a matter of concern in that the British government, which had long shown itself sympathetic to Mussolini, officially recognised the fascist 'conquest' of both Ethiopia and Albania, and in a war directed primarily against Nazi Germany, was unwilling to withdraw such recognition.

This reluctance was the more disturbing, Sylvia felt, in that the British government had for half a century been party to treaties recognising Italian dominance in East Africa. An agreement of 1906, to which Britain was a signatory, had thus partitioned Ethiopia into Italian and other European 'spheres of influence' while the Anglo-Italian treaty of 1938 expressly recognised Mussolini's 'conquest'. Sylvia also recalled that Britain, a colonial power, had consistently refused to treat Ethiopia, an independent African country, as on a par with sovereign states in Europe. Statesmen of the 'civilised countries', she noted, were moreover accustomed to use African territories as bargaining countries in the settlement of inter-European disputes, as had happened in the case of Italy before, during and after World War I. There was therefore nothing to preclude the British government, whose good faith in matters Ethiopian had so often proved wanting, which still recognised Victor Emmanuel as Emperor of Ethiopia, and which included many friends of the Italian monarchy, from concluding a compromise peace in which Italy would be allowed to retain its colonial empire – which officially still included Ethiopia.

N.T. & E.N. therefore pressed the British Government to make specific commitments: (1) to withdraw recognition of the Italian 'conquest' of Ethiopia, and to recognise the country's right to full independence; (2) to accept Ethiopia as an ally, and to accord the Emperor's government in exile the same status as given to European refugee governments from countries occupied by Nazi Germany; (3) to commit itself to the total dismantling of the Italian colonial empire; and (4) to recognise the complete independence of Albania.

Besides writing numerous articles on the subject in the paper, Sylvia bombarded the British government and its ministers with letters, corresponded in the national press, and drafted a series of Parliamentary questions for several MPs to ask in the House of Commons.

The first, asked by Geoffrey Le Mander on 19 June 1940, was of considerable importance. It induced the Foreign Office to agree that, because of Italy's 'unprovoked entry' into the European war, Britain was 'entitled to reserve full liberty of action' in respect of earlier undertakings regarding Italy's position in the Mediterranean, North and East Africa, and the Middle East. A second question, asked by Colonel Wedgwood on 11 July, committed Britain to recognise the Emperor's government as 'the lawful Government of Ethiopia', with the 'status as an ally'.

Notwithstanding this Parliamentary reply, the British government was remarkably reluctant to implement this assurance. Evidence of this crystalised in the BBC's unwillingness to include the Ethiopian national anthem in its Sunday evening recital of the 'National Anthems of the Allies'. This was a question on which Sylvia agitated for many months, and was the subject on much correspondence with the BBC, the Foreign Office, and several MPs.

The British government and the BBC procrastinated for almost a year, and, despite the Parliamentary statement of 11 July, 1940, did not play the Ethiopian anthem until the evening of 11 May, 1941 – a full ten months later.[8] This delay was not fortuitous, but characteristic of the British government's unwillingness to treat Ethiopia, then virtually the only independent African country, on equal terms, or to welcome it wholeheartedly into the international community.

'FASCISTS AT LARGE, ANTI-FASCISTS INTERNED'; THREATS TO SYLVIA'S LIFE

Another matter resulting from Italy's entry into the European war arose from the malfunctioning of the British Home Office – and doubtless some Conservative sympathies with fascism. It was soon apparent that the authorities dealing with enemy aliens in Britain failed to differentiate adequately between Italian fascists and anti-fascists. Those interned included many lifelong anti-fascists, among them Ani Anzani, secretary of the Italian section of League of the Rights of Man, and a contributor to *N.T. & E.N.*, and several former members of the International Brigade who had fought in Spain, as well as Jewish refugees from Mussolini's racial laws. Not a few prominent fascists, including the founder of the London *Fascio*, were on the other hand left at large. This miscarriage of justice, which seemed to Sylvia symptomatic of the British government's bumbling and far from resolute attitude to fascism – had tragic consequences: Anzani and other anti-fascists were drowned when the *Arandora Star*, the boat on which they were being shipped to detention on the Isle of Man, was sunk by a German submarine.

To obtain justice for the survivors the paper for many weeks published biographical data of Italian residents, in a series of articles entitled 'Fascists at Large, Anti-Fascists Interned'. Not untypical was the case of an anti-fascist artist Aldo Cosomati. Though married to an English woman, he had been interned in the Isle of Man, where one of his anti-fascist cartoons was seen by the fascist inmates who beat him up and left him bleeding. After months of such exposure by the paper, reinforced by letters to ministers, most injustices were redressed – though the government, despite the tragedy of the *Arandora Star*, never admitted that any injustice had been committed.

As a result of her espousal of anti-fascist causes Sylvia now received two threatening letters. The first, despatched by a Nazi supporter in Rochester, declared that Hitler would be in Britain 'very soon', and that, if she did not stop publishing her paper, it would 'find itself without an Editor'. The second, from 'Italian London Fascists' – incensed by the 'Fascists at Large' articles,[9] likewise threatened that 'the invasion of England will take place in a few days', after which 'You will pay with your life'. That these letters were not entirely fanciful became apparent at the close of the war with the official disclosure from German records that Sylvia's name was among those the Gestapo was to arrest after an anticipated German occupation of Britain.

THE FASCIST COLLAPSE IN EAST AFRICA, AND THE FATE OF THE ITALIAN COLONIES

The Allied campaign for the liberation of Italian East Africa, which began in January 1941, was the subject of several eye-witness accounts published in the paper, one of the first under the heading:

> ITALIANS FIGHTING TO BE ENSLAVED!
> When Will They Revolt?
> ETHIOPIANS FIGHTING TO BE FREE!
> The Drums of Victory Are Heard

The Allied advance was so successful – and Italian resistance so half-hearted[10] – that Addis Ababa fell after less than three months. Sylvia now made efforts to press Italian anti-fascists to commit themselves to the principle that a future post-fascist Italy must renounce any claim to Ethiopia. One of the few who did so was Professor Salvemini.

The collapse of the fascist empire meanwhile inevitably raised the question of the future of the Italian colonies in Africa, and, as far as Ethiopia was concerned, most specifically that of Eritrea. This colony, founded only half a century earlier, had been the springboard for two successive Italian invasions of Ethiopia, in 1895-6 and 1935-6. Most of the territory, including the highlands, where the capital, Asmara, was situated, had formed an integral part of Ethiopia since time immemorial, and was historically and culturally more Ethiopian than many parts of Ethiopia itself. Despite the advent of Italy the Ethiopian government had never regarded Eritreans as different from other Ethiopians; many inhabitants of the colony had gone to work in Addis Ababa, and Eritrean youngsters, denied education by the fascists, had entered Ethiopian schools, the most promising being sent abroad for study, like other Ethiopians, and, on returning, had risen to important positions in Ethiopian government service.

Several of Sylvia's closest friends among the Ethiopians in London were from Eritrea. They included Lorenzo Taezaz, who had drafted Haile Sellassie's speech to the League and had travelled secretly to Italian-occupied Ethiopia to meet the patriots; Ephrem Tewelde Medhen, who had served in the Ethiopian Foreign Service; and, at a less exalted level, Mr Tedros, who had settled in London as a waiter, and who, with his wife and children, was amongst *N.T. & E.N.*'s most loyal supporters.

Sylvia, like her Eritrean friends, believed that the Italian colony should be reunited to the rest of Ethiopia from which it had been carved only within her lifetime. This opinion was first expressed in a *N.T. & E.N.* editorial at the end of March 1941 – four days before the Allied occupation of the Eritrean capital, and well before the Emperor raised the question of the colony's future. The article recalled that the colony had been twice used by the Italians for the invasion of Ethiopia, and declared that Italy should therefore forfeit the territory. 'With Italy removed Eritrea with its seaboard should return to Ethiopia.' A subsequent leader, in mid-May, emphasised Ethiopia's need for 'access to the sea, by the recovery of at least some part of her ancient coast'.

The future of the Italian colonies was also discussed in the paper in a series of articles entitled 'The Post-War World I Want'. Professor A. Berriedale Keith, a frequent contributor, urged that 'Eritrea and Italian Somaliland should be given the opportunity of joining Ethiopia', and that 'Ethiopia should have Jibuti', while C. I. Matthews, from the West Indies, urged that Ethiopia should be returned the neighbouring colonial territories, that is Eritrea and the Italian, French and Italian Somalilands, which had been 'filched from her in past decades'. Ethiopia should thus have her seaboard restored. The paper meanwhile continued to indict Italian colonialism, and began serialising an eye-witness account of 'Ethiopia under Mussolini's Rule', written by a Hungarian physician using the pseudonym Ladislas Sava. It contained a heart-rending description of the Graziani massacre.

Eritrea was at that time administered by Britain as Occupied Enemy Territory, and fascist legislation – and racial laws – remained in force. Any form of political manifestation was prohibited.

BRITISH ATTEMPTS TO CURTAIL ETHIOPIAN INDEPENDENCE

By the autumn of 1941 it became evident to Sylvia – after talks at the Foreign Office, as well as with Colonel Orde Wingate and Sir Philip Mitchell, both newly returned from East Africa – that the British government, whose forces were then in occupation of most of the former Italian empire, so far from following the unselfish policy she had urged in her first wartime editorial, was attempting to replace the Italians as the *de facto* rulers of the Ethiopia. British officials, unbeknown to the British public, seemed bent on turning Ethiopia into a virtual protectorate, and were also seeking to annex large parts of the country. Sylvia concluded that the struggle for Ethiopia's independence was far from completed – and that the paper must now fight for the country against its supposed liberators.

The new situation was reflected – to the surprise of many readers – in the issue of 27 September, which carried the heading:

INDEPENDENCE OF ETHIOPIA IN DANGER
All Her Friends Must Be On The Alert
REASSERT YOUR FAITH IN FREEDOM'S CAUSE

The leading article, headed 'Justice to Ethiopia Still Refused, Independence Endangered', analysed two articles in the London *Times*, which revealed that there was 'an attempt to reduce Ethiopia to the status of a protectorate,"as part of a larger territory"' governed by a British Agent, and so-called advisers in the provinces, who would be, not the servants of the Emperor, his Government and provincial administrators, but their masters'. Contrary to the assumption that Ethiopia had been liberated, the fact was that:

No Ethiopian Government is yet permitted to function. The Emperor and his ministers are still prevented from resuming their beneficial work of development in education and public health, in agriculture, industry, communications and transport. The oft-proposed loan to Ethiopia to repair war damage and accelerate development has not been accorded. The Ethiopian Government is not yet even permitted to draw revenue, to levy taxes, or to make financial arrangements for the Ethiopian State.

Despite the earnest wish of the Emperor to co-operate in the common struggle against the Axis, no Treaty of Alliance with his Majesty's Government in the United Kingdom has yet been signed.

British recognition of the Italian conquest has not yet been formally annulled.

British *de jure* recognition of Ethiopian independence, with the Emperor Haile Selassie as rightful sovereign, has not yet been accorded.

Efforts are being made to disarm and disband, or as 'The Times' puts it, discard the patriot armies and to substitute military and police forces under British officers . . . British judges are presiding over Ethiopian courts.

This and other articles, reinforced by appeals to members of the British Government and MPs, led to Parliamentary questions being put notably on 1 October by Mr Noel-Baker, Mr Wedgwood and Mr Mander, which drew only evasive replies from the Foreign Secretary, Anthony Eden. It thus became apparent that the British government, which had failed Ethiopia at the time of Mussolini's invasion, and had later recognised the fascist 'conquest', was seeking to take a leaf from the Duce's book by itself trying to dominate the country. The days of imperialism, Sylvia concluded, were far from dead. Many of her readers shared this view, and continued to support – and raise funds for – the paper in its continued anti-colonialist struggle.

The seriousness of the situation was further underlined a fortnight later, in an article headed 'GRAVE NEWS FROM ETHIOPIA' which reported that 'the promised Ethiopian independence is far from being obtained. The British army of occupation prevents any effective Government by the Emperor and his Cabinet or the provincial officials appointed by them'. Sylvia's opposition to this policy was shared by Professor Berriedale Keith, who wrote several polemics on the question. A front-page editorial article was headed: 'ETHIOPIAN INDEPENDENCE NOT YET RECOGNISED . . . Vigilance and Active Support Still Needed'.

The paper's political demands were reiterated in an editorial early in November which urged the British government to:

(1) Rescind British recognition of King Victor Emmanuel as Emperor of Ethiopia, and declare null and void all agreements made with Italy and France to exercise control or influence in Ethiopia.

(2) Give formal recognition to Ethiopian independence, with the Emperor Haile Selassie as sovereign *de facto* and *de jure* . . .

(3) Abandon all claims to administer or exercise authority in Ethiopia, and facilitate immediate resumption of control by the Government of Emperor Haile Selassie I.

(4) Conclude a Treaty of Alliance and Friendship with Ethiopia, affording mutual support against Axis aggression.

(5) Restore to Ethiopia Eritrea and the port of Massawa formerly held by Italy as a shield against Italian aggression . . . .

Not long after this it became apparent that British officials were scheming not only to obtain quasi-protectorate control over the country, but also to annex several provinces. Early in December *N.T. & E.N.* headlines read: 'GRAVE DANGER TO ETHIOPIA: British Project to Continue in Occupation of Boran and Ogaden'.

The background to these manoeuvres was further publicised in a series of articles entitled 'ETHIOPIAN MYSTERY', which appeared in January 1942. They told of British attempts to annex parts of Ethiopia, as well as to 'the Emperor's Fight with his Liberators'. The extent of Ethiopian discontent was underlined in a fourth 'Ethiopian Mystery' article. Written by 'a well informed correspondent' – in fact Abebe Retta, a scholarly patriot later attached to the Ethiopian Legation in London – it declared that whereas Ethiopians 'associated' their country's liberties 'with the exploits of Wingate and the Ethiopian armies of which he was in command', other British officers and colonialists had 'their eyes upon various morsels of Ethiopian territory'.

THE FIRST ANGLO-ETHIOPIAN AGREEMENT, AND THE PRINCESS TSEHAI MEMORIAL HOSPITAL

In Ethiopia meanwhile the diplomatic struggle between the Emperor and the British continued unabated. Haile Selassie was forced, by the continued British occupation, to sign an Anglo-Ethiopian Treaty, on 31 January, 1942. It was a compromise which recognised Ethiopia's independence, but imposed a system of exclusively British advisers, and left Britain in occupation of vast stretches of the country. Professor Berriedale Keith trenchantly commented that the agreement had the merit of destroying the 'wholly discreditable attempt' to establish a British protectorate, but it was 'impossible to find any legal or moral justification' for Britain's attitude. Sylvia agreed, writing that the treaty was 'merely a step on the road' to 'real Ethiopian independence', and the result of 'hard-bargaining' with the British who had sought to impose a 'Colonial solution'. Particularly disturbing, she added, was the 'failure to guarantee Ethiopia's territorial integrity', which was 'particularly unfortunate in view of the persistent agitation to dismember her', and the absence of any reference to the 'restoration to Ethiopia of her ancient ports'.

To commemorate Britain's belated recognition of Ethiopian independence – and to expose the limitations placed on the country's actual freedom – the paper early in March organised a Commemoration at the Institute of Archaeology in London. The gathering was embarrassing to the British government in that it was attended not only by long-standing supporters, but also by foreign diplomats, to whom it was brought home that Ethiopia, often referred to as the first country to be freed from Axis domination, was still largely under foreign control. Speakers included two Parliamentary friends, Mr Mander and Lord Wedgwood, as well as Mr Alfonso de Rosenweig Diaz, the ambassador of Mexico, a country which had never recognised the Fascist occupation, and representatives of both China and Albania. Messages of support were read out from the Archbishop of Canterbury, Dame Elizabeth Cadbury, Professor Catlin, Eleanor Rathbone MP, Viscount Cecil, Camille Huysmans of Belgium, and others. A second conference was held four months later, at Cowdray Hall. Addressed by Lord Davies, J.H. Greenwood, and Harold Moody of the League of Coloured Peoples, it was attended by numerous representatives of United Nations Associations, and Women's Cooperative Guilds – and passed resolutions demanding the restoration to Ethiopia of the Ogaden (which had formed part of the country prior to the Italian invasion), and Ethiopia's right to access to the sea.

Growing interest in the future of the Horn of Africa meanwhile lead to the publication of a succession of articles on the subject, notably a series by Sylvia herself, entitled 'Ethiopia and Europe on the Horn of Africa', as well as a leading article in which she declared that the colonial era was 'closing'. The paper's continuing antifascist stance was reaffirmed by an ongoing feature 'Oppression and Revolt' chronicling resistance throughout Axis-occupied Europe.

The death, on 17 August, 1942, of the Emperor's daughter Princess Tsehai, who had served in Britain as a nurse, led Sylvia to initiate plans for the founding in Addis Ababa of the country's first modern hospital, to be built in the princess's name. A Princess Tsehai Memorial Hospital Council was established under the chairmanship of Lord Davies, with a number of Vice-Presidents, including Sylvia's old suffragette friend Emmeline Pethick Lawrence, Colonel Orde Wingate's widow, Lorna, John Murray, Principal of Exeter University, and Professors Sydney Chapman and J.E. Weiss. Sylvia was the honorary secretary. There were two Hon. Treasurers, first Isabel Fry, and later the British royal physician Lord Horder.

THE FUTURE OF ITALY

By the spring of 1943 Allied victories in North Africa caused *N.T. & E.N.* to become increasingly preoccupied with the future of Italy, which was the subject of many articles, notably by 'Crastinus' and Professor Angelo Crespi. Numerous articles on Albania – many by its great friend Miss M.E. Durham and by Albanians in exile – also appeared, as well as others on Romania, in which Sylvia had taken a keen interest since her visit a decade earlier, and on the Balkans more widely.

The successful Allied landing in Sicily, in July, and the fall of Mussolini a few weeks later, gave the question of Italy's future greater urgency, and prompted the paper to run the headline: 'NO! TO FASCISM, WITH OR WITHOUT THE "DUCE"'. Reacting to the establishment by the Allies of a collaborationist government under Marshal Badoglio – who had been responsible for the use of poison-gas and the bombing of the Red Cross in Ethiopia – an editorial declared that 'Badoglio, "Duke of Addis Ababa", Must Go, Too'. The paper published numerous indictments of the general, as well as of the King of Italy, who had called Mussolini to power and still claimed the titles of 'King of Albania and Emperor of Ethiopia'. *N.T. & E.N.* campaigned for the overthrow of the monarchy, and for an Italian republic.

Badoglio's maintenance in power also had significant implications for Ethiopia, where he was named as a war criminal. To avoid his being charged, Ethiopia was excluded from the United Nations War Crimes Commission. The result was that though the Allies later staged highly publicised trials of German and Japanese war criminals not one Italian fascist was indicted for crimes committed in Ethiopia.

N.T. & E.N. also ran many articles on Ethiopian history and culture. These included a serialisation of the seventeenth-century German scholar Ludolf's *New History of Ethiopia* (which the present writer as a youth copied out each week for the printer), and an anonymous English translation, by Abebe Retta, of the writings of a supposed[11] Ethiopian free-thinker philosopher Zara Yaqob.

THE OGADEN AND 'RESERVED AREA'

As the end of the European war – and the ensuing Peace Treaty – approached, British officials in Ethiopia intensified their efforts to annex parts of the country. These moves were denounced by *N.T. & E.N.*, in particular in two articles in March 1944. The first bore the headlines:

GROSS BREACH OF FAITH!
INTRIGUES TO DISMEMBER ETHIOPIA
Plan for Faked Plebiscite by British Military Authorities in the
Reserved Area

The second article was entitled:

ANOTHER DISCREDITABLE PROJECT TO GRAB ETHIOPIAN
TERRITORY!
Sudan Colonials Demand Tigray Province, Historic Centre of
Ethiopian Culture . . .

These articles – and in particular the first – incensed two Conservative MPs, Mr Petherick and Mr Stanley Reed, who, like their colleagues, had received complimentary copies of the paper directed

'To be delivered in the House'. The two accordingly asked Parliamentary questions, on 15 March. Petherick asked whether the government would 'take steps' to stop such 'propaganda'; and Reed whether it would 'cease giving facilities' for the paper's publication. The Minister of Information, Brendan Bracken, replied that he had read the articles, but felt that Britain's record could stand up for itself. Miss Rathbone thereupon intervened to declare that *N.T. & E.N.* had been 'a very useful watchdog in the interests of Ethiopia', and that, if the allegations objected to were 'unjustified', the 'best way' to deal with them would be 'to give a definite assurance that no such plebiscite has been arranged or is contemplated'. This the Minister refused to do, merely commenting: 'This paper contains attacks on England which are worthy of Goebbels. It has insulted the British troops who have rescued Ethiopia, and in my opinion it is a poisonous rag'. Bracken's reluctance to go into the specifics of the charges was scarcely surprising, for before long a British Foreign Secretary, Ernest Bevin, would openly propose the annexation of the territory to which the article referred.

THE BEGINNINGS OF ERITREAN UNIONISM; SYLVIA'S FIRST VISIT TO ETHIOPIA

The defeat of the Italians in Eritrea had led meanwhile to the emergence, partially under the auspices of the Ethiopian Orthodox Church – and in defiance of the British Military Administration – of a strong Eritrean nationalist and anti-colonialist movement demanding reunion with Ethiopia. Some of the first of many reports on this movement appeared in *N.T. & E.N.* in April 1944. Opposition to an Italian return to the colonies was later expressed by Professor Angelo Crespi, who observed that though Fascism was dead, the 'amoral self-centred and aggressive nationalism of a politically ignorant and arrogant ruling class' which had engendered Italian colonialism was still very much alive. The paper also published texts of British wartime leaflets dropped in 1941 promising the ex-Italian colony reunion with Ethiopia.

The future of Eritrea was also discussed in many articles. Correspondence in *The Times* between Professor Jevons of the Abyssinia Association and others was reproduced in January 1944, while Miss M.E. Durham rebutted Italian claims – and recalled that an old Albanian guide had once said of the Great Powers: 'They are just like brigands. By night they go out robbing together, and by day they quarrel about the booty'.

N.T. & E.N.'s parliamentary friends meanwhile scored a signal success when one of them, Mr Barstow, asked the Foreign Secretary, on 4 October, whether Great Britain was 'opposed to the return of the colonies to Italy, and whether the Italian empire was irrevocably lost'. Mr Eden replied, 'Yes Sir'. This was an important commitment – even though attempts were soon made to renege on it.

Towards the end of the year Sylvia paid her first visit to Ethiopia to inspect the site for the Tsehai Memorial. She travelled by way of British-occupied Eritrea where she met the Unionist leader Tedla Bairu, and the Asmara Native Council which presented her with a bouquet of flowers in the Ethiopian national colours, green, yellow and red. She also met – and had some exchange of words with – sundry British colonially-minded officials who were strongly opposed to Eritrean nationalist-cum-Unionist aspirations. On arriving in Addis Ababa she met many Ethiopian friends who had been in exile in Britain. She wrote a series of articles on schools, hospitals and other institutions, and broadcast over Addis Ababa radio, describing the country's reconstruction as she saw it.

THE SECOND ANGLO-ETHIOPIAN TREATY

Her visit coincided with the signing, on 19 December, 1944, of the second Anglo-Ethiopian Agreement, which, though granting Ethiopia greater independence, still left Britain in control of a large amount of the country. Commenting on this, she wrote that she had read the text with 'profound grief and serious misgiving', for she was convinced that 'a great injustice' was being 'obstinately perpetrated'. Pointing out that Britain was still to occupy a third of Ethiopia – the Ogaden and 'Reserved Area', she observed autobiographically:

> After nine years of struggle to secure Justice for Ethiopia and to induce the Government of my own country to act with justice, to fulfil its pledges and honour the principles it has professed on our national behalf, I must declare my intention to oppose this policy which removes from Ethiopian jurisdiction a third of the country . . .

To challenge this continued occupation N.T. & E.N. called a conference, at Alliance Hall, in April 1945. The meeting, addressed among others by Val McEntee MP and the Mexican minister, heard a lengthy report by Sylvia on her visit to Ethiopia – and about her concern at the curtailment of the country's independence. The gathering passed a series of resolutions, two of them on the political future. The first declared:

> As it would be contrary to international justice to deprive Ethiopia, who was not an aggressor but the victim of a cruel and unprovoked aggression, of any part of her national territory, and a violation of British principles and pledges to annex any territory at Ethiopia's expense, this Conference declares that an early date should be fixed for the withdrawal of British Military Administration . . .

The other resolution, moved by Jomo Kenyatta, declared: 'This Conference demands that the ex-Italian colonies, Eritrea and Somalia, be returned to Ethiopia'.

This period, which coincided with the paper's tenth anniversary,[12] witnessed publication of further articles on Fascism, Ethiopian history, and the Italian colonies. Prominence was given to an Ethiopian government memorandum on their future, as well as to articles, by an Eritrean author Alazar Tesfa Michael, entitled 'Eritrea Today'. Subsequently republished as a pamphlet, they showed that the British military authorities had kept fascist legislation in force, so that the colour bar[13] was still in operation. An article on the first 'Ethiopian Cooperatives', then being organised by David Hall, an Ethiopian of partial German descent, was likewise issued as a pamphlet. The paper also published several other pamphlets, three of them by Sylvia herself. These comprised critiques of British colonialist ambitions in and around Ethiopia, in *British Policy in Eritrea and Northern Ethiopia* and *British Policy in Eastern Ethiopia and the Ogaden*, and a survey of Ethiopia and her claims to the ex-Italian colonies, in *The Ethiopian People, their Rights and Progress*. The paper also produced a gruesome account, largely financed by the West Indian Pan-Africanist T.R. Makonnen, of *Italy's War Crimes in Ethiopia*.[14] It featured photographs of Fascist atrocities taken by the perpetrators themselves.

THE PEACE TREATY WITH ITALY

With the approach of the post-war settlement, the movement to deprive Ethiopia of the Ogaden gained political momentum. This prompted *N.T. & E.N.* to address 'An Open Letter to Mr. Bevin' which appeared in May under the banner headlines:

HANDS OFF ETHIOPIA!
NO ANNEXATION OF OGADEN PROVINCE
Restore Italian Colonies to their Ethiopian Motherland

Bevin's own plan, which included the creation – mainly at Ethiopia's expense – of a 'Greater Somalia', was attacked in the paper in the following month. A few weeks later Sylvia drafted a letter on the subject to *The Times*. It was signed by many of Ethiopia's friends, and was followed by a pro-Ethiopia meeting at Livingstone Hall, addressed among others by Isabel Fry, the Rev. W.E.C. Partridge, the Rev. Gordon Milburn, T.R. Makonnen, and the South African author Peter Abrahams.

The Paris Conference, convened to draft the peace treaty with Italy, opened at the end of July 1946 – and was marred by news of a massacre in Asmara where Sudanese soldiers employed by the British Administration ran amok. Sylvia travelled to Paris to lobby and report proceedings for the paper. She found the Italians actively canvassing to return to Africa, and circulating a booklet in praise of the fascist occupation of Ethiopia. Their delegation included Enrico Cerulli, a sometime fascist colonial official who had earlier advised the fascist delegates at Geneva. By way of reply *N.T. & E.N.* circulated copies of its pamphlet *Italy's War Crimes in Ethiopia*. At the end of the conference Italy formally agreed to renounce its colonies, and promised to return all loot[15] taken from Ethiopia – but immediately announced a diplomatic initiative to return to Africa.

This period witnessed the arrival in London of the first Ethiopian students to study in Britain after the war. Six became Sylvia's wards, while others wrote articles in the paper. They included two future Ethiopian Prime Ministers, Endalkachew Makonnen and Mikael Imru, and the future Ethiopian dramatist Menghestu Lemma, who became her close personal friend.[16] Pictures and cartoons by Afewerk Tekle, later the country's foremost artist, whom she regarded as a son, were frequently published.[17]

THE GROWTH OF THE ERITREAN UNIONIST MOVEMENT

In Eritrea meanwhile there was a great expansion of the Unionist movement, as well as the emergence of several smaller rival parties. Perhaps the most influential had the support of the Italian settler population and of Eritreans drawing Italian pensions. It demanded the return of Italy. Much space in *N.T. & E.N.* was devoted to these developments. The paper (then printed in Manchester) continued to give the Unionist movement its support. On the eve of the Conference of Foreign Ministers called to discuss the future of the Italian colonies it held a conference at Caxton Hall. Chaired by Sylvia, it was attended by delegates from United Nations Associations, Women's Cooperative Guilds, the Labour and Liberal Parties, and trades unions, as well as the Union of Democratic Control and the League of Coloured Peoples. Resolutions were passed in favour of Ethiopian reunion and the British withdrawal from the Ogaden. Support for these policies was also voiced in a letter to *The Times* signed by Sylvia, together with Mrs Corbett Ashby, the Rev. Canon Douglas, Isabel Fry, two Labour Members of Parliament, Peter Freeman and Fred Longden, Dr Maud Royden Shaw, Fred Woods, general secretary of the Clerical and Administrative Workers Union, and the Pan-Africanist writer George Padmore.[18]

The Conference of Foreign Ministers, unable to decide on the future of the former Italian colonies, decided to despatch a Commission of Enquiry to Libya, Eritrea and Somalia. It was composed of representations of the four Great Powers, Britain, France, the USA and the USSR. As far as Eritrea was concerned the commissioners formed two factions. The British and Americans were sympathetic to the Unionists, whom they recognised as having massive popular following, while the French and Soviets gave their support to a then largely Italian-based independence block.

These developments – which seemed to herald a possible return of Italian colonialism to Africa – greatly disturbed Sylvia and other Ethiopian sympathisers in Britain, and resulted in a flurry of activity. The signatories of the earlier letter to *The Times* despatched an Open Letter to the Foreign Secretary, Ernest Bevin, in which they were joined by the Dean of Gloucester, the Rev. Dr. H. Costley White, Lorna Wingate, the editor's old suffragette comrade-in-arms[19] Baroness Pethick Lawrence, Professor H.E. Roaf, and five other MPs, including the indomitable Mrs Braddock. Lady Pethick Lawrence also wrote a letter to *N.T. & E.N.* in which she attacked the British occupation of the Ogaden, declaring: 'I regard any alienation of the Provinces of Ethiopia as a very great scandal and a cause of deep shame'. The paper also held a poster parade outside the Houses of

Parliament: those taking part included Sylvia, Mrs Tedros, the West Indian wife of the above-mentioned Eritrean resident in Britain, Mary Downes, and the present writer. Publicity in the paper was also given to Italian opposition to the Italian government's then insistent demand for the return of the former colonies, as well as to Eritrean demonstrations for unity with Ethiopia. Many articles were devoted to the ex-colonies. Serialisation thus began of editorial studies of 'Italian Colonisation', and 'Ex-Italian Somaliland',[20] as well as a work by Alazar Tesfa Mikael, entitled 'Eritrean Heroes' – all of whom, like most educated Eritreans of that time, considered themselves Ethiopians. Numerous statements on the former colony, mainly by the Emperor and the Ethiopian Foreign Minister, Ato Aklilou Hapte Wold, were also reproduced.

Continued efforts were also made to raise funds for the Princess Tsehai Memorial Hospital, by then being under construction. Activities included postal appeals to members of various professions, as well as bazaars and fetes and a Central Hall Concert, believed to have been the first occasion on which Verdi's 'Hymn to the Nations' was played.

THE THREATENED RETURN OF ITALY TO AFRICA

Though the Italian government had renounced all claim to Italy's colonies by the Paris Peace Treaty of 1946 it launched a major diplomatic campaign three years later to regain them.[21] The architect of this manoeuvre, the Italian Foreign Minster Count Sforza, succeeded in winning the diplomatic support of many Catholic UNO member states, particularly in South America, and was therefore able to marshal considerable voting power. This initiative was recognised by *The Times* which in 1949 gave its support to a proposal whereby Eritrea would be placed under joint British, French and Italian control. This scheme, which would have left the large Italian settler community firmly entrenched, was castigated by Sylvia in an article headed: 'THE PLAN EXPOSED: ANGLO-FRANCO-ITALIAN TRUSTEESHIP PLOT MERELY CLOAKS ITALIAN TRUSTEESHIP'.

Later issues were likewise devoted to opposing the Italian initiative. One carried the slogan 'ITALY MUST NOT BE ALLOWED TO RETURN TO AFRICA', and an account of the Italian colonies by the

American civil servant James Burns, with the heading 'INEFFI-CIENCY and CORRUPTION'. The reminiscences of Italian-occu-pied Ethiopia, by the Hungarian physician Sava, were again serial-ised. Prominence was also given to a letter in *The Times* in which Sylvia, Isabel Fry, the Socialist academic Professor G.D.H. Cole and five British MPs urged that 'the decision . . . that Italy must renounce all title to her former colonies be upheld'. Opposition to the Italian claims was also voiced in many subsequent articles, including two heartfelt appeals by an Eritrean author, Seyoum Berhané.

Many young Eritreans, angered by the possibility of a return of Italian colonialism, had by then taken up arms to fight for reunion to Ethiopia, as a result of which a banner heading reported, at the end of August: 'LIFE AND DEATH STRUGGLE IN ERITREA'. The same issue ran the slogan: 'UNO must NOT sanction an Italian Return to Africa'.

A few weeks later, on 21 November, 1949, the UN General Assembly, after intense bargaining in which the South Ameri-can and Arab states formed a united block, came to the remarkable compromise that Libya should become independent after three years, and that Somalia be placed under Italian trusteeship for ten years, while a decision on the future of Eritrea was postponed pending the despatch of another commission of enquiry. It was to be composed of representatives of Burma, Guatemala, Norway, Pakistan and South Africa. In view of the pro-Italian stance of the South American states, the partitionist and anti-Christian bias of Pakistan, the racist charac-ter of South Africa, and uncertainty as to the position of Burma, it appeared that Norway would perhaps be the only country to give the unionist case a fair hearing. It therefore seemed that Italy, the aggressor of Mussolini's war, who had already returned to Somalia, might well obtain control of both the former colonies from which it had launched its invasion fifteen years earlier, while Ethiopia, the victim, might be left once more without access to the sea.

Alarmed at this possibility, *N.T. & E.N.* organised another poster parade from Fleet Street to the Houses of Parliament. Some of the posters read '1940 Britain urged Somali people to fight for freedom; 1949 Britain voted at U.N.O. for Italian forces to return to Somaliland', and 'Power politics at U.N.O. instead of Justice. U.N.O. Commission packed four to one against Ethiopia going to Eritrea'. Sylvia also despatched further letters to the press. One, in *The Times*, was signed by three professors, G.D.H. Cole, H.E. Roaf, and F.E. Weiss, and nine Members of Parliament, as well as the Dean of Gloucester, Canon

Douglas, Dorothea Layton, and Gordon Selfridge's daughter Princess Rosalie Viazemski.

THE FUTURE OF ERITREA AND THE OGADEN SETTLED

The propaganda struggle over the future of the former colonies continued throughout most of 1950. In January *N.T. & E.N.* published a letter on the 'Eritrean Crisis' written by a long list of Eritrean patriots, and an article by Bereketab Habte Sellassie, one of the Eritrean students educated in England at Ethiopian government expense, who recalled the vast number of leaflets which had been dropped over Eritrea by the RAF during the war, promising that Eritrea 'should be united with their brothers and their Motherland', Reports that the British administration of Eritrea was offering rewards for the capture of Eritrean patriots fighting for their freedom led Sylvia and Lady Pethick Lawrence, as sisters-in-arms since suffragette times, to publish a joint protest, headed 'BLOOD MONEY'.

The paper meanwhile held another conference in April which was convened by Peter Freeman in a House of Commons Committee Room, and was attended by many United Nations Association, Labour, Cooperative and African delegates. A resolution was passed urging the British government to 'honour the pledge made to Ethiopia during World War II to return Eritrea to Ethiopia'. The gathering also 'deeply regretted the decision to permit the Italians to return to the former Somaliland Colony'. This theme was the subject of an Open Letter to Ernest Bevin, drafted by Sylvia, and signed by seventeen Labour MPs.

In the spring of 1950 the second commission of enquiry went to Eritrea. This prompted *N.T. & E.N.* to organise its last conference on the ex-colonies. Held in a House of Commons Committee Room, in July, it pressed for the return of Eritrea to Ethiopia, and the speedy termination of the Italian Trusteeship in Somalia.

A few months later the long diplomatic struggle came to an end, when the UN General Assembly, following the recommendations of Norway, Burma and South Africa, finally decided, on 2 December, 1950, that the ex-colony should be federated with Ethiopia, under the Ethiopian crown.

The Princess Tsehai Memorial Hospital Council in London, which by the summer of 1950 had raised some £48,000, meanwhile continued to hold fund-raising functions. These included a bazaar and fete at Kingsway Hall in December 1949, and a series of garden parties in the spacious grounds of Bedford College, addressed by such notables as Lord Winster, Brigadier Parkinson, Canon Douglas and Isabel Fry, the actor Donald Wolfit, and the exiled Chief Seretse Khama.

Sylvia, who was invited to attend the opening of the hospital in Addis Ababa, paid a second visit to Ethiopia at the end of 1951 which led to a further series of articles on institutions and places in Ethiopia. These included a vivid description of the Asmara slums, and an account of the 'Wanton Destruction', of the docks at the Eritrean port of Massawa, carried out by the British administration of Eritrea – the subject also of a *N.T. & E.N.* pamphlet by the editor, entitled *Why are We Destroying the Eritrean Ports?*[22] The paper also serialised a number of historical articles which were later incorporated in Sylvia's 747-page tome *Ethiopia. A Cultural History* which contained an introduction by Canon Douglas. Other articles dealt with Ethiopian history, as well as that of neighbouring countries Kenya[23] and Uganda.

Sylvia's opposition to the British occupation of the 'Reserved Area' of Ethiopia – by then the only part of the country under foreign control – found expression in numerous articles, as well as in another letter to *The Times* in January 1953, which she signed with Lady Pethick Lawrence, three Members of Parliament, Stan Awbery, Peter Freeman and Arthur Henderson, two divines, the Rev Canon Douglas and the Rev. J. Scott Lidgett, and Professor G.D.H. Cole. The paper's stance led to opposition from some British colonialists, as a result of which *N.T. & E.N.* was declared a 'Prohibited Publication' in the British Somaliland Protectorate. The occupation of the 'Reserved Area' finally came to an end, however, in 1954, after which Sylvia felt that, with the restoration of national sovereignty throughout Ethiopia, *N.T. & E.N.*'s mission was at last drawing to a close.

THE END OF THE PAPER

The paper finally came to an end on 5 May, 1956, after twenty years of publication.[24] The last issue announced that it would be followed by a new publication entitled *The Ethiopian Review* – a name subsequently changed to *Ethiopia Observer*. Also reproduced was a poem by the editor entitled 'O Addis Ababa, O Fair New Flower'.

Sylvia shortly afterwards moved permanently to Addis Ababa where she helped to found a Social Service Society, and for the next four years edited her new monthly publication, which, like *N.T. & E.N.* before it, was printed in Manchester. Each issue, a large proportion of which she wrote herself and involved much travelling, was devoted to a separate aspect of Ethiopian life. On her death, on 27 September, 1960, at the age of seventy-eight, the publication became a quarterly, and was edited for the next sixteen years by her son and daughter-in-law. Like Sylvia's more famous weekly out of which it had been born, it thus spanned a generation.

NOTES

1. On this period see also R. Pankhurst, *Sylvia Pankhurst, Artist and Crusader* (London, 1979), pp. 179–211.
2. The letters here quoted are reproduced in full in R.K.P.P., 'The Years of Appeasement', *N.T. & E.N.*, 10 and 31 October, 7 November, 26 December, 1953, and 2, 9 and 16 January 1954.
3. For a brief account of the newspaper see also R. Pankhurst, 'New Times and Ethiopia News', *Quarterly Yerkatit* (Addis Ababa, 1987), XI, No. 1, pp. 32–6.
4. Quoted, together with other African correspondence of the time, in R.K.P.P., 'A Continent Aroused, Africans Rally to Ethiopia', *New Times and Ethiopia News*, 30 February 1954.
5. For subsequent confirmation of the continued use of poison gas during the occupation see the Ethiopian Ministry of Justice publication, *Documents on Italian War Crimes* (Addis Ababa, 1950).
6. Confirmation of the veracity of this report is implicit in the Duke's remarks to Mussolini's son-in-law Count Galeazzo Ciano, recorded in the latter's diary, *Diario 1937–1943* (Milano, 1980).
7. For confirmation that such was in fact Fascist strategy at this time see *inter alia* R. Pankhurst, 'The Ethiopian Patriots: The Lone Struggle, 1936–1940', *Ethiopia Observer* (1970), XVIII, No. 1, pp. 40–56.
8. On efforts to have the Ethiopian National Anthem played with the other anthems of the Allies, and the procrastination encountered, see R. Pankhurst, 'The Ethiopian National Anthem in 1940: A Chapter in Anglo-Ethiopian Wartime Relations', *Ethiopia Observer* (1971), XIV, No. 3, pp. 219–25, and *idem.* 'The Ethiopian National Anthem in 1941', *idem* (1972), XIV, No. 1, pp. 63–6.
9. There is reason to believe that this letter was sent by an Italian fascist resident in London who was still residing there in 1989. – R.P.
10. On the disintegration of Italian fascist morale and defection among Italy's 'colonial' soldiers – both significant features of the campaign –

see R. Pankhurst, 'The Ethiopian Patriots and the Collapse of Italian Rule in East Africa', *Ethiopian Observer* (1969), XII, No. 2, p. 92–127.

11. Though then unknown to either the translator or the editor, the Ethiopian authorship of this work has been contested by several prominent foreign scholars, whose views have in turn been opposed by others, notably by two professors of Addis Ababa University, Amsalu Aklilu and Claude Sumner.

12. On 5 May 1945, the tenth anniversary of publication, the paper included an anthology of excerpts from articles in earlier years.

13. On these laws see R. Pankhurst, 'Fascist Racial Policies in Ethiopia: 1922–1941', *Ethiopia Observer* (1969), XII, No. 4, pp. 272–86.

14. On this individual, a keen supporter of the paper and its activities, see Ras Makonnen, *Pan-Africanism from within* (London, 1973), especially pp. 115, 145.

15. Though some loot was duly returned no effort was made to return the Aksum obelisk which stands to this day in Rome. On this see R. Pankhurst, 'Ethiopia and the Loot of the Italian invasion: 1935-6', *Présence Africaine* (1969), No. 72, pp. 9–20.

16. See also R. Pankhurst, 'Menghestu Lemma'. *Journal of Ethiopian Studies* (1988), XXI, 200–13.

17. On this artist, and the drawings he produced for *N.T. & E.N.*, see R. Pankhurst, *Afewerk Tekle, Short Biography and Selected Works* (Addis Ababa, 1987).

18. On this writer see G. Padmore, *Pan-Africanism or Communism?* (London, n.d.), especially pp. 145, 365.

19. Emmeline Pethick Lawrence wrote about Sylvia and their old suffragette days in her foreword to E.S. Pankhurst and R.K.P. Pankhurst, *Ethiopia and Eritrea, The Last Ten Years of the Reunion Struggle, 1941–1952* (Woodford Green, Essex, 1953), pp. 11–12.

20. This was later issued as a paperback pamphlet, and shortly afterwards as a hardback published in London in 1951 by Watts & Co., with a foreword by Peter Freeman, MP.

21. For a detailed account of the manoeuvres of the four Great Powers, meetings of the UN on Eritrea, and Commissions of Enquiry, see E.S. Pankhurst and R.K.P. Pankhurst, *op. cit.* This work also includes an account of *N.T. & E.N.*'s involvement in the propaganda struggle.

22. This work, which was published by *N.T. & E.N.*, included Sylvia's description of Asmara, entitled 'Asmara: the Heart Disease of a Lovely Modern City'. The work likewise appeared as a hardcover book, with the title *Eritrea on the Eve, The past and future of Italy's "first-born" Colony, Ethiopia's ancient Sea Province* (Woodford Green, Essex, 1952).

23. These formed the basis of the present writer's book *Kenya: The History of Two Nations* (London: Independent Publishing Company) with a foreword by Professor Harold Laski's widow Frida Laski.

24. Though *N.T. & E.N.* had thus come to an end it is interesting to recall that in Ethiopia one of the principal Amharic newspapers, named in 1941, still bears the name *Addis Zemen* (literally 'New Times').

7

Sylvia Pankhurst's Papers as a Source

M. WILHELMINA H. SCHREUDER

Sylvia Pankhurst's papers were given to the International Institute of Social History (IISH) in Amsterdam upon her death in 1960, by her son Dr Richard K.P. Pankhurst. The bulk arrived there in 1961, while a smaller addition was sent in 1970. The files of newspapers and the books in the collection were transferred to the library. Of the remainder, a short description was drawn up.

My involvement with the papers started in 1965, when I was appointed Secretary to the Director and for part of my time was employed in rearranging and classifying the Institute's extensive collection of British, Irish and North American pamphlets. At the time I was looking for a subject for a PhD thesis. One of my colleagues suggested that I should look at Sylvia Pankhurst's papers with this aim in view. Consequently, I began drawing up a superficial inventory of the various boxes as a spare time activity. In the end the doctoral thesis remained unwritten, partly owing to lack of time, but largely as a result of the complexity of the subject.

I hope to illustrate the possibilities for research offered by the collection, as well as the problems one is bound to encounter in the process.

The collection is quite bulky (four running metres) and covers a period of roughly one hundred years, as well as a wide field of activities. This became clear in the course of the first investigation and inventorising, when it also became apparent that there was no inherent order. The chief principle of arrangement seemed to be that of size, probably as a result of the collection's having been shipped twice, from London to Addis Ababa and from Addis Ababa to Amsterdam. Consequently, it was decided to draw up a new arrangement, bringing together the papers of Sylvia herself, as far as possible in chronological order, and putting the documents concerning her parents, other members of the family and so on, under a separate heading.

Chronologically, the first sources for research are the items concerning Sylvia's father, Dr Richard Marsden Pankhurst, her mother, Emmeline Goulden Pankhurst, and some of their relations. These provide information about their lives and activities. Those of Dr Pankhurst contain a number of books of newspaper clippings (1863–98), from which one might gain an idea of his interests. There are also a number of letters, several from Lydia Becker, about the early women's movement in Manchester; manuscript notes, apparently for speeches or lectures, and finally, tributes from the constituencies for which he stood as a parliamentary candidate.

The amount of material of and about Emmeline Pankhurst and her relatives is smaller; chief among it are letters by Ursula Bright about the Women's Franchise League and a minute book (1896–7) of the Executive Committee of this organisation. The information in these documents, could be used to confirm and, possibly, add to what has already been published about the movements concerned, as well as on the roles of the Pankhursts in them.

The papers of Sylvia Pankhurst herself cover a period of almost eighty years from her birth in 1882 to her death in 1960. The strictly personal papers contain the earliest documents: her birth certificate, a school report, a share in the Clarion Cyclists' Club (and those of other members of the family), diplomas, documents about scholarships and a certain amount of correspondence. The last is rather tantalizing as a source, since it is very scattered and leaves large gaps of information.

An interesting aspect of the letters that are available is that some of them are clearly connected with the books Sylvia wrote. Examples of this are the letters (1907-10) from Mrs Wolstenholme Elmy, which provide information about the early women's movement, used in the writing of *The Suffragette* (1911) and a folder of letters from various organisations, for example the ILP, confirming dates of membership of her parents and so on, information used for *The Suffragette Movement* (1931). The sketches and drawings vary: work Sylvia did as a child; a number of studies, probably done while attending classes, and a number of designs and sketches, among them the designs for Pankhurst Hall. Some postcards are to be found under the heading WSPU, while others were photographed and are in the picture department of the Institute.

Sylvia Pankhurst's writings are the largest part of the collection. They have been divided into typescripts and manuscripts, while a further distinction has been made between writings of a journalistic nature and fiction and poetry. In quantity the manuscripts dominate, while at the same time they are the most complicated to consult. One reason is that they are very difficult to date, except very roughly by the subject dealt with. Moreover, most of them are in fact exercise books, in which a number of subjects are dealt with. Sometimes, one is written about back to front, another front to back, both being interspersed with draft letters, poems, or notes of a quite different nature. To make things even more difficult, the handwriting varies a lot, sometimes so much that it seems parts have been written by another person. Nevertheless, a study of manuscript material and comparison with typescripts and/or books and articles published could be well worthwhile. It might show an interesting light on the way in which Sylvia's ideas developed while she was writing. Most of the material in the manuscripts is also found in the typescripts in the collection or in the books published.

In quantity, the typescripts are second only to the manuscripts. Many of them are available in two, or even three, different versions, that sometimes are clearly amended and improved. I have tried to find out if the best versions were ever published, but this effort was unsuccessful. On the basis of this failure and of the fact that no typescripts are there of the books that were published (*The Suffragette Movement, The Home Front, Save the Mothers*, the books on Africa, and so on), I have been led to the conclusion that the typescripts in the collection have not been published. This is supported by the existence of discarded chapters of *The Suffragette Movement* among them.

It seems a pity that no-one ever read these pieces, for some of them present an interesting view of the subject treated. For instance, the articles about working women in the north of England, written about 1905, paint an impressive picture of the hard work, and difficult lives of these women. Similarly, the articles made out of the descriptive letters Sylvia wrote to Keir Hardie from the United States around 1910 give a very personal view of the circumstances she encountered there. The same could be said about the planned book *In the Red Twilight*, even though part of this was published as a serial in the first few issues of the *New Times and Ethiopia News* (1936).

From the correspondence, it does not become clear if and why these items were not published; it is one of the questions to which the collection does not contain the answer.

The manuscripts and typescripts put under the heading 'fiction' do not seem to have reached the stage of publication either. They are even more difficult to put a date to, with the exception of the two suffragette plays and a few poems about special occasions. With some of the poems a printed clipping is available, so they were probably published in the the *Dreadnought*. Checking this is difficult, because the clippings are undated, while there are very many manuscript and typescript poems. Moreover, some of them may have been included in the collection *Writ on a Cold Slate*. Quite apart from the literary value of this material, the content of the story outlines and the poems would be worth studying to learn more about Sylvia's ideas and feelings, for example in the stories about British girls marrying foreigners, or the poems about the people and things around her.

In the *Inventory*, papers from and about Sylvia's work in several movements and associations have been put under the heading 'Activities'. A large part of these are concerned with her work in the East End, starting as a branch of the Women's Social and Po-litical Union, to further the struggle for the vote. This part of the collection is best known and has been consulted most frequently. First of all, there are the minute books of the East London Federation of the Suffragettes, later Workers' Suffrage Federation and after 1917, Workers' Socialist Federation; its Council; Finance Committee and General Members' Meetings (May 1913–20). They give an idea of the way in which the movement was run, how the work was shared out among the members, how it reacted to the problems arising from the First World War in the East End and how it developed into one of the constituent bodies of the Communist Party of Great Britain.

Of Sylvia's work for the WSPU before the establishment of the East End Branch, the collection contains chiefly printed matter: some programmes and pamphlets, and a few letters. To this period belong some forms from Holloway Prison, giving information about Sylvia's health while there. The most interesting documents of the WSPU are the letters Emmeline and Christabel Pankhurst wrote to Sylvia, telling her it would be better for her to make the East End Branch into an independent body and suggesting suitable names for it, thus in effect throwing her out of the WSPU (late 1913, early 1914).

About the East End work, a number of other documents are available: some annual reports, a certain amount of correspondence, and some other minute books of committees in which a number of groups co-operated to keep the cause of the workers and of the vote alive in war-time.

In addition to her work in the ELFS and with its members, Sylvia Pankhurst instigated several projects to help working-class women earn a living, provide meals for them and their families and care for young children. On one of these projects, a toy factory, a quantity of material has been brought together for a lawsuit brought by one of its workers, Mrs Hercbergova, because she felt insulted by what Sylvia wrote about her in *The Home Front*. Both the minute book and a number of other documents give information about the projects and about other activities of Sylvia's to improve the pay and conditions of soldiers' and sailors' wives and children.

After the Russian Revolution of 1917, the WSF and the *Dreadnought* took the part of the revolutionaries in Russia and hoped for a similar development in other countries, including Britain, hence the change of names into Workers' Socialist Federation and *Workers' Dreadnought*. Both the minute books and the paper clearly show this turn of events, while at the same time the pacifist views that had found expression in the *Dreadnought* right from the beginning of the war were more sharply put in its opposition to the conscription law. Among the correspondence, some letters show the trouble this caused the printer of the paper, so that a replacement had to be found, while other documents tell about the police raiding the office.

Quite a number of documents about Marxism, Soviet Russia and its organisation, its leaders and ideas, most of them translated from Russian, have found a place in the collection, some of them published by the Russian Information Bureau or by the Hands Off Russia Committee, others as proofs or typescripts. About Sylvia Pankhurst's role in the foundation of the CPGB, which was constituted by a number of left-wing socialist parties, among them the WSF, and her being thrown out of the party quite soon afterwards, a number of documents give information. Here again some questions remain unanswered.

Of the *Dreadnought* files on other subjects a few remain; for instance, one about Ireland and the Easter Rising. One folder contains Sylvia Pankhurst's appeal against a six months' prison sentence for articles in the *Dreadnought* (1920). After the discontinuation of the

Dreadnought in 1924, until the 1930s, no organisational activities have left their traces in the collection.

After 1930, Sylvia became active in a number of anti-fascist organisations: for example in 1932–3 the Women's International Matteotti Committee. 1933 has left a file on the Van der Lubbe case in Germany, and there remain a number of documents such as agendas or reports. Part of these activities was her support for Ethiopia and its Emperor, of which a number of documents give an impression. Another interesting file is that of the correspondence about Italian refugees, sponsored by the Friends of Free Italy.

Among the papers marked 'Family and others' a number of letters addressed to Silvio Corio can be found, some of them also concerned with Italian refugees. This is the only trace of the part he played in Sylvia's life, and it tells us nothing about their relationship. A similar vagueness exists about Sylvia's relationship with Keir Hardie, of which a number of postcards and letters, and the letters from the USA mentioned before, are the only witnesses. It is difficult to know how a few words from around 1910 which suggest love should be interpreted into the language and behaviour of the 1990s.

Originally, the collection also held a large number of photographs: family portraits, photos of demonstrations and other activities of the suffragette movement; of Sylvia's designs for the Women's Exhibition in the Skating Rink; of the work in the East End; of women working in men's jobs during the war (1914-18); of the poverty suffered in the East End; of the Spanish Civil War; of Ethiopia and Ethiopians, and a number of other subjects. Like the posters, postcards and other things Sylvia designed for the WSPU, most of the photographs were transferred to the collection of pictorial material in the IISH, in order to render their use by the public easier. A list of these has been added to the collection. A number of photographs were left with the papers, either because they could not be identified or were not considered relevant for social history. Among these are a considerable number of photographs taken on the occasion of Sylvia's visit to Romania in the 1930s, which may have gained relevance after what happened in Romania recently. The same might be true for the pieces Sylvia wrote about that country, which as far as can be ascertained were never published.

I have tried to give an impression of the possible sources for research to be found in Sylvia Pankhurst's Papers. For a more detailed description, one should consult *Inventory of the E. Sylvia Pankhurst Papers, 1866–1960* by Wilhelmina H. Schreuder and

Margreet Schrevel, Working Paper No. 8, published by Stichting Beheer IISG Amsterdam in 1989, to which I acknowledge my debt in preparing this brief introduction to the Papers.

Over the years during which I worked on them, the Papers brought me in touch with a fascinating woman. I hope that others will be encouraged to consult them to seek a closer acquaintance for themselves.

Sylvia Pankhurst's Publications

The Suffragette. The history of the women's militant suffrage movement 1905-1910 (New York: Sturgis and Walton, 1911)

Rebel Ireland. Thoughts on Easter Week. (London: Workers' Socialist Federation, n. d.)

Education of the Masses (London: Dreadnought Publications, 1918)

La grande conspiration contre le socialisme russe et allemand (Petrograd, 1919)

Die grosse Verschwäring gegen den russischen und den deutschen Sozialismus (Petrograd, 1919)

Education of the Masses (London: Dreadnought Publications, 1921)

Soviet Russia as I Saw It (London: Workers' Dreadnought Publications, 1922)

Writ on Cold Slate (poems) (London: Workers' Dreadnought Publications, 1922)

The Truth about the Oil War (London: Workers' Dreadnought Publications, 1922)

India and the Earthly Paradise (Bombay: Sunshine Publishing House, 1926)

Delphos, or the future of international language (London: Kegan Paul, 1927)

Is an International Language Possible? A lecture (London: Morland Press, 1928)

[With I Stefanovici] *Poems of Mihail Eminescu* (London: Kegan Paul, 1930)

The Life of Emmeline Pankhurst. The Suffragette struggle for women's citizenship (London: T. Werner Laurie, 1930)

Save the Mothers. A plea for measures to prevent the annual loss of about 3,000 childbearing mothers and 20,000 infant lives in England and Wales (London: Knopf, 1930)

The Suffragette Movement: an intimate account of persons and ideas (London: Longmans, 1931)

The Home Front. A Mirror to Life in England during the First World War (London: Hutchinson & Co., 1932)

British Policy in Eritrea and Northern Ethiopia (Woodford Green: Sylvia Pankhurst, 1945)

British Policy in Eastern Ethiopia 1, the Ogaden and the reserved area (Woodford Green: Sylvia Pankhurst, 1945)
Education in Ethiopia (Woodford Green: New Times and Ethiopia News Book Department, 1946)
The Ethiopian People: their Rights and Progress (Woodford: New Times and Ethiopia News Book Department, 1946)
Is an International Language possible? A lecture delivered before the Annual Conference of the Société de Philologie, Sciences, et Beaux Arts (London: Morland, 1947)
Ex-Italian Somaliland (London: Watts, 1951)
Why are we destroying the Ethiopian Ports? With a historical retrospect 1557–1952 (Woodford Green: New Times and Ethiopia News Book Department, 1952)
Eritrea on the eve: the past and future of Italy's 'first born' colony, Ethiopia's ancient sea province (Woodford Green: New Times and Ethiopia News Book Department, 1952)
(With Richard Pankhurst) *Ethiopia and Eritrea. The last phase of the reunion struggle 1941–52* (Woodford Green: Lalibela House, 1953)
Ethiopia. A cultural history (Woodford Green: Lalibela House, 1955)
Communism and its tactics, edited and introduced by Mark Shipway (Edinburgh: Shipway, 1983)

Articles in collections by others are not easy to trace. Two that have been mentioned in this book are:

'Some autobiographical notes, by E. Sylvia Pankhurst. With an introduction by Dr Jane de Iongh', in *Jaarboek/Yearbook International Archives for the Women's Movement*, vol I (Leiden: E. J. Brill, 1937) pp. 89–98.
'Sylvia Pankhurst' in *Myself When Young – by famous women of today*, edited by the Countess of Oxford and Asquith (London: Frederick Muller Ltd, 1938) pp. 259–312.

Sylvia Pankhurst edited the following newspapers and journals:
The Woman's Dreadnought (1914–17)
The Workers' Dreadnought (1917–24)
Germinal (1923)
Humanity (1932)
New Times and Ethiopia News (1936–56)
Ethiopia Observer (1956–60)

Index

Abrahams, Peter, 184
Accademia di Belle Arti, 7
Action Feministe Internationale, 161
Addis Ababa, 155, 158, 160, 173, 182, 190–1, 192
adult suffrage, 61–3, 68–9, 75–6, 96, 111, 113, 124, 126, 130, 134–5, 143
African nationalism, 158
African Service Bureau, 161
All-Workers Industrial Revolutionary Union, 143
Alston, Mr, 27
America *see* USA
Amsterdam Sub-Bureau (of Comintern), 122, 142
Anderson, Sir Kenneth, 16, 25
Anglo-Ethiopian Treaty (1942), 178
Anglo-Ethiopian Treaty (1944), 182–3
Anglo-Italian agreement (1938), 162–3, 168–9
anti-conscription campaign, 93–100, 123–4
anti-fascist movement, xv, 149–75
anti-fascists interned during Second World War, 172–3
Anti-Suffrage Review, 60, 82
appeasement, xii, 162–4
Anzani, Ani, 172
Appleton, W. I., 94
anti-imperialism, 146, 151, 165
'anti-patriotic' meeting (in Brighton), 129
anti-war agitation, 88–100
anti-parliamentarism, 122, 138–40, 143–6
Aosta, duke of, 162
Arandora Star, the sinking of the, 172–3
Araquistain, Louis, 168
Artists' Suffrage League, 51, 55
art works by Sylvia Pankhurst: angel motif, 50, 52; banners, 51,

55–6; calender for 1910, 50–1; dancing girls sketches, 55; Berwickshire agricultural workers series, 48; Black Country portrait of an old woman, 44; 'Feed My Lambs' postcard, 41; 14 July (1912), 55–6; Glasgow cotton mill series, 49; 'In a Pot Bank' *see* Potteries series; Kent landscapes, 53; Oberammergau sketchbook, 54; Parten Kirchen sketchbook, 54–5; Pankhurst Hall decorations, 40–1; 'pit brow' girls series, 46; portraits of Keir Hardie, 33, 41–2; Potteries series, 46–7; prison sketches, 1906, 43; self-portraits, 54; Scottish fisherwomen series, 47–8; suffragette tea service, 50; Venice watercolours, 32, 40; Women's Exhibition decorations, 52–3, 55; women shoemakers' series, 45–6; *Workless and Hungry* poster, 41; WSPU membership card, 44; WSPU prisoners' illuminated address, 51–2
Arts and Crafts Movement, 2, 37
Ashby, Mrs Corbett, 162, 185
Asmara, 181, 183, 188; massacre at, 183
Asquith, H. H., 76–8, 97, 103
Astor, Lady Nancy, 108
Avenol, Mr, 160
Awbery, Stan, MP, 189

Badaglio, Marshal, war crimes of, in Ethiopia, 153, 179–80
Bairu, Tedla, 182
Bancroft, Elias Mollineaux, 4, 38
Bands, Cllr J., 104
Barstow, Mr, MP, 182
Bax, Ernest Belfort, 60, 82
Beamish, Miss, 96

Beaufort-Palmer, Francis, 156
Becker, Lydia, 193
Benson, W. A., 33
Berhané, Seyoum, 187
Berrier, Count Hilaire du, 157
Besant, Annie, 61
Best, Nellie, 95, 99
Bevin, Ernest, 181, 183, 185, 188
Billington-Greig, Teresa, 65, 67, 83, 84
Black Country, Sylvia Pankhurst's visit to, 44–5
Blackfriars Press, 131
Blatchford, Robert, 33 *see also The Clarion*
Bologna Conference (of PSI), 141
Bolsheviks: demand peace and power to the soviets, 126–7; relatively unknown in Britain, 127–9; seize power, 132–3; dissolve Constituent Assembly, 137–40; abandon Communism, according to Sylvia Pankhurst, 143
Bondfield, Margaret, 63
Boran, province of, 177
Bouvier, Eugenia, 95
Boyce, Emma, 89–90, 95, 102
Bracken, Brendan, 181
Brackenbury, Georgina and Marie, 55
Braddock, Mrs, 185
Brailsford, H. N., 165
Brighton, 'anti-patriotic' meeting at, 17 May 1917, 129
British Policy in Eritrea and Northern Ethiopia (1945), 183
British Policy in Eastern Ethiopia and the Ogaden (1945), 183
British Socialist Party *see* BSP
British Workers' and Soldiers' Council, 130–1
Brittain, Vera, 165
Brogan, Hugh, 128
Brown, Professor, 16, 20
Browning, Amy, 52–3
Bryant, Louise, 140
BSP, 94, 98, 103, 111–13, 122, 130
Bukharin, Nilolai, 140

Burston school strike, 100

Cadbury, Dame Elizabeth, 178
Cadness, Henry, 5, 13
Call, The, 112, 117
Campbell-Bannerman, 12
Carruthers, Leslie, 156
Cartlidge, Mr, 15
Castle, Barbara, 117–18
'Cat and Mouse Act', 73–4
Catlin, Professor, 178
Cecil, Lord, 162, 178
Cerulli, Enrico, 184
Chamberlain-Mussolini agreement, 162–4
Chambers, Mr, 16, 18, 25, 27
Chaplin, Charlie, 154
Chapman, Professor Sydney, 179
Chelsea Polytechnic, 20
Chew, Ada Nield, 79, 82, 83
Chkeidze, N. S. (first president of the Petrograd Soviet), 125
Clarion, The, 134, 193 *see also* Blatchford, Robert
Clements, Mr, 28
Clyde workers' revolt, 100, 128, 138
Cockerell, Mr, 16, 21, 27, 28
Cockermouth by-election (1906), 64
Cole, G. D. H., 136, 187, 189
Cole, Henry, 1
Comintern *see* Communist International
Comintern Sub-Bureau (Amsterdam), 122, 142
Communist International xi, 121–2, 141–2
Communist Party (British Section of the Third International), 142, 148
Communist Party of Great Britain, 123, 142–3, 195, 196
Communist Workers' Movement, 143
Communist Workers' Party (of Germany) *see* KAPD
Connolly, James, 75, 113, 114
conscientious objectors, 112, 124
conscription, 93–100, 123–4

Constituent Assembly, dissolution of, 137–40, 145–6
'constitutional crisis' (1910–11), 134
Contagious Diseases Act, the, 93
Cooper, Selina, 83
Corio, Silvio, 156, 169, 179, 197
Cornish Guardian, The, 153
Cosomati, Aldo, 173
cost price restaurant, 104, 108, 123
CPGB *see* Communist Party of Great Britain
Cradley Heath, 44
Crane, Lancelot, 25
Crane, Walter, 5, 7, 32, 33, 37
'Crastinus' *see* Corio, Silvio
Crawfurd, Helen, 97
Crespi, Professor Angelo, 156, 179, 181
Cromer, Lord, 60
Cunard, Nancy, 165
Currie, John S., 14–17, 20–7, 30, 34
Czechoslovakia, 163

Daily Express, 131, 151
Daily Herald, 75, 94, 129, 151, 154
Daily News, 13
Daily Telegraph, 151, 152
Darwin, Robin, 31
Davey, Cllr Mrs J., 167
Davies, Lord, 177, 179
Davison, Emily Wilding, 78
Defence of the Realm Act, the *see* DORA
Defaux, M. and Mme, 6
De Gaulle, Charles, 170
De Leonism, 128
democracy (*see also* direct democracy; referendum; soviets); lack of in WSPU, 65–6, 75; in ELFS and its successors, 72–3; Sylvia Pankhurst's commitment to, 132–3, 144–6; in Russia, 125, 132–3
Derby Scheme, the, 95
Despard, Charlotte, 65–6, 75, 76, 82, 94
dictatorship of the proletariat, 122, 145
direct democracy, 133–6, 137–8, 144

Dollan, Agnes, 97
DORA, 92–9, 123, 131, 141–2
Douglas, Rev. Canon, 185, 187–8, 189
Downes, Mary, 156, 162, 186, 189
Drake, Charlotte, 95, 96, 97, 98, 103
Dreadnought, the, 77, 84, 86, 101, 102, 105, 114, 115, 123, 124, 126, 127–30, 131–2, 140–2, 146, 154
'dual power' in Russia, 126
Dublin lockout, 75
Durham, Miss M. E., 179, 181
Dutch *Women's Yearbook*, 57

East End Deputation, 1914, 77–8
East London Federation of the Suffragettes (*see* ELFS)
East London Observer, 95, 117
Eastman, Crystal, 70
Easter Rising, the, 113–14, 115, 134, 196
Eden, Sir Anthony, 176
ELFS, xi, 73–8, 84–5, 88–91, 93–6, 99–103, 106, 112, 123, 195, 196
Emergency Conference of Anti-Parliamentary Groups, 142
Emerson, Zelie, 72
Emerson & Co., 1, 6, 7, 39
Eminescu, Mihai, 165
English, Edward, 16
equal pay, 109–10
Eritrea, 150, 175, 184–9; post-war 'Eritrea crisis', 188–9
Ethiopia: invaded by Mussolini, 150; Sylvia Pankhurst takes up the cause of, 150; Italian atrocities in, 153, 155–7, 159–60, 164, 183, 184; Britain recognises Mussolini's 'conquest' of, 161–4, 171, 176; status of in Britain, 172, 190; 'spheres of influence' in, 171; playing of national anthem of by the BBC, 172, 190; is 'liberated', 173–5; British imperialism and, 175–7, 180–9
Ethiopia. A Cultural History (1955), 189
Ethiopian People, their Rights and Progress, The (1946), 183

Ethiopian Review, 189
Ethiopia Observer, 189–90
'Eye of Moscow', 141, 146

Fabian Society, 49, 134
Fascio, 172
fascism, xii, 146, 149–75
Fawcett, Millicent, 76
Federation of Peace Councils, the, 161
feminism, 62, 69, 71, 79–82, 87–8, 100–7, 110–13, 115–16
Flynn, Elizabeth Gurley, 70
Ford, Isabella, 63, 77
Foster, W. Arnold, 164
Fourth International, 123, 142
Franco, xii, 164
Frankfurt, Comintern conference in, 142
Freeman, Peter, MP, 185, 188, 189
Free Trade Hall incident (1905), 65
Friends of Abyssinia (Ethiopia) League of Service, 156
Friends of Free Italy, 197
Friends' Peace Council, 161
Fry, Isabel, 161, 179, 184, 185, 187, 189
Fulham ILP, 63

German Communist Workers' Party *see* KAPD
'German gold', 132
Gilbert, Professor Sir Alfred, 11
Gillett-Gatty, Mrs, 161
Glasier, Bruce, 60, 64
Gojjam, province of, 158, 162
Gollancz, Victor, 162
Gore-Booth, Eva, 96
Gorter, Herman, 143
Grayson, Victor, 79
Graziani massacre, 159–60, 175
'Greater Somalia', 184
Great Scourge and How to End it, The, 67, 83
Greenwood, J. H., 178
Guild Socialism, 136
Guistizia e Libertà, 156, 160

Hall, David, 183

hammer and sickle, the, 146
'Hands Off Russia Committee', 91, 141, 196
Harburn, Mrs E. F., 165
Hardie, James Keir, 63, 74, 78, 80, 133; meets Pankhurst family, 3, 61–2; *Open Letter to the King*, 5; relationship with Sylvia Pankhurst, 11, 14, 59, 63, 68, 69, 84, 194, 197; asks parliamentary questions on Royal College of Art, 11, 13; death of, 124
Harrison, Brian, 82–3
Harvey-George, Miss, 30, 34
Haverfield, Elvina, 88
Hayward, Mr, 20, 29
Henderson, Arthur, MP, 189
Hercbergova, Mrs, 108, 196
Hicks, Margaretta, 195
Hitler-Stalin pact, 166
Hobhouse, Emily, 99
Hobson, G. A., 135
Hockney, David, 31
Home Front, The (1932), 97, 115, 118, 121, 146, 194, 196
Horder, Lord, 179
Hornes, Miss, 15
housewives, demand for inclusion in 'soviets', 130
Hugenholtz, the Rev. Dr, 161
'human suffrage', 96, 124, *see also* adult suffrage
Hungarian Exhibition (Earl's Court) 1908, 13
Huysmans, Camille, 178
Hyde, Robin, 165

ILP, 3, 7, 60, 62, 88, 89, 90, 92, 97, 100, 130, 133, 193
ILP News, 64
Imru, Mikael, 184
Independent Labour Party *see* ILP
Indian National Congress, 161
India League, 161
industrial unionism, 138, *see also* syndicalism
Industrial Workers of the World *see* IWW
initiative, the *see* referendum

Institute of Ethiopian Studies, 158
International Institute of Social History, Amsterdam, xvi, 57, 75, 84, 85, 115, 135, 147, 192–8
In the Red Twilight, 147, 148, 194
Iredell, Rev. E. O., 163
Iskra, 127
Italian East Africa, threatened post-war return of to Italy, 184, 186–9
Italian Socialist Party, 141
Italy: Sylvia Pankhurst in Venice 1902–3, 6–7, 36, 39–40; Bologna (PSI conference in, 1919), 141
IWW, 70, 91

Jeffries, Richard, 13
Jevons, Professor, 181
Jibuti, 159, 161, 174
Johnson, Wallace, 161
Jones, Lucia, 116, 148
Jus Suffragi, 92
Justice, 119

KAPD, 121, 142–3
Keir Hardie (*see* Hardie, James Keir)
Kenney, Annie, 11, 54, 62, 65, 68, 83
Kenya Association, 161
Kenyatta, Jomo, 161, 163, 183
Kerensky, Alexander, 125, 126, 132
Kollantai, Alexandra, 143
Koo, Wellington, 161
Krivitsy, General, 168
Kropotkin, Prince Peter, 61
Kvostoff, General, 127

Labour and the New Social Order, 136
Labour Leader, The, 78
Labour Party, 61, 62, 65, 76, 77, 100, 110, 112, 113, 133, 143 *see also* Labour Representation Committee; Labour Party Conference
Labour Party Conferences, Belfast 1907, 63; 1912, 76; 1917, 98; 1918, 98
Labour Representation Committee, 62
Lady Whitworth Scholarship, 6, 39

Langdon-Davis, John, 165
Langdon-Davis, Mrs, 115
Lansbury, Edgar, 97, 104
Lansbury, George, 68, 73, 74, 75, 76, 94, 100, 117, 130–2, 146
Lansbury, Minnie, 97, 105, 118–19
Lanteri, Professor Edward, 11, 28
Larkin, James, 75
Lawrence, Susan, 108
Layton, Lady Dorothea, 163, 188
League of Coloured Peoples, 161, 178, 185
League of Nations, 150–5
League of the Rights of Man, 172
League of Rights for Soldiers' and Sailors' Wives and Relatives, 105
Leeds Soviet Convention, 130, 132, 126, 144
Left Communists, 121–3, 141–6
'Left-Wing' Communism, an Infantile Disorder, xi, 121–2, 142, 146
Le Mander, Geoffrey, MP, 171, 176, 178
Lemma, Menghestu, 184
Lenin, V. I., xi, 121–2, 142, 146
Liddington, Jill, 65, 76, 85
Lidgett, Rev. J. Scott, 189
Liebknecht, Dr Karl, 114, 127
Litvinov, M., 140–1
Lloyd George, David, 80, 93, 110
London Labour Council for Adult Suffrage, 135
Longden, Fred, MP, 185
Lucas, Professor F. L., 156, 163
Ludolf's *New History of Ethiopia*, 180
Luxemburg, Rosa, 143
Lytton, Constance, 50

Macarthur, Mary, 108
MacDonald, James Ramsay, 10, 130, 132
McEntee, Val, MP, 183
Mackay, Walter, 103
McKenna, Reginald, 74
Mclean, Inspector, 131
Maclean, John, 93, 100
McMillan, Margaret, 61

Maddox Brown, Ford, 5
Makonnen, Endalkachev, 184
Makonnen, T. R., 183–4
Malatesta, 162
Manchester: Art Museum, 1, 35;
  High School for Girls, 4; Munici-
  pal School of Art, 5–6, 38–9;
  Whitworth Institute, 5
Manchester Guardian, The, 150, 151,
  152
Manion, Mrs, 91
Mann, Tom, 61
March, Cllr S., 103
Marsden, Dora, 82
Martin, Azaj Warqneh C., 156
Marx, Karl, 80
Massawa, 177; destruction of, 189
Mathews, C. I., 174
Matteotti, Giacomo, xii, 150, 160,
  168, 170, 197
'Maximalists and Leninists', 126
Medhen, Ephrem Tewelde, 174
Menczer, Bela, 157
Menon, Krishna, 161
Michael, Alazar Tesfa, 183, 186
Michel, Louise, 61
Milburn, Rev. Gordon, 184
milk centres, 106
Milwaukee, Sylvia Pankhurst in, 71
Mitchell, Hannah, 62, 83
Mitchell, Sir Philip, 175
Modigliani, Dr G. E., 156
Moira, Professor Gerald, 9, 13, 27,
  30
Montefiore, Dora, 68, 74
Moody, Harold, 178
Morning Post, The, 128, 131
Morris, William, 5, 33, 61
Moss, W. F., 131
'Mothers' Arms', the, 106, 123
Munich Crisis, 163
Munitions Act, 93, 96, 99, 123, 128
Murray, John, 179
Mussolini, 146, 149, 153, 161–2;
  enters Second World War,
  167–71; fall of, 179–80
Myself When Young, 42, 56, 57, 94

Napier, Helen, 156

'National Anthems of the Allies',
  172
National Council of Adult Suf-
  frage, 113
National Distress Bureau, 105
National Examinations Scheme, 8
National Register Act, 93, 109, 113
National Union of Women's
  Suffrage Societies *see* NUWSS
National Women's Council, 94, 103
Negro Welfare Association, 161
Nehru, Jawarhlal, 161
Nevinson, Henry, 165
New English Art Club, 37
News Chronicle, The, 151, 152
New Statesman, The, 76, 85
New Times and Ethiopia News, 56,
  149–200; Amharic editions,
  158–9; bookshop, 164–5; a
  'prohibited publication', 189
No Conscription Fellowship, 95
Noel-Baker, Francis, MP, 161, 163,
  176
Norris, Jill, 65, 76, 85
NUWSS, 49, 76–9
  fighting fund, 76–7

October Revolution *see* Bolsheviks
Ogaden, province of the, 177–8,
  180–5, 187

Padmore, George, 185
Pall Mall Gazette, 13, 43
Pankhurst, Christabel, xi, 4, 7, 12,
  39, 51, 58–9, 63–4, 66–7, 69, 71,
  75, 80–1, 83, 85, 87, 91, 100
Pankhurst, Emmeline, xi, 1–2, 4–5,
  6, 7, 36, 39, 40, 62–4, 66–7, 69, 71,
  80–1, 87, 91, 100, 159, 193, 195
Pankhurst, E. Sylvia: arts works by,
  see under art works; books by, *see
  under* titles; poems by, 14, 189,
  194, 195; homes of, in London, 1,
  2, 10, 12, 16, 42, 54; imprison-
  ments, 14, 43, 44, 67, 73, 142, 196;
  relationship with Keir Hardie,
  11, 14, 59, 63, 68, 69, 84, 194, 197;
  scholarships of, 6, 8; studies in
  Venice 1902–3, 6–7, 36, 39–40;

visits USA, 14, 70–1; clandestine journeys by, xi, 141–2; threats to life in Second World War, xii, 172; in Ethiopia, 182, 189–90 death, 190
Pankhurst Hall, Salford, 7, 40, 193
Pankhurst, Harry, 11, 53
Pankhurst, Richard Keir Pethick (son of Sylvia Pankhurst), 57, 185, 190
Pankhurst, Richard Marsden (father of Sylvia Pankhurst), xi, 1, 3, 4, 36–7, 40, 59, 62, 68, 193; death of, 4, 59; influence on Sylvia of, 36–7, 59, 62, 68
Paris peace treaty (1946) 184, 186
Parkinson, Brigadier, 189
Parsons, Mrs, 78
Partridge, Rev. W. E. C., 184
Patriot movement in Ethiopia, 157, 164–5, 167, 176
Payne, Jessie, 78, 88
People's Russian Information Bureau, 141, 196
Petherick, Mr, MP, 180, 181
Pethick-Lawrence, Emmeline, 51, 54, 67, 68, 71, 78, 85, 113, 179, 185, 188, 189, 191
Pethick-Lawrence, Fred, 68, 71
Petroff, Irma and Peter, 165
Phillips, Mary, 102
Philips Price, 140
poison gas, use of by the Italians in Ethiopia, xii, 153, 155, 157, 160, 163, 179, 190
Prince Kessie of Ashanti, 165
Prince's, Skating Rink, exhibition 1909, 14, 50, 53, 197
Princess Tsehai Memorial Hospital, 177–9, 186, 188–9
Prison and Prisoners, 50
Pritt, D. N., 162
Proctor Travelling Scholarship, 6, 39

Queen's Hall, 51
Queen Mary's Workshops *see also* sweated labour, 107

racism, 55, 70, 183, 187
radical suffragists, 65, 74, 83
Ransome, Arthur, 132–3, 140
Ras Abbebe Aregay, 164
Ras Imru, 160
Rassagna Sociale dell' Africa Italiana, 167
Rathbone, Eleanor, MP, 161, 163, 178
Rathbone, Nellie, 118–19
Rebels' Social and Political Union, 104
recall *see also* referendum, 133, 135–6, 144, 147–8
Reed, John, 140
Reed, Stanley, MP, 180
referendum (and initiative), 114, 133–6, 137–8, 139, 144
Registration Act, *see* National Register Act
Renson, I., 90
'Reserved Area', 180–1, 182, 189
Retta, Abebe, 177, 180
Rhondda Socialist, The, 99–100
Ricardo, Halsey, 16, 21, 26, 28
Richmond, Sir William, 19, 25
Roaf, Professor H. E., 185, 187
Robertson, Margaret, 77
Robeson, Paul, 162
Roe, Mrs, 10, 11
Romania, 197
Romero, Patricia, 59, 68, 71, 78, 82, 84
Rosen, Count Carl von, 157
Rosen, Andrew, 66, 82, 83, 84
Rosenweig Diaz, Alfonso de, 178
Ross, Betty, 165
Rosselli, Carlo, 59, 156, 157, 159, 168, 169; murder of, 59, 168, 170
Rothenstein, William, 32
Rothstein, Theodore, 141
Rothwell, L., 94
Rowbottom, Sheila, 60, 82
Rowley, Charles, 5
Royal College of Art, Board of Education enquiry at (1909–11), 14–35
Rugby Housewives Committee, 103

Runciman, Walter, 110
Russian Revolution, 80–1, 196;
   outbreak of (February/March)
   and Sylvia Pankhurst's response
   to, 115, 125; early support for
   Bolsheviks by Sylvia Pankhurst,
   115, 125–7; support for Constituent Assembly, 125, 132; support
   for dissolution of Constituent
   Assembly, 137–40

Salvemini, Professor Gaetano, 157,
   173
Sanger, Margaret, 70
Santos, Albert, 145
Sassoon, Siegfried, 114, 131
Sava, Ladislas, 177, 187
Savoy, Mrs, 78
Schulze-Gaevernitz, Dr Ruth, 157
Scurr, John, 74
Scurr, Julia, 78, 94, 103, 108
SDF, 60, 134
Sedgwick, Mr, 15, 16, 29
Sellassie, Bereketab Habte, 188
Sellassie, Haile, Emperor of
   Ethiopia, 157, 168–9, 175–7
Sennett, Maud Arncliff, 106, 111
Seretse Khama, Chief, 189
Sforza, Count, 186
Sharpe, Edith, 94
Shaw, George Bernard, 134
Shaw, Dr Maud Royden, 185
Sheehy Skeffington, Hannah, 102,
   118
Short, Professor Frank, 21
Smillie, Robert, 100
Smith, Cicely Fox, 6
Smith, F. E., 129
Smyth, Norah, 88–9, 94, 96, 112,
   131
Snowden, Philip, 60, 64
Social-Democratic Federation *see*
   SDF
socialist feminism, 79–82, 87–8,
   100–7, 110–13, 115–16
Socialist Labour Party, 115
Social Revolutionary Party/Social
   Revolutionist Party *see* SRs, the
socialist Sunday schools, 90

Social Services Society, 189
Solidarity, 115
Somalia, 150, 175, 184–5, 187, 189
Sorensen, Rev. Reginald, 163
soviets, 122, 126, 128, 130–2,
   139–46
Spanish Civil War, xii, 158–9, 164,
   197
Spare, Austin Osman, 10, 16, 20, 21,
   23, 30
Spare Rib, 91, 117
Sparrow, Walter C., 38
Speaker's Conference on Electoral
   Reform, 134
Spencer, Augustus, 10, 13, 20,
   23–7, 29, 31, 32
Spencer, Beckwith, 19, 29, 31
Spencer, Colonel Maurice, 156
SRs, the, 127, 139
Stanley, Venetia, 78
Starkie, Enid, 165
Stead, W. D., 43–4
Steer, George L., 165
Stephens, Jessie, 90
Students' Union (at RCA), 25, 26
Suez Canal Company, 151, 153
Suffragette, The (1911), 14, 68, 70, 73,
   84, 85, 193, 194
Suffragette Crusaders, 94
suffragette movement *see* WSPU
   and Women's Freedom League
Suffragette Movement, The (1931) 33,
   56, 57, 58, 68, 69, 70, 82, 83, 84,
   85, 193, 194
Sukloff, Marie, 127
Swanwick, Mrs, 99
sweated labour, 94, 107
syndicalism, 70, 91, 128–9, 138–9
*Sylvia Pankhurst: Artist and Cru-
   sader*, 34, 190
Sylvia Pankhurst Papers (Amster-
   dam) *see* International Institute
   of Social History
*Sylvia Pankhurst: Portrait of a
   Radical*, 59, 82, 84

Taezaz, Lorenzo, 174
Taylor, Cllr, 96
Tchaykovsky, Dr Barbara, 89, 96

Tedros, Mr and Mrs, 174, 185
Tekle, Afewerk, 184
Third International, *see* Communist International
Thring, Lillian, 192
Thorne, Will, 74
Tigre, province of, 162, 180
Times, The, 131, 151, 181, 184, 185, 186, 187, 189
Tonks, Professor, 20
toy factory, 32, 108, 196
trade unions, 45, 61, 62, 70, 73, 74, 75, 77, 91, 94, 96, 100, 101, 103, 109, 110, 121, 124, 128, 129, 133, 138, 140, 143, 161, 162, 185
Trafalgar Square, rallies in: 19 May 1906, 12; August 1913, 74; 26 September 1915, 124; 8 April 1916, 95–6; 1938, 163
Tsehai, Princess, xii, 48, 162, 178, 181
Turner, Cecil, 156

Union of Democratic Control, 185
United Nations Association, 178, 185
United Nations War Crimes Commission, 180
United Suffragists, 94
USA, 14, 70–1, 84, 133–5

Verdi's *Hymn of the Nations*, 186
Viazemski, Princess Rosalie, 188
Victor Emmanuel, King of Italy, 169, 171, 177
Virgin, General Eric, 157
Votes for Women, 44, 49, 50, 57, 68, 69, 84

Walker, Malvina, 92, 95, 96, 101–2, 110
Wallhead, R. C., 7
Walling, William English, 127
Walts, Mrs, 96
Ward, Bessie, 94
Warner, Mr, 16
Warren, A. H., 103
Watkins, Elsie, 78
Waugh, Evelyn, 159

Wazir Ali Baig, 159
Webb, Beatrice, 76
Wedgwood, Colonel, MP, 172, 176, 178
Weinholt, Arnold, 167
Weiss, Professor, J. E., 179, 187
Westminster Review, 13, 42
White, Dr H. Costley, Dean of Gloucester, 185
Wingate, Colonel Orde, 175, 177
Wingate, Lorna, 179, 185
Winslow, Barbara, 70, 80, 84
Winster, Lord, 189
Wold, Ato Aklilou Hapte, 186
Wolfit, Donald, 189
Wollo, province of, 162
Woman's Dreadnought, *see* the *Dreadnought*
Women Artists, Society of, 37
Women Painters of the World, 38
Women's Charter (of ELFS), 123
Women's Convention Against Conscription, 97
Women's Co-operative Guild, 94, 161, 178, 185
Women's Exhibition (Prince's Skating Rink, Knightsbridge, 1909), 14, 50, 53, 197
Women's Franchise League, 193
Women's Freedom League, 65–6, 70, 76, 77, 85, 118
Women's International League, 98–9
Women's International Matteotti Committee, xii, 149–50, 196
Women's Labour League, 94, 110
Women's Liberal Association, 49
Women's League of North Dakota, 70
Women's Movement of Today and Tomorrow, The, 75
Women's Party, the, 81
Women's Social and Political Union (*see* WSPU)
Women's suffrage poll (of ILP), 62
Women's Trade Union League, 94, 110
Women's War Emergency Council, 167

Woodford, 155, 168
Woods, Fred, 25
Woolway, Mr, 25
Workers' and Soldiers' Council of
     Great Britain, 130–1 *see also*
     Leeds Soviet Convention
Workers' Dreadnought, see the
     Dreadnought
Workers' Socialist Federation *see*
     WSF
Workers' Suffrage Federation *see*
     WSF
WSF, 88, 89, 91, 95–8, 100, 107,
     109–16, 121, 125, 129–30, 135, 195
WSPU, 7, 11, 12, 13, 32, 42, 49–53,
     55–6, 62–6, 68–71, 72, 75–6,

78–81, 87, 195; foundation of, 7,
     62; autocratic running of, 65–6,
     75; hostility to Labour of, 63–4,
     69, 75–6; discouragement of
     working-class women in, 66, 68,
     78, 195; supports First World
     War, 80; attacks Keir Hardie's
     pacifism, 80
Women's Year Book, 1930, *see* Dutch
     Women's Year Book

Yaqob, Zara, 180, 190–1

Zahkind, 141
Zinoviev, G., 140